Chek Yang Foo

Grief Play Management

Chek Yang Foo

Grief Play Management

A Qualitative Study of Grief Play Management in MMORPGs

VDM Verlag Dr. Müller

Imprint

Bibliographic information by the German National Library: The German National Library lists this publication at the German National Bibliography; detailed bibliographic information is available on the Internet at http://dnb.d-nb.de.

Cover image: www.purestockx.com

Publisher:
VDM Verlag Dr. Müller Aktiengesellschaft & Co. KG , Dudweiler Landstr. 125 a, 66123 Saarbrücken, Germany,
Phone +49 681 9100-698, Fax +49 681 9100-988,
Email: info@vdm-verlag.de

Zugl.: Perth, Curtin University of Technology, Diss., 2006

Produced in USA and UK by:
Lightning Source Inc., La Vergne, Tennessee, USA
Lightning Source UK Ltd., Milton Keynes, UK
BookSurge LLC, 5341 Dorchester Road, Suite 16, North Charleston, SC 29418, USA

ISBN: 978-3-639-06191-8

TABLE OF CONTENTS

LIST OF FIGURES

LIST OF TABLES

ACKNOWLEDGEMENTS

This study on grief play which has culminated into a publication would not have been possible without the contribution and participation of several individuals.

A first mention must be made of two persons who got the project started. Dr. Heinz Dreher of Curtin University of Technology, my Ph.D supervisor, who when reading my proposal for a short research paper on MMORPG game communities in 2000, remarked "this looks like it has the potential for a Ph.D". Also, I thank Assoc. Professor Khong Chooi Peng of Nanyang Technological University. She provided the 'push' of encouragement that convinced me to leave a comfortable position teaching software engineering in Singapore to pursue a Ph.D driven by keen interest as opposed to career advancement.

As I searched for my focus, Assoc. Professor Edward Castronova of Indiana University upon reviewing my ideas suggested that I choose grief play as the topic of study. Also, Dr. Helen Merrick of Curtin University, my co-supervisor, encouraged me to look at virtual communities to get a sense of what had already been said about bad behavior online.

Along the way; Elina Koivisto of Nokia Research Center in Finland, my co-author for my first several papers on grief play; Jonas Heide-Smith of IT University of Copenhagen, Ren Reynolds, an independent researcher, and Matthew McGee who was my co-guild manager in *EverQuest*; and of the gaming industry, Damion Schubert and Alexander Macris; all of whom helped with ideas on perspectives to take on grief play. The many players, developers and game managers who participated in the study also need to be acknowledged—the study stands on the insights each took the time to share.

The final mention is reserved for Ling, my fiancée during the Ph.D. Her constant affirmations and daily prayers provided assurance that a Ph.D on *gaming* was worth doing. With her, the completion of this thesis has additional meaning—that there is indeed life, *after* the Ph.D.

January 2006

INTRODUCTION TO THE STUDY

Massively Multi-player Online Role-Playing Games (MMORPGs) are large online worlds on the Internet where players create and play characters alongside other participants. Many MMORPGs are commercial ventures: they are designed by game development houses, and distributed and managed by game operators. MMORPGs make use of a 'client-server' model. A copy of the software is purchased by each player and installed on their client computers. Once properly configured, players connect to the game worlds running on servers maintained by game operators, and typically pay a recurring subscription fee for access into the game world.

When played on modern computers, the game worlds are graphically rendered in realistic fashion. Complemented with attractive visual and audio effects, MMORPG game worlds can be seen, heard and played from a 'first person' perspective. This lends itself to an immersive experience for players. MMORPGs allow participants to play characters from a range of professions. Some professions are peaceful—for example, a blacksmith who manufactures weapons, amour or other equipment for sale to other players, or a fishmonger who sails in his[1] own boat to fish in the sea and returns to dock to sell his catch. Other professions are more combative, for example, adventurers who band together to defeat computer-controlled 'monsters' or fight each other for fame and glory. Many MMORPGs are populated with large numbers of players. One MMORPG is *EverQuest*. Operated by Sony Online Entertainment, *EverQuest* has an active subscriber base of 460,000[2] players, of which as many as 118,000 can be online at any one time (Sony Online Entertainment Inc. 2003). Some MMORPGs in Asia are played by millions of players even.

Players also spend large amounts of time in these game worlds. Studies of player habits have found that the average *EverQuest* player spends 21.9 hours per week in the game, with others spending upwards of 50 or more hours per week (Yee 2001). MMORPGs are designed to accommodate the different activity preferences players may have. Some players prefer to socialize; others prefer to explore the environment. Through playing, players grow in social standing among their peers, individual play skill, and their characters progress in prowess. For some players, they play to

---

[1] For consistency, the masculine form will normally be used when referring to participants of MMORPGs.
[2] See http://www.mmogchart.com.

continually advance their characters in levels of power so that new and additional play areas become accessible to them.

The range of activities to perform and ways to do them generates both discussion and debate among enthusiastic players. Much of these discussions occur in either game operator-managed or fan discussion forums. These discussion forums become an extension of the virtual community that already exists in the game, and are filled with daily postings of player experiences. For example, there are numerous postings on how players encountered and defeated a challenge in the game. Other postings relate their satisfaction or displeasure in some aspect of the game, or their interactions with other players. Players of MMORPGs invest a lot of time in the characters they play, and are interested in the game worlds they reside in. Their interest in the game extends to such public discussion, providing a wealth of data for researchers investigating MMORPGs.

MMORPGs are persistent game worlds. Every player can act on and influence the game environment, and the environment continues operating in its changed state even when players are logged off the game (Papargyris & Poulymenakou 2004, p. 44). MMORPGs are also designed to encourage interaction among players (Axelsson & Regan 2002). With a high degree of interactivity possible among players in these large multi-player environments, inevitably, actions carried out by players impose on one another. One tenet of game design is to increase the value of a game resource or content by making it scarce. Hence, in many cases, players compete with each other for game resources and content. The majority of players appear to get along harmoniously, and many impositions are treated as a normal part of game play. However, some players appear to play in ways that intentionally disrupt other players' gaming experiences. This type of player behavior[3] has been called 'grief play', and grief players are commonly known as 'griefers'. The following remarks are made by players: the first is one perception of griefers, and the second is a reaction to a grief play incident:

> Some people just get their kicks out of making other people miserable. In real-life we call 'em bullies, in games we call 'em griefers.

> It's just a game.

---

[3] The term "player behavior" is used in a general way in this study, and refers to the manner in which players conduct themselves. Play styles refer to specific activities that players engage in.

These are just two common reactions from players on grief play. Grief play has also affected various aspects of MMORPGs. They include player attitudes, how they respond to each other as members of the larger player community, and their expectations of the game. Grief play has also affected the game operation, both in the design of games and how the game operator responds to player complaints on the disruption of their play experiences. Grief play is problematic for game operators because when players are distressed by griefing, they will take their unhappiness to public platforms and demand that game operators act on griefers. While End-User License Agreements in MMORPGs may insulate game operators from players initiating lawsuits over service issues, there are still real business concerns when players are unhappy. Players who are sufficiently unhappy with the game may leave the game.

If managing grief play on the part of the game operator was a simple matter, there would be no cause for concern. However, there is a strong interplay between grief play and what is allowed and disallowed by game rules. Generally speaking, while rules can disallow certain types of play activities, determining when an activity becomes grief play and hence actionable is difficult. One difficulty faced is that many MMORPGs inherently include a degree of violent play. Attempting to distinguish between an aggressive act of grief play which may be disallowed and normal and allowable game play can be difficult. Many players who grief do not regard their activities as non-normative game play. A second difficulty faced is that players make use of their own standards of etiquette when determining if an act is grief play. These player norms are not always congruous with what is allowed or disallowed by game rules. Hence, a player who believes his play experience has been intentionally disrupted by another may demand action from the game operator, even if the game does not explicitly disallow such activities. A third difficulty is that while developers continually devise new mechanisms to manage grief play, these mechanisms can come at some cost to the types of player interactivity permissible.

There is a large amount of data available in the form of discussion postings from players and interviews with game developers on mechanisms to manage grief play. However, there has been limited study of this player behavior. Hence, this study is intended to explore grief play, with its research objective as follows: "To investigate grief play and its management mechanisms." The study is explorative in view of the limited body of scholarly work on grief play. Its five operationalized objectives are:

1. To investigate what grief play means.

2. To investigate what motivates players to engage in grief play.

3. To investigate how grief play affects the game.

4. To investigate what players expect from grief play management.

5. To investigate grief play management.

The study was conducted from September 2002 to January 2006. Its conduct kept in mind several considerations. Firstly, disputes regarding what is grief play observed in discussion forums prior to the commencement of study suggested that there were differing view points among participants on the meaning of grief play. Secondly, grief play itself can be a subjective experience. It was observed in discussion forums that some players reacted badly to an activity while other players when subjected to the same activity were less bothered by it. Thirdly, a good amount of data was already available in textual form, which lent itself to qualitative methods. With these considerations in mind, a qualitative modus operandi was chosen. The study drew upon semi-structured interviews with players and developers of MMORPGs, and discussion postings from players. It was interpretivistic, and viewed through my perspectives of having been a player of several MMORPGs since 1997, and my own subjective experiences of grief play. It also drew upon existing literature on virtual communities and bad behavior to provide a broader context for the investigation.

With the overall goal of the study decided upon, the research objective was next divided into five objectives. Each of these is dealt with in a separate chapter in this book, and these five substantial chapters are framed by overview, literature review, methodological, and concluding chapters.

The book first presents an overview titled *MMORPGs and grief play*. It begins with a discussion of one popular type of computer game, the computer role-playing game (CRPG), which has its roots in tabletop role-playing games (RPGs) like *Dungeons and Dragons*. Sessions of these tabletop RPGs are participated in by small groups of players with a facilitator who describes and manages the proceedings of each encounter. The basic tenets in CRPGs are similar—except that a player can now 'see' and experience the encounter on their computer screens, complete with audio-visual effects.

Small-scaled multi-player CRPGs can be participated in by a limited number of players who are often known to each other. The session of play is intimate. MMORPGs in comparison are very large multi-player CRPGs played on the Internet, and the game can comprise hundreds of thousands of players. Few players know each other outside this virtual world. With such large numbers of people at play and the immediate layer of anonymity from the game being situated online, 'bad' behavior can occur. The chapter describes grief play as a form of bad behavior, and introduces two considerations that pervade the study: the issues of role-playing and what is perceived as 'normative' game play, and the rules which govern what is allowed and disallowed in the game.

There is little study on grief play in MMORPGs. However, MMORPGs are also virtual communities, and grief play is comparable to bad behavior that can occur in other virtual environments or in the real-world. Hence, an initial selection of literature surrounding these foundational areas of the topic was sought early on in the study. Further sources were investigated when grief play was better understood after the first year of data collection. The *Literature review* chapter presents a survey of material pertaining to areas of studies on virtual communities and computer-mediated communication. It discusses how the reduction of social cues in online environments can lead to anti-normative, disinhibited behavior and anonymity. One particular example of bad behavior took place in a Multi-user Dungeon (the predecessor of the MMORPG), and aroused interest among researchers of virtual communities. Early data collected also revealed that some players believe there is similarity between grief play and the concepts of bullying and teasing. Literature regarding both types of behavior is included. Lastly, some players perceive acts that benefit the individual but inconvenience or hurt the collective to be grief play. The chapter looks also at "the tragedy of the commons", one model of such behavior.

The *Research design* chapter discusses the research paradigm, data collection methods and issues surrounding the manner in which the study was conducted. Since experiences with grief play were drawing different reactions from participants and this was a relatively new area of research, the study employed grounded theory. Grounded theory allows the researcher to have 'hunches' on where areas of interest may lie, but demands that he does not have preconceived theories in mind before the study commences. Rather, theory is to surface from data through the course of the research. Data existed primarily as text and subjective experiences, and were collected as discussion postings and through semi-structured interviews with players and developers. There were some challenges to deal with in the use of these two data collection methods. Some methods of validating data were built into the investigation to ensure that the data collected was reasonably representative of the perceptions from each participant.

The next five chapters each centre attention on one of the five objectives. *Defining grief play* explores what grief play means to participants. In particular, while many players define grief play in a similar way to that published in literature, further investigation exposed circumstances where players view an act as grief play even when it does not meet the criteria posed in literature. Key to this is their perceptions of implicit rules and norms of behavior in the game. Player perceptions are compared to the game operator's, who base their determination using game rules. The variance of perception between both participant groups leads to a re-evaluation of the definition of grief play, and the chapter proposes a new term for the more subtle forms of grief play.

The next chapter, *Grief player motivations,* investigates the factors that can cause players to engage in grief play. Factors are either 'reasons' that expedite grief play, or 'motivations' that can compel or drive a player to grief. MMORPGs as games also comprise several facets: they are role-playing games, they are played on the computer, and they involve large numbers of players. Player models surrounding each of these facets are presented. Comparisons of griefer motivations are made to these models, alongside motivations of people who bully and tease.

Impacts of grief play next investigates the consequences of grief play on the game world. It looks at how grief play affects player experiences, game design and operation. Subsequent analysis of these impacts leads to two outcomes. Firstly, the question of whether grief play constitutes problematic behavior or not is examined. Secondly, the impacts of grief play on players are shown to be be influenced in several ways: including the expectations players have of the game operation, and the ability of players to respond against griefers.

The first of these two influences are discussed in *Player expectations.* This chapter presents player expectations of the game operation, particularly in the management and control of grief play. It also notes that while players can be unhappy with grief play and dissatisfied with the game operator if they fail to respond to expectations, players in reality are limited in their ability to effect change. Moreover, the expectations players have of the game operation may not be congruous with what is intended by the operator. The chapter looks at two possible reasons for this incongruity: that it can be due to player ignorance of the game operator's stated expectations for their game, or that players do not adjust to those expectations.

The last of the five substantial chapters, *Grief play management,* investigates several methods for managing grief. Some of these methods have been implemented while others have seen limited use or are hypothetical. Game operator-driven methods are investigated as well as player-driven methods. The second influence on the impacts of grief play—the ability of players to respond against griefers—is one such player-driven method. Each method poses its own pros and cons, and these are discussed in the chapter.

The last substantial chapter is followed by *Study outcomes.* This chapter presents a review of the five research objectives of grief play, and the general observations on grief play made in the course of the study.

The significance of this research lies with its two segments of intended readership. The primary group of readers comprises the players, developers and operators of MMORPGs, many of whom feel the impacts of grief play, and have expressed interest in the outcome of this study. The other group comprises social and computer-mediated communication researchers. The large number of people participating in MMORPGs forms a rich field of opportunities for investigation into persistent environments, and this project's exploration of social disruption and conflict management in role-playing virtual communities will be of interest to social researchers.

CHAPTER 1: MMORPGS AND GRIEF PLAY

Early computer games were primarily played by single players. Many computer games created today are still designed as single-player experiences. Making use of algorithms in the game code, the computer controls the opponents that the human gamer will play against. Advances in artificial intelligence make computer opponents increasingly humanlike. For example, computer opponents can respond to some situations apparently in ways that a human person would. However, playing with or against real opponents continues to be attractive to many players. One reason for this is cited by Morningstar & Randall (1991, p. 279) in their commentary of Lucasfilm's *Habitat*[4]. They note that no one has yet figured out how to create an automaton that can simulate the complexities of real human beings. Playing against human beings can provide a higher level challenge than that of computer-controlled opponents. In non-cooperative multi-player games, for example combat-centric ones where players 'fight' each other, there is an adrenaline rush and sense of achievement in beating other human beings. Virtual worlds that allow players to fight each other are more exciting than those which do not allow their players to do so (Bartle 2004, p. 410). Even in cooperative multi-player games, players can communicate with other players to accomplish a task, and foster social relationships when doing so. In both cooperative and non-cooperative multi-player games, the potential for collaboration and sharing of experiences is significant (Manninen 2002).

One popular type of game is the computer role-playing game (CRPG). To discuss this, the concept of role-playing needs to be introduced first.

Role-playing games

To 'role-play' means to deliberately assume or 'act out' a role. Where reading a book and watching a show at the theatre are arguably passive experiences, role-playing is interactive and requires active engagement from its participants. The role-playing of characters from a historical setting has been used as a way of encouraging students in classroom education to be aware of how people in different times "felt, thought, believed and behaved differently" (Luff 2000, p. 9). Role-playing, in other words, can help participants experience differing points of view.

---

[4] *Habitat* was one of the gaming industry's first attempts in creating a multi-user virtual environment (Morningstar & Randall 1991).

One popular type of game is the role-playing game (RPG). In an RPG, participants create characters consistent with personas in that setting. They will then assume, play and maintain their characters over an extended period of play time (Williams & Skoric 2005, p. 221). While role-playing can be based on a historical setting, RPGs are commonly based on fictional and fantastic worlds. In 1974, the first widely popular RPG was Gary Gygax and Dave Arneson's *Dungeons & Dragons* (D & D) (Hallford & Hallford 2001, p. 39). D & D was a union between traditional board war games and interactive storytelling (Bartle 2004, p. 71). In D & D, one player becomes a 'Dungeon Master', who is the 'controller' of the session. Other players will assume roles of fictional characters in the setting that is decided upon. D & D was inspired by popular fantasy fiction, for example J. R. R. Tolkein's *The Lord of the Rings*. Fictional characters that could exist in this setting include spell-casting wizards, dragon-slaying warriors, or club-wielding trolls who deal with problems using brute strength. Playing on tabletops, the Dungeon Master becomes the story-teller, and describes to players what they see, hear and feel. The Dungeon Master also describes the range of actions available to the characters controlled by players in the session. Players will then decide on actions. For example, when faced with a fearsome dragon, players may attack, retreat, stall, or engage in conversation with the dragon. Dice would be used to determine the outcome of their decisions. Like other games, rules exist to govern how its players interact with each other and also the setting. The Dungeon Master is expected to be familiar with these rules, so that he can rule on whether an activity is permitted by players or not.

D & D was successful and gained a strong following. It did not take long for other game publishers and enthusiastic players to create their own settings and game systems. CRPGs appeared soon enough. The game software installed on the computer now becomes the Dungeon Master and controller of the proceedings. CRPGs offer many advantages over traditional D & D type of games played on the tabletop. A computer-controlled Dungeon Master is not subject to human limitations of fatigue or arbitrary application of game rules. These computer games also allow players to play on their own time, without having to organize sessions where players can attend at the same time, as a D & D session would require.

At first, CRPGs were single-player, with other characters in the setting controlled by the computer. Computer technology became increasingly integrated with networking, and it became possible for multiple people to play together. Some of these early online games were text-based games played on Bulletin Board Systems (BBS). Multi-user Dungeons/Dimensions/Domains (MUDs)[5] had already made their appearance, with textual descriptions of objects, characters and creatures in the virtual world displayed on the computer screen (Ito 1997, p. 90). With MUDs, not only were participants anonymous, they were role-playing (Beaubien 1996, p. 181). These are two distinguishing characteristics of MUDs compared to face-to-face social rituals that Lin & Sun (2003, p. 70) identify[6]. Players of MUDs played with each other freely on BBS and university computer networks, and attracted academic attention in the early 90s. Some of the early scholarly studies include Bruckman's (1992) study of emerging social and psychological phenomena and Curtis' (1992) similar study of social phenomena in MUDs. The emergence of virtual communities on the Internet from the mid-90s also led to the publication of literature on these communities. These include Rheingold's (2000) "*The Virtual Community: Homesteading on the Electronic Frontier*," and Kim's (2000) "*Community Building on the Web*", the latter which delves into mechanisms of building and running an online community. MUDs as a form of virtual community in particular attracted attention. Aarseth (1997, p. 149) notes that from the perspective of textual aesthetics, MUDs were seen as the most interesting of new digital network media. Their importance is also noted by Rheingold (2000), who regards them as vehicles for studying the impact of virtual communities.

From the mid-90s onwards, computer technology continued to advance, and MMORPGs appeared. Unlike MUDs, descriptions of the world and its inhabitants in MMORPGs are no longer textual but graphical (Axelsson & Regan 2002). The visual depictions are also complemented by audio effects that further immerse players into believing "they are there". Unlike MUDs, many MMORPGs are also commercial ventures that adopt subscription-based models of revenue generation. Players pay an initial cost for the purchase of the game product, and an ongoing fee for continual access.

In general, multi-player games today range from small-scaled games played by two persons (for example online chess played on Yahoo!), somewhat larger multi-player games of several dozen players (for example in a first-person shooter where players are divided into two sides), to large and massive multi-player online games (MMOGs) like MMORPGs.

---

[5] MMORPGs are regarded as the descendants of MUDs (Ducheneaut & Moore 2004, p. 360; Williams & Skoric 2005, p. 221).

[6] As the study will show later in Chapter 5, these two characteristics can also be influences to a player's propensity to grief.

MMORPGs

Some differences distinguish MMORPGs from its smaller-scaled brethren and single-player games. Firstly, there is a wide range of activities possible in MMORPGs. Games like online-chess played by two persons or a first-person shooter played by a small group of players are focused in their scope. For example, the tasks expected from one group of players in a multi-player session of id Software's first-person shooter *Quake* could be to decimate the ranks of their opponents within allotted time, and if successful that group wins (Oliveira & Henderson 2003, p. 186). MMORPGs are designed to emulate living worlds where the activities permissible to a player are similar to that in the real-world. These player activities can extend beyond violent conflict with each other. Depending on the game, players can take on crafting professions, create fine wares from raw materials, then advertise and sell them to other players who may need them for their own advancement. Many MMORPGs have in-game economies where players transact services and goods with each other, using virtual money unique to the game as a form of currency. Secondly, activities undertaken by players have a persistent effect on the rest of the world. This effect lasts even when the player has 'logged off' or retired from the session. For example, in Electronic Art's *Ultima Online*, a player can buy a house, customize it, and open it to public access for other players. His establishment will continue to stand in the virtual world after he has logged off to return to the real-world. Thirdly, many MMORPGs are designed to stretch a player's interest and span of commitment. Many single-player games can be 'won' or completed in 40 to 50 hours of play time. Players of MMORPGs can spend dozens of hours in a single week playing. It can take several months of accumulated play time for their characters to advance to a reasonably 'powerful' state. For example, a player who creates a new character in a combative profession could take months—or thousands of play hours—to advance his character to an experienced level of progress capable of wielding powerful items or weaponry. Many players also form themselves into player communities, some of which persist from one game to another. Through the continuous introduction of new game content from the game operator[7], players can play MMORPGs for years. For example, several respondents from *Ultima Online* have played the game since 1997. They still

---

[7] MMORPGs are constantly evolving in terms of content and rules. This in turn poses difficulties for MMORPG researchers, as rules or game mechanisms studied at one point could very well have changed by the time their work is published. In fact, one (very) large difficulty experienced in this study was the continually changing game rules in several MMORPGs. The fluid nature of these game rules forced repeated revisions to arguments in this study making use of or citing a game rule.

actively play as a result of new content that has been added, and enjoy the community of friends and fellow players they have gotten to know over the years of play.

Large numbers of players subscribe to MMORPGs. An ongoing project tracking Massively Multi-player Online Games (MMOGs) at http://www.mmogchart.com reports that more than 3 million players subscribed to NCsoft's *Lineage* in 2003. Other successful titles that are studied in this project include *EverQuest* which enjoys 454,000 subscribers at the time of writing, Mythic Entertainment's *Dark Age of Camelot* with 175,000 subscribers, Sony Online Entertainment's *Star Wars Galaxies* with 255,000 subscribers, and *Ultima Online* with 157,000 subscribers. An even larger MMORPG is Blizzard Entertainment's *World of Warcraft*. In December 2005, Blizzard Entertainment (2005b) reported that this MMORPG surpassed the 5 million subscriber mark.

With such participation, public interest in MMORPG has grown. One study of player demography in MMORPGs is Nicholas Yee's *The Norrathian Scrolls* (Yee 2001). Yee's study centered on *EverQuest*, and he collected data from 4,000 players between September 2000 and May 2001 through the use of online questionnaires. His results reveal a number of statistics. For example, in *EverQuest*, the average age of an *EverQuest* player is 25.6 years, and about 84% of *EverQuest* players are male. *EverQuest* players also spend an average of 21.9 hours per week playing the game. His research is ongoing[8]. More studies of MMORPGs are also noted in Chapter 2.

Key terms

There are terms in an MMORPG that describe specific activities, play styles or constructs in the game world. Some of the more commonly used terms and those referred to in this study are as follows.

Table 1: Key terms

Term	Description
Player attributes	
Class	A profession chosen by the player. Classes may be combative—for example a spell-casting wizard—or non-combative, for example a tradesperson or skilled artisan.
Level	A discrete stage of advancement for a player. A higher level player is a more powerful player.

---

[8] See http://www.nickyee.com/daedalus/gateway_intro.html.

Term	Description
Experience	Advancement rewards that players gain, which when accumulated will enable them to progress to higher levels of prowess.
Constructs and objects	
NPC	Stands for 'non-player character'. These are computer controlled characters in the game world that players interact with, for example to further progression of a task.
Mob	Stands for 'mobile object'. These are NPCs in the game, but are usually hostile and intended for players to fight and defeat. Mobs that are 'contested' usually refer to high-level mobs that award powerful items, and thus are sought after by advanced players.
Actions and activities	
Camp	To camp for an item or mob means to wait in a game area where the item or mob is known to appear. Camps can involve dozens of hours of waiting.
Pickup	Describes how a group of players assembled for an event. As opposed to player community groups, pickup groups comprise players who are unknown to each other, and are usually formed ad-hoc.
Raid	An event where multiple groups of players organize themselves to defeat a particularly difficult encounter.
Loot	Monetary or item rewards that players gain, for example from defeating mobs or completing a game event. Also, to 'loot' means to take these rewards.
Emote	Refers to an action in-game that expresses an emotion. Some games will render an emote visually, while other games will display the emote a player is acting as a visible text message. An example of a text emote is: "Tom waves hello to Jane."
Respawn	When players die, they will 'reappear' in some part of the game world. The 'respawned' player will usually be temporarily weakened, and in many games, also suffer some temporary loss of character prowess.
Player interactions	
PvP	Stands for 'player versus player', and refers to activities where players engage in opposition against each other (Bartle 2004, p. 407), for example in combat. In this study, PvP refers to player versus player interactions of the combative kind.
PvE	Stands for 'player versus environment', and refers to activities where players engage in opposition against constructs of the game world, for example mobs.
PK	Stands for 'player-kill', or when a player engages in an activity—usually combat—that results in the 'death' of another player's character. Player-killing when taken literally is a normal aspect of PvP. However, the word as commonly used has negative connotations; for example the victim was killed in a particularly aggressive manner, or that the act of killing was non-consensual[9].

[9] See Chapter 7 – 'Game design'

Term	Description
Organization	
Zone	A distinct game area. The game world (on each server) of an MMORPG like *EverQuest* or *Star Wars Galaxies* is separated into many 'zones'.
Server	The large number of players in the game is typically distributed among 'servers', which often hold identical copies of the game world. All players are still playing the same game. However, players who play on different servers cannot play with each other, although they may still be able to chat across servers. Occasionally, servers may use different rule sets. For example, a game can largely comprise non-PvP servers but still supports one PvP server.
Player community	Players seek out and socialize with other players of similar aims and goals. Often, they organize themselves into groups of persistent nature, and many develop distinct identity and structure (Papargyris & Poulymenakou 2004, p. 43). They enjoy the use of identity tags to show their affiliation, and have access to member-only chat channels. These player communities are known by different names in different games. For example, player communities are known as guilds in *EverQuest* and *Ultima Online*, and player associations in *Star Wars Galaxies*.

There are other terms used in the study, for example 'training', 'kill-stealing', and 'ninja-looting'. Many of these denote grief play activities, and will be explained in Chapter 4.

Challenges in MMORPGs

Players are attracted to MMORPGs for several reasons. Firstly, the online role-playing game is an avenue for many people to get out of their normal lives and live out a fantasy through the characters they create. While watching a fantasy movie at the theatre may provide the same visual experience, they are non-interactive. Role-playing games allow participants to interact and 'become' the characters they play. It is an attractive proposition to be some great warrior or wizard who is able to slay powerful and evil monsters. MMORPGs are seen by some as the preferred virtual experience (Oliver 2002). Secondly, these games do not have high barriers of entry. Being online, geographical and national boundaries are transcended and MMORPGs can be played from anywhere in the world. All that is required is a copy of the software, a means of payment for subscription, and access to the Internet. MMORPGs are accessible in this sense.

MMORPGs have become profitable ventures for game operators. However, it has also introduced challenges for game operators to counter. Three such challenges are described below.

Game exploitation

Some players view an MMORPG not only as an avenue to play an alter-ego in a large social world, they also find ways to 'beat' the game by taking advantage of game code[10] that is erroneous, or of other loopholes accidentally introduced by game design. The term exploitation is often used to describe actions where poorly written game code has been taken advantage of, or a game mechanic has been used by players to their advantage in a way that had not been anticipated. An example of an exploit is 'gold duping' (Grimmelmann 2005), which is the creation of large amounts of virtual money in ways that have not been anticipated or intended by game design. Occasionally, such acts of exploitation are facilitated by third party programs that change how the game works. For example, third party programs can be used to empower an exploiter's characters with unusual abilities or equipment that would be otherwise unavailable to him. In other instances, exploiters have used such programs to handily defeat other players. For example, at one point, exploiters in *Ultima Online* could use these programs to crash the game client of another player. When players lose connection to the game, their characters become stuck in 'limbo' in the game world and are vulnerable. This allows the exploiter to kill the character with ease[11]. The engagement of activities to play a 'game' different to that intended by design is commonly known as metagaming[12].

The existence and exploitation of program bugs to engage in unintended activities is the subject of much debate. Anecdotal evidence from discussion postings reveal that there is often argument over whether a feature used in an unintended way is exploitative, or just innovative and harmless. This is the more so when players themselves are not always privy to the inner workings of a game mechanism, which can make it difficult for them to know whether a game mechanism is really working as intended.

Having said this, some game operators will still treat the use of any bug as cheating, although taking advantage of bugs is regarded as a lesser offence compared to intentionally changing the way code works (Scholder & Zimmerman 2003, p. 216). When bugs are used in exploitative

---

[10] The term "code" as used here refers to the statements in a software program that instruct computer hardware. Code in the software program governs the actions a user is permitted, which can explain Lessig's (1999) remarks that "Code is law" in *The Industry Standard*.

[11] *Ultima Online* has a history of such exploitation, but recently has been successful in eliminating many of these exploits.

[12] Metagaming refers to the existence of a game system within another game.

fashion, players can become upset, particularly those who are unaware or refuse to use the bug on ethical grounds. Some particularly upset players may leave the game, which directly affects the business (Yan 2003). In severe cases, servers have to be brought down and code corrected with rollbacks to 'non' buggy states. While MMORPG developers constantly plug these loopholes and action is taken against such exploiters when they are discovered, these games are complex in design and code. Bug discovery and remedy action are difficult, and bugs in game code can continue to exist.

eBaying

Another challenge that has surfaced is eBaying. A character's prowess can limit the activities permitted. In *EverQuest* for example, prowess is measured in part by the quality of the equipment that character possesses. Often, this equipment is attained through involved adventures within the world. For example, upon the completion of a long and difficult task, the character may be awarded a sword that would endow him with improved capabilities.

Not every player wants to invest in the time and effort required to complete these tasks in order to gain these rewards. When there is a demand for such items to be gained without accomplishing the tasks normally required of it, there will be a supply to meet that demand. Since items can be traded among players in many games[13], situations where such virtual assets are sold for real-world cash have risen. The most common virtual asset sold is game money, which is the currency used in the game for a variety of tasks, including the purchase of equipment. A small sum of game money can be sold for hundreds of real-world dollars. The price of game money can be particularly high when it is scarce, for example when the game is in its infancy and the majority of its players are just starting out as low-level characters. These secondary markets have been estimated to range from USD100 to USD800 million a year in trade volume (Sony Online Entertainment Inc. 2005)[14]. The term eBaying in the context of MMORPGs has come about through the use of online auction houses of eBay and Yahoo! by players to expedite such transactions. Today, there are many web

---

[13] Some games do not allow certain items to be exchanged among players. For example, some items in *EverQuest 2* are marked 'No-trade'. The item may have been awarded only to the player who completes the quest, and cannot be traded away thereafter.

[14] In April 2005, Sony Online Entertainment announced plans to formally incorporate player selling of items for real-world dollars into selected game servers (Sony Online Entertainment Inc. 2005).

sites, for example http://www.playerauctions.com and http://www.ige.com, that specifically allow players of various MMORPGs to sell virtual assets for real-world money.

The large amount of money exchanging hands has resulted in some players playing the game for the express purpose of acquiring game currency which they sell for real-world money. Some players do this by camping[15] an area with the intent of acquiring an item repeatedly for resale[16]. At times, this is expedited through one person subscribing to multiple accounts which let him play multiple characters simultaneously. Playing multiple characters simultaneously is normally difficult, but there are third party programs that run scripted series of actions. This has the effect of automating tasks in the game that would not be possible or at least easy without the use of such programs. Using such programs, an *individual* can undertake tasks or defeat mobs that would normally require a *group* of characters played by individual persons. To best optimize the time investment and reward returns, this player will situate himself in a single location in the game world, repeatedly engage the same mob, and obtain its reward which he sells back to other players for game currency. These characters are known—and not in polite fashion—as 'botters'[17].

Many players feel that trading virtual assets for real-world cash "breaks the spirit of the game" (Lastowka & Hunter 2004), and many players dislike eBayers (Taylor 2002, p. 231). Botters are similarly disliked, as observed from discussion postings, but sometimes for a different reason. Assets within the game—for example prized items such as rare or powerful swords and amour pieces—are already scarce by game design. Competition to attain them can be fierce. A botter group which repeatedly 'harvests' the mobs for these items makes it difficult for other players to acquire the same item, as the mob is now monopolized by the botter group. This creates unhappiness among other players, and they frequently demand that the game operator take action. Some players also call such monopolization grief play. Game developers implement mechanisms to stop such programs from working, and game operators also attempt to catch botters and discipline them appropriately. Some game operators even work actively with auctioning sites to stop

---

[15] See Chapter 1 – 'Key terms'.

[16] This can occasionally lead to area monopolization and kill-stealing. See Chapter 4 – 'Greed play'.

[17] The term 'botter' is a derivative of 'bot'. Usage of the term bot varies, but it is often used to denote computer-controlled characters in first-person shooter games. Many bots are custom created by player enthusiasts. The bot carries out actions dictated in its instruction script. An MMORPG botter is a player who makes use of external programs that execute a pre-prepared series of instructions, and in so doing allows him to run multiple characters without the usual human participation.

transactions involving assets within their games from exchanging hands on those sites. For instance, in 2000, Sony Online Entertainment was successful in securing cooperation with eBay and Yahoo! to stop players of *EverQuest* from transacting their in-game assets on these sites (Taylor 2002, p. 230).

Bad behavior

Kolbert (2001) in her commentary for *The New Yorker* notes that MMORPGs from the start were supposed to have been 'self-policing' and not require direct attention from game operators. It is not easy for developers to create code that can fully deal with the large range of player behaviors and play styles. The high degree of player interactivity invariably creates situations where players impose on one another. Moreover, when there is conflict of behavior and play styles, disputes and arguments can occur. Players lodge 'petitions' requesting attention from customer service representatives (CSRs) of the game operator. When in-game, these employees are called 'game masters', and are trained to rule and mediate player disputes[18].

A third challenge that has surfaced is bad behavior in MMORPGs. Davis (2002) contextualizes bad behavior as perceived by users in the environment, and defines it as:

> Any aversive behavior users felt did not belong in a particular online environment.

According to this definition, grief play is one form of bad behavior since it disrupts the gaming experience of other players. However, it is not in the intention of this study to presuppose that grief play constitutes problematic behavior. Rather, the term 'bad behavior' is merely a suggestion that there are players who perceive the behavior as such. The choice of research methods employed in the study took into account the need to explore if grief play is indeed a problem[19].

Grief play

Bad behavior in online gaming worlds in itself is not a new phenomenon. Studies of MUDs from the early to mid-90s, for example Bruckman et al. (1994) and Reid (1994), note that antisocial behavior existed even then. In 1993, Dibbell's "*A Rape in Cyberspace*" (1993) reported an antisocial act in a MUD that resulted in widespread shock and outrage.

---

[18] See Chapter 6 for a further discussion of petitions and customer service.

[19] See Chapter 3.

The American Heritage Dictionary of the English Language defines 'grief' as "a source of deep mental anguish", "annoyance or frustration". What grief play is can be determined through the existing definitions of griefers. Mulligan & Patrovsky's (2003, p. 475) definition of a griefer is:

> A player who derives his/her enjoyment not from playing the game, but from performing actions that detract from the enjoyment of the game by other players.

Lin & Sun's (2005) definition contains similar elements to the above:

> A grief player engages in playing to disrupt or distress other players' gaming experiences, and derives enjoyment from such behavior.

In scholarly work, there seems to be consensus about the general characteristics of activities that a griefer engages in, and these characteristics are accepted as a working definition of grief play. Specifically, grief play is seen to be intentional and disruptive to players affected by it, but enjoyable to the player who perpetrates it. Grief play is comparable to online troll behavior found in virtual communities (Smith 2004, p. 12). Online 'trolling' is described as deceptive behavior where a member of the community intentionally deceives and enjoys the disruption and damaging of trust within the community (Donath 1999, p. 45). Sage (2003, p. 90) further describes the effects a griefer can cause on players and the game operator. In *Ultima Online*, one griefer who killed players in-game caused over 50 calls for CSR attention every night. The calls came from irate players complaining against the griefer. According to Goslin et al. (2003), players can have a low tolerance for grief play (p. 14).

Grief play can also be associated with teasing and bullying. The motivation of griefers in some of their activities, for example, 'newbie-killing'[20] (Foo & Koivisto 2004, p. 248), apparently stems from a desire to demonstrate power and superiority over weaker participants. This desire to dominate is consistent with observations made in teasing and bullying (Land 2003, p. 155). Besag (1989) and Galloway (cited in Bosworth et al. 1999, p. 342) also characterize bullying as actions with the deliberate intention of causing distress to others. These characterizations are similar to grief play, and are elaborated in Chapter 5.

---

[20] Foo & Koivisto (2004, p. 248) define newbie-killing as the killing of new and frequently inexperienced players of the game. Newbie-killing as a form of grief play is discussed in Chapter 4.

Grief play in an MMORPG is further exemplified by several characteristics. Firstly, there is contention over the type of activities that should be classified as grief play. Literature suggests that grief play is intentional, but early investigation in the study noted that in some circumstances, players may regard disruptive activities as grief play even if the perpetrators may not have been intending to disrupt their gaming experience (Foo & Koivisto 2004, p. 246). Furthermore, some griefers attempt to excuse their activities by claiming it is role-playing on their part.

Secondly, griefers are adept at adjusting their play styles around rules. Certain types of activities can be made impossible through code. However, even though MMORPGs often include statements in the End-User Licensing Agreement (EULA), Terms of Service (TOS), or Rules of Conduct[21] (ROC) that disallow players from playing in ways that disrupt the enjoyment of others, in practice, game operators often take action against griefers only when their intention to disrupt is explicitly demonstrated. Players themselves employ their own norms of behavior when assessing the permissibility of an activity. An explanation of rules in an MMORPG will be presented in a later section of this chapter, and the issues regarding intention in relation to player and developer perceptions will be elaborated upon in Chapter 4.

Thirdly, the effects of griefer activities can be considerable. This is even though the number of griefers in an MMORPG may be quite small—Pizer (2003, p. 431) notes that just 3 percent of players grief. One player [R27] describes an incident where a large scale player-run event in *Ultima Online* was disrupted by a small number of players:

> We had a circumstance recently … in which an in-game RP (role-playing) event was griefed by about 5 players. Two guilds were formed to represent the pirates attacking Trinsic and the Trinsic defenders, respectively. This involved about 100 players and was to last about three hours with about 5 battles. … At the time the event was to start, one griefer decides to destroy all our defenses by breaking up the weighted boxes we had made to stop the attackers. Other griefers joined the defenders guild and spent the first 10 minutes stealing from the crafters and supply persona and then went into the opposing guilds 'safe area' killing and looting them. Looting was not allowed. As a result, the event was called (off) after about 15 minutes.

This incident is known as the "Trinsic incident", and is cited in later chapters.

---

[21] The Rules of Conduct (ROC), Terms of Service (TOS), and End-User License Agreement (EULA) are documents supplied in the game. They may be displayed prominently in the game manual, on the game's web site, or displayed as an information screen each time a user logs into the game. For simplicity purposes, these documents will be collectively referred to as the ROC in this book.

Two of these characteristics of grief play need to be elaborated upon before a full discussion of grief play can begin. They are role-playing, and rules in MMORPGs.

Role-playing and grief play

Role-playing a fictional character in an MMORPG means that, ideally, the player should adopt behavior and mannerisms that are consistent with a character in that setting. For instance, a player who role-plays the club-wielding troll in a fantastic setting should not engage in intelligent discourse on how magic is cast in the world. In traditional tabletop role-playing games, the Dungeon Master can be expected to enforce rules of player behavior. He could simply state "that behavior is not allowed by your character", and that would be the end of discussion. In comparison, while rule sets exist in today's MMORPGs (see next section), governing player behavior is more difficult. For example, game mechanics can be created where characters of different races are unable to communicate with one another. Words spoken by participants playing elfish characters would appear as gibberish to participants playing troll characters since they are of different races and speaking different languages (in the game). However, it is much harder to create code to stop characters of a similar race from engaging in abusive behavior against each other. Code can filter offensive words so that they do not get displayed on the player's screen, but abuse can still happen without the use of offensive words.

The early MMORPGs used rules that gave players leeway in the kind of activities they could impose on one another. *Ultima Online* for instance allows a player to steal items from another player. It also allows PvP as a form of player activity, and even explicitly warns players that they can be attacked by others when they leave the safe havens of urban cities. In essence, one could argue that these are 'role' playing games after all. In principle, players should be able to role-play unsavory characters (like thieves and murderers) alongside players who role-play morally upright characters (like virtuous knights). However, some players began to take player versus player combat to the limit. They relentlessly killed new players, or engaged in types of behavior that other players found abusive or distasteful[22]. Some players engaged in these behaviors because of a

---

[22] Games can be designed to discourage or stop players who are powerful compared to their targets from repeatedly attacking their victims over and over again. For example, code disallowing a high-level player from attacking a low-level one can be written. However, levels are not the only indicators of player ability—other indicators could include individual skill. Code can only go so far in distinguishing levels of prowess; it would be hard to write code to stop a highly skilled player griefing another at the same level.

genuine desire to role-play their characters in a fashion that is consistent with its type. Moreover, the context of a fantastic role-playing game suggests that violence is legitimate. It has been argued that it is a reasonable expectation that one's character in an RPG will be at some point "abused, violated, dismembered and exterminated" (Powers 2003, p. 197). Reid (1999, p. 123) further argues that player-killing for some adds depth to the virtual world. However, even despite such premises in a fantastic role-playing game, few players in early *Ultima Online* at least liked having their characters killed repeatedly or in abusive fashion. For them, it was tantamount to harassment and unwarranted abuse. Based on their experiences of having been victims, many players believed that the intention of the players engaging in repeated player-killing and abusive behavior was to grief. Role-playing or not, such behavior was intolerable for them.

For some, role-playing refers more to how a character should be developed in terms of his skills and abilities that will in turn determine his responsibilities in team situations (Oliver 2002). This is as opposed to role-playing that demands a player interacts with other players in ways that are consistent with the character type, as described earlier in this section. A journalistic article in *LA Times* in 2002 cites two examples of griefers; one claimed he fed on the negative reactions of other players when he succeeded in ruining their experiences, and another claimed it gave him a feeling of empowerment over his victims (Pham 2002). The sentiments expressed by the griefers in this article corroborate with that observed in discussion postings by griefers. Some players question if a true role-player should be deriving such enjoyment from causing other players misery and seeing them suffer, as opposed to deriving enjoyment from playing a particular character type with certain skills and abilities. The motivations to grief are an important aspect of the study, and are discussed further in Chapter 5.

In some games, game masters seem reluctant to intervene when these incidents happen. PvP combat is an allowed game mechanism in some games. The manner in which players are killed could be merely an issue of individual style for an accepted activity. The producer of *Ultima Online*, Richard Garriott, when interviewed in 1998 by *Wired News*, remarked that *Ultima Online* was designed to support the role-playing of evil characters (Kim 1998). In addition, in response to players who were complaining about grief play, he maintained the importance of player self-policing by remarking that:

> Those who have truly learned the lessons of the Ultima games should cease their complaining, rise to the challenge, and make Britannia[23] into the place they want it to be.

Whether these play styles are intended to be genuine manifestations of role-played behavior or not, player-killing and other abusive behavior in *Ultima Online* upset a lot of players. In a later commentary published in *The New Yorker* (Kolbert 2001), it was reported that griefers in *Ultima Online* succeeded in tormenting the players so much that the game world was split into half just so to separate griefers from the other players. Clearly, the effects of grief play can impact the game operation. The expectation of the game operator is for players to resolve disputes on their own. Alongside the expectations of players on grief play management, these are key interest areas in the study, and will be discussed in Chapter 7.

Rules in an MMORPG

Preece (2001, p. 349) notes that the existence of policies in virtual communities contributes to good sociability. In fact, the governance that emerges from these policies is a requirement for a virtual community (de Moor & Wagenvoort 2004), and such policies, along with its members, are typically key areas of interest for researchers (Preece & Maloney-Krichmar 2005). These policies, or rules as they will be known in this book, can be formal or informal, but they all provide a basis to govern the community. When players report on grief play incidents, there is often debate over whether the activity is allowed or disallowed by rules. Hence, a second consideration in MMORPGs is its rules. While problematic behavior may be rule-breaking, any discussion of such behavior will also need to take into account rule making and rule enforcement (Sternberg 2001, p. 266). In the context of an MMORPG, such a tripartite consideration is important as bad behavior typically breaks rules (whether formal or informal ones), while rule making and enforcement stipulates the response on the part of service providers and how such behavior will be regulated.

On rule making, Järvinen (2003) proposes a topology comprising multiple types of rules, each governing a different game element. Other authors also describe rule models that distinguish from one type to the next. For instance, Salen & Zimmerman (2004, p. 139) use a model comprising three levels—constitutive rules which are the "abstract, core mathematical rules", operational rules which are the "rules of play" that players follow, and implicit rules which are the "'unwritten rules' of etiquette and behavior". A similar set of rules is cited in Sternberg's (2001) work on virtual

---

[23] The name of the fictional world in *Ultima Online*.

communities: that rules can be technical, formal, and informal (p. 280). In this study, Salen & Zimmerman's (2004) model has been adopted to form a taxonomy of rules:

1. 'Law of code' or what has been written into program code.

2. Rules found in the ROC accompanying MMORPG titles, which are referred to as 'game rules' in this study.

3. Implicit rules which are the loosely defined, social rules of fair-play and etiquette expected by players.

An example of Law of code is code that governs whether players can engage in non-consensual PvP activity against each other. An example of a game rule is a rule that governs whether players are allowed to 'train' (see below) mobs on other players. An example of an implicit rule is the expectation for players to share a contested mob that spawns infrequently in a zone.

Law of code rules are sacrosanct in a game and normally impossible to break (Lastowka & Hunter 2004), and in this sense they can enforce rules of play. Program code that governs sensitive aspects of the game is especially protected. This is in contrast to a MUD like *LambdaMOO* which allowed users with appropriate programming skills to write their own subprograms; one user was able to commit virtual rape by writing code to give himself additional powers over other users (Beaubien 1996, p. 187). However, depending on the resilience of game code in the MMORPG, it may still be possible to employ third party programs that modify game logic, as described in an earlier section. Alternatively, given the complexity of code in these games, an existing loophole that has been overlooked in game design may be exploited. Taking the example in the taxonomy of rules above, players cannot normally engage in PvP unless they have consciously taken some predefined action in the game consenting to such activity. If such an activity is still inflicted on players who have not consented, it could be through the use of third party programs or code exploitation. Game operators often disallow both methods of changing the game as it is designed and intended. For example, the EULA of *Dark Age of Camelot* (Mythic Entertainment Inc. 2001) states the following:

> You may not use your or third-party software to rewrite or modify the user interface or otherwise manipulate data in such a way as to use the System to acquire items, currency, objects, character attributes or beneficial actions not actually acquired or performed in the Game.

Game rules are complementary with Law of code, and can formalize rules of play that are too complex to code. In the example above, mobs may be designed through code to automatically

17

acquire new players to attack when an existing target they are chasing resets. This happens if the mob's initial targets run too far or teleport themselves away to escape. The other players in the vicinity can thus be attacked by a mob that did not 'belong' to them. During the chase, other nearby mobs may also become aggressive against nearby players. This results in a 'train' forming as a chain of mobs chases players across a play area. While such a game design element may have been intended to increase the level of challenge experienced by players, it can also be used by players to grief others. It may be possible to reduce or even eliminate through code the occurrence of trains altogether. However, when no such code exists, rules forbidding intentional trains from forming would be stated in game rules to disallow such behavior.

Implicit rules in an MMORPG can be likened to community norms. These norms, or the standards of behavior that players believe are appropriate for the game, influence the expectations players have of each other. Smith (2004, p. 4) notes that the intense debates among players regarding these rules often gravitate towards the "spirit of the game". Breaking implicit rules do not always mean that game rules are also broken (outside a possible general game rule stating that players must 'play nice'—see Chapter 4). Consider an analogy: there is usually no law in the real-world demanding that a person must stand in line to use a public telephone if there is already a queue. But there would be a societal expectation that people should queue up to use the telephone. Cutting in line is rude under such an expectation. This analogy can be applied to implicit rules in MMORPGs. For example, there may not be game rules demanding players share contested mobs, and it may be impossible for Law of code to enforce sharing. However, implicit rules may still expect players to share. Implicit rules are not usually made explicit by the game operator. Rather, many implicit rules operate on the basis of decency and courteous behavior among players. They are extensions of behaviors that are already present in the real-world, and thus rarely communicated by the game operator or among players. For instance, the sharing of contested mobs is identical to the real-world equivalents—for example waiting in line at the telephone queue or taking turns to play with playground equipment—but such rules are rarely put into statements. The more complex implicit rules without immediate real-world equivalents tend to be communicated among players through word of mouth. Whether implicit rules should be formally stated by the game operator is debatable. In non-PvP game environments at least, there are usually general game rules in MMORPGs requiring players to play in ways where they are not abusive to each other.

There is a strong interplay between rules—both game and implicit—and grief play. For game masters ruling on incidents, whether intentionally disruptive play activities are disallowed or allowed and to what degree ultimately depend on what game rules state. Even then, where game rules may disallow such activities, enforcement is still difficult. Moreover, some players rely on implicit rules and can perceive a disruptive activity to be grief play and demand responses from the game operator, regardless of what the game rules might say. The book will address these issues, alongside rule-breaking in Chapter 4.

This chapter has introduced MMORPGs, explained some of its key terms, and discussed the role-playing and rule considerations surrounding these games. The next chapter looks at the existing body of knowledge related to grief play.

CHAPTER 2: LITERATURE REVIEW

This chapter investigates areas of knowledge related to grief play. Keeping in mind that the study was explorative, some areas of interest could be identified early, for example bad behavior and computer-mediated communication. Other areas of interest only surfaced after some data was collected and analyzed. Reference to research in emerging areas was made at several junctures throughout the study. These new areas included teasing, bullying, and Hardin's (1968) "the tragedy of the commons".

The chapter begins with an overview of current MMORPG research. There have been several studies of social and cultural aspects of MMORPG players and communities, but little on grief play itself. However, there is abundant literature on computer-mediated communication (CMC) and virtual communities. The definition of virtual community adopted for use in this work emphasizes the presence of shared interests among participants. In particular, two experiences that draw people to virtual communities are focused on: identity play, and mastery over the environment; these two experiences will be related to motivations for players to grief. The chapter will also present literature pertaining to bad behavior that occurs on the Internet. In particular, it discusses a well-reported and researched incident in *LambdaMOO* MUD, called "*A Rape in Cyberspace*".

The reduction of social cues and anonymity are commonly cited as factors in contributing to antisocial behavior online. These factors and research of disinhibition and dissociative anonymity are also considered. The chapter next discusses the governance and management of virtual communities. Also, since grief play has been related to teasing and bullying, literature surrounding these behaviors will be presented. Finally, a model known as the tragedy of commons that pertains to the use of scarce resources in communal environments is presented.

MMORPG research

Online gaming did not always attract the same level of attention it does today. Ducheneaut & Moore (2004, p. 360) note that it took almost 15 years after the creation of the first MUD for the first serious examination of social interaction in MUDs, even though these games had been designed with social interaction among participants in mind.

Today, there is growing interest in the study of MMORPGs. This is shown by the increasing amount of research and initiation of projects studying various areas of interest, and also the establishment of research communities centered on MMOG research. One such community is Terra Nova at http://terranova.blogs.com, which focuses on social aspects of online gaming communities. Another vibrant community is MUD-Dev, short for "Discussion of MUD system design, development, and implementation" at http://www.kanga.nu/lists/listinfo/mud-dev, which is participated in by MUD and MMORPG game developers. There is also a continuous generation of publications investigating various aspects of MMORPG design—for instance, its usability aspects (Cornett 2004).

There are also other quantitative projects studying player demography and behavior. They include Yee's *The Daedalus Project* at http://www.nickyee.com/daedalus which has surveyed 35,000 MMORPG players since project initiation in 1999, and *Project Massive* at http://www.projectmassive.com, conducted by a team of researchers from the Human-Computer Interaction Institute at Carnegie Mellon University. There is also a third well-known project which tracks MMOG subscriptions at http://www.mmogchart.com.

Of particular interest in this study is the investigation of socio-cultural aspects of MMORPGs, since grief play is largely a social issue[24]. Brown & Bell (2004) argue in their study of multi-player games as collaborative virtual environments that:

> Games are not just an intriguing application of collaborative technology: massive multi-player games feature new and surprising complex forms of online social organization. (p. 350)

One of the most well-known social studies conducted of MUDs that has influenced today's research of MMORPGs is Richard Bartle's 1996 paper on player types. While his model of player types was created 10 years ago, it is still widely referenced today by MMOG researchers studying player behavior and motivations. Bartle's 1996 work was extended upon in his more recent 2004 book on the design of online games. His findings are related to grief play in Chapters 4 and 5. The investigation of the communal aspects of MMORPGs is also of interest in this study. Jakobsson & Taylor's (2003) study of social networking among players reveal the importance of reputation and social capital in player communities. Another study is Koivisto's (2003) paper on how MMORPG communities can be supported through game design. In it, she identifies chat mechanisms, house establishments, and tools for the organization of player communities as mechanisms put into

---

[24] See Chapter 8 – 'Discussion'.

MMORPGs to support such communities. MMORPGs have also been investigated as learning environments (Delwiche 2003; Papargyris & Poulymenakou 2004). Delwiche (2003) cites the use of role-playing as particularly effective in this regard, since they require the participant to view the environment through different perspectives. In so doing, he argues that perspectives on broader theoretical and professional aspects of MMORPGs can be gained.

Despite the existence of work investigating various socio-cultural aspects of MMORPGs, there has been relatively little research on grief play. This is despite the abundance of data generated about it in discussion forums. Players often post emotionally-charged accounts of incidents when they were griefed, for instance into public discussion forums like rec.games.computer.ultima.online in the case of *Ultima Online*, or discussion forums managed by the game operator. Interestingly, while disruptive play styles existed in MUDs, there is no indication where or when the term grief play was first used to describe these play styles. However, an investigation of Usenet newsgroups revealed that the term grief play as used occurred in *Ultima Online* as early as 2000, even though disruptive play styles have existed in the game since inception in 1997. The literature review revealed that there is an occasional mention of grief play in news or popular media, and griefers are cited in published literature; for example as a player type in Bartle's (2004, p. 167) work. There is also a smattering of research papers on grief play, for instance Lin & Sun's (2005) work on griefers in Taiwanese MMORPGs. Beyond this, there is little formal research on grief play and how it should be managed. As far as I am aware, this work is the first substantial study of grief play.

CMC and virtual communities

Since MMORPGs are a form of virtual community making use of CMC, literature on this subject was reviewed early in the study. CMC can encompass any communication that is facilitated through computer technology. One definition of CMC is as follows:

> Any form of interpersonal communication that uses some form of computer technology to transmit, store, annotate, or present information that has been created by one or more participants. (Wolz et al. 1997, p. 51)

Many computer-based tools of communication fall within this definition of CMC. These tools include e-mailing, Internet messaging, discussion forums, and interactive computer games. Computer-based communication expedites the exchange of information and ideas. Virtual communities allow a person to seek out another with similar ideas or knowledge (Igbaria 1999, p. 68). The term virtual community is commonly used to describe instances of CMC where a group of people meet, discuss and converse in settings of persistence. Individuals in the virtual community can engage in commercial transactions, discussion of shared interests, or socialization (Porter 2004). Rheingold (2000) famously posits that virtual communities:

> ...are social aggregations that emerge from the Net when enough people carry on those public discussions long enough, with sufficient human feeling, to form webs of personal relationships in cyberspace.

Key to the existence of these communities is the shared interest they are oriented around (Gotved 2002, p. 406; Ridings et al. 2002, p. 271). Of the many definitions of a virtual community offered by scholars, Porter's (2004) definition has been adopted for use in this study. Her definition emphasizes the presence of shared interest in the activity the community engages in, and notes that they can be operated as business interests:

> A virtual community is defined as an aggregation of individuals or business partners who interact around a shared interest, where the interaction is at least partially supported and/or mediated by technology and guided by some protocols or norms.[25]

Roberts (1998) provides an interesting point on the word 'community'. She argues that this word does not have a specific meaning as it has been used in a "metaphorical sense" for a long period of time (p. 361). Some authors (for example Ridings et al. 2002, p. 272; Andrews 2004, p. 64) argue that communities are no longer defined as physical places, but by the social relationships that exist among people in it. The use of the word indeed seems general, because a community according to the literal sense of the word and as used in the online context could comprise every person who is connected on the Internet. In other words, every person online is a member of a larger Internet community. On the other hand, Bakardjieva (2003, p. 292) recognizes that there are many variations of "virtual togetherness"—or the different ways people can engage one another while online. Hence, she argues that it is not appropriate to use the term virtual community to describe all the social activities that people conduct online. This is where the idea of 'shared interests' noted by Gotved (2002, p. 406) and in Porter's (2004) definition comes in. In this study, the word community will normally be used to denote smaller sized groups more focused in purpose. Specifically, player communities[26] in this study refer to persistent groups organized in a game, and

---

[25] A distinctive characteristic of the virtual community is in its residence as an online environment. I use the term 'online environment' in this study generally to mean areas where interaction is expedited through CMC, particularly in reference to the Internet.

[26] See Chapter 1 – 'Key terms'.

its members can number from a dozen to several hundred people. These communities possess dimensions similar to other virtual communities, including: purpose around a shared interest, cohesion and a sense of collective identity, interaction among community members, and self-policing (Roberts 1998, p. 361).

Also of interest is how virtual communities compare to real-world communities. It has been argued (for example in Bakardjieva 2003, p. 293) that virtual communities should not be seen as inferior representations of interactions among people just because they lack a face-to-face dimension. Indeed, modern real-world communities can possess characteristics not so dissimilar to those found in their virtual cousins (Wellman & Gulia 1999, p. 187), since communication in real-world communities can be similarly mediated and imagined. An example of this is the use of telephones to maintain ties among members of the community. Turkle (1995) echoes a similar sentiment—that the virtual world need not be perceived as separable from the real-world. In fact, the interactions of members in a virtual community can offer a model of social change that a virtual community makes on real lives (Rheingold 2000). Another element of virtual communities that is of interest in this study is social capital, which "encourages collaboration and cooperation between members" (Preece 2004, p. 37). Social capital can also act as a cushion against the emergence of conflict (de Moor & Wagenvoort 2004).

People are drawn to virtual communities in different ways. Bromberg (1996, p. 147-149) cites major social functions that users can experience. Users who are isolated find comfort in interactive CMC. Upon getting online, some even isolate themselves from earthly environments in favor of virtual ones. Another function is identity play, which allows users to explore and adopt alternate or preferred identities, occasionally even identities that they do not express in the real-world (Suler 2002, p. 456). Bromberg (1996) also notes the erotic appeal some users find in virtual communities—not only in the engagement of "netsex" but also in the very transcension from the physical to the virtual world. Lastly, the mastery—for example technological—over the virtual environment is appealing to some users, as it gives them a sense of power. Such mastery of the environment and the sense of power attained is similar to motivations exhibited in MMORPGs: some players play to achieve (Bartle 1996), and a sense of power can be attained through the accomplishment of in-game objectives.

Having defined virtual communities and taken a look at the experiences that draw people to them, the next section turns to bad behavior in virtual communities.

24

Bad behavior in virtual communities

According to Herring (2004, p. 30), the demography of CMC users is changing. Today's users are younger and less technically skilled than the first users of CMC. She argues that this has led to an overall decline in the quality of discourse, resulting in publicly accessible CMCs that are "more noisy, fragmented, and contentious" (p. 30) than private domains. While the lower quality of discourse and the increasing noise should not be immediately attributed to bad behavior, it does hint that online environments may be contentious places. Finn (2004, p. 470) notes the presence of risk-taking and asocial behavior in online environments. Some behavior people on the Internet demonstrate when they talk to one another has been described as 'primitive' and 'childish' (Holland 1996). One scholar whose work is frequently referenced is Suler (1997). He wrote a lengthy treatment describing the various forms of online bad behavior and different approaches to management. In the context of online gaming, studies conducted reveal that the presence of bad conduct online is common. Davis' (2002) quantitative study of bad behavior in online multi-player games notes that 75.4% of respondents in his study had personally experienced bad behavior.

Sternberg (2001, p. 13) uses the term 'misbehavior' in her work on online behavior, defining it as "behavior which does not conform to norms and which breaks rules." Whilst recognizing that other authors make use of synonymous terms to describe bad behavior, she argues that the word misbehavior is neutral compared to words like antisocial behavior, which implies intent. Similarly, she notes that the term deviant behavior implies "moral pervasion" (p. 13). However, for the purpose of this study on grief play, the use of the word misbehavior to describe grief play could have posed a problem—because grief play does not always break rules instituted by the game operator. In fact, in some cases, grief play does not even break community rules (although the behavior will still be perceived by the afflicted as unpleasant). Hence, another word had to be chosen. The term decided upon is 'bad behavior', with the term 'bad' taken to mean something that is unpleasant, disagreeable, or disturbing. Davis' (2002) definition of the term bad behavior has been adopted for operational reasons, and is again:

Any aversive behavior users felt did not belong in a particular online environment.

His definition avoids the implication that grief play—as a form of bad behavior—breaks rules instituted by the provider. Also, this definition emphasizes that bad behavior is predicated on the perception of users. This is an important consideration in grief play, and will be discussed in Chapter 4.

Of interest here is also research on behavior in MUDs, since MUDs are the predecessors of MMORPGs. In particular, one study of bad behavior in MUDs should be mentioned. This incident is "*A Rape in Cyberspace*", as reported by Dibbell in 1993. In this incident, a user who obtained additional privileges by writing special code in the *LambdaMOO* MUD was able to take over another user's character. He then narrated a variety of sexually-oriented activities on that user's character (Dibbell 1993).

Dibbell's account has been studied by many authors. Among them is MacKinnon (1998). In his analysis of the incident, MacKinnon poses questions that relate directly to the subjectivity of activities that occur online. In the incident, the perpetrator had not uttered the word rape and it is only by interpretation of the incident did one conclude that rape had occurred (p. 152). Dibbell (1993) himself notes that the incident had taken place in the "realm of the symbolic". No one suffered any physical harm per se, although Huff et al. (2003) provides a contrasting point in this regard (see below). Moreover, MacKinnon (1998) posits that virtual environments allow participants to selectively attribute meanings and significance to events that occur there (p. 152). This points to the subjectivity of participant perception in the interpretation of activities in virtual communities.

However, whilst the rape took place in a virtual environment, scholars argue that the kind of distress and harm that can still result from actions online should not be trivialized. Dibbell (1993) in his article revealed that the victims were distressed by the incident. Huff et al. (2003, p. 15) in their own analysis note that virtual characters do not act unless the physical individuals behind them act. They remark that these actions have effects on both virtual characters and on real people. The act of rape in this case had been what Williams (2000, p. 95) calls a re-engineering from a physically manifested act into a textual but still harmful performance[27]. Powers (2003) has a similar sentiment: that the actions of perpetrator of this rape incident constituted "real moral wrongs" (p. 191). With reference to the rape incident, he writes:

---

[27] Williams (2000, p. 96) has an additional and interesting comment on virtual criminality and the real-world systems to deal with it. He remarks that real-world legal systems have yet to catch up with what he calls "sub-criminal" behavior in virtual communities. One reason he cites is that virtual communities tend to favor their own methods for conflict management. This in turn nudges research on conflict management into media and communication disciplines of study, which he believes currently suffers from a lack of adequate understanding in "criminological matters of deviance, regulation and forms of online justice."

> ... We should begin by acknowledging that there were real actions by members of this virtual community, and not merely virtual actions by the characters on a screen. (p. 193)

It is on this basis that the virtual rape incident aroused interest in the bad behavior of participants in virtual communities, as scholars recognized that the hurt and injury caused could be real to the victims. In the context of online games, the lack of consequences is a factor in encouraging game players to behave in the worst possible way, as Pritchard (2000) notes in a commentary on hackers and cheaters for *Gamasutra.com*. When a player is caught—for instance, for using hack programs—to beat his opponents, normally, real-world punishment like paying fines cannot be meted out for his behavior. He may be rejected by other players, but it is not difficult to return to the game in a new identity, and no one will know better. Jensen et al. (2002, p. 447) also posit that policing systems that exist in online spaces are reactive by nature—they are not as effective in prevention[28].

The relation of rules to bad behavior is also critical in any discussion. Sternberg (2001) notes the existence of 'rules' and 'norms' in the regulation of misbehavior in virtual communities. The propensity of bad behavior depends on the permissibility of that environment, and whether or not stated rules are enforced and punishment meted out for rule breakers. If there are no consequences, participants will misbehave (Pritchard 2000).

Also of interest are the causes that lead people to exhibit bad behavior online. Preece (2004, p. 58) highlights some underlying reasons: they include unintentionally annoying ways of communicating, a lack of sensitivity towards another person's feelings, and simply malicious behavior. Joinson & Dietz-Uhler (2002, p. 279) also posit that the Internet itself seems to be an ideal playground for people with sociopathic tendencies. They argue that psychiatric illness in the real-world could be a possible reason for people engaging in attention seeking and deceptive types of activities. Furthermore, advances in modern communication technology make it possible for the common person to have easier access to nearly everyone else. Also, some individuals derive greater enjoyment from competitive activities than others, and will be drawn to games which include such situations where they can challenge and beat their opponents (Vorderer et al. 2003, p. 5). However, such competition can also be a precursor to aggression and hostility in games (Williams & Clippinger 2002, p. 496). This is echoed by Davis (2002), who remarks that the competitive nature

---

[28] Discussion on policing and response systems to grief play will be presented in Chapter 8.

of online games, coupled also with the age of players, leads to bad behavior among players. The reasons cited in literature here—ignorance, competition, and the circumstances of the environment—are related to motivators that can compel a person to grief, and will be discussed in Chapter 5.

Reduced Social Cues

Having discussed the presence of bad behavior online and in MUDs and also why it occurs, initial observations of data on grief play also revealed that many players believe bad behavior stems in part from anonymity. The common argument lies in that a reduction of social cues (from being anonymous) leads to a loss of inhibition, and is a possible precursor for bad behavior. This section reviews literature pertaining to the loss of social cues, and the anonymity that can result.

Collins (1992) describes social cues as:

> The various geographic, organizational, and situation variables that influence the content of conversation among persons.

Cues can be static or dynamic (Sproull & Kiesler 1986, p. 1495). Static cues are produced from a person's appearance and artifacts, and dynamic cues are produced from a person's nonverbal behavior, which may change over the duration of the interaction. The physical world is filled with cues of both types (Gupta & Pu 2003, p. 245), with communication media varying in how rich or minimal these cues are (Sproull & Kiesler 1986, p. 1496). A face-to-face conversation can be rich in contextual cues as participants receive visual and auditory sensory information on the nuances of the message. These cues in turn help manage the communication exchange (Kiesler et al. 1991, p. 333). These cues are minimized in written communication like letter writing, and particularly in computer-mediated communication, for example emailing or discussion forum posting. In the context of MMORPGs, there are usually no visual cues for players to draw on. There is some limited use of audio facilities, but normally only to support collaborative types of game play, for example a raid[29] event.

There are important effects arising from the minimization of social cues in CMC. Some users of CMC find it difficult to discuss matters that may evoke strong reactions or feelings among

---

[29] See Chapter 1 – 'Key terms'.

participants (Adrianson & Hjelmquist 1999, p. 180). Other authors point to less restrained behavior. For example, Siegel et al. (1986, p. 161) argue that CMC reduces "feelings of embarrassment, guilt, and empathy for others", and Kiesler et al. (1991, p. 339) in their study of student groups note that the participants in CMC demonstrated behavior that was more uninhibited than those who were making use of face-to-face communication. The cause for this seems to be a loss of concern from the message originator on how recipients will respond to the message (Lee 2005). The absence of some social cues can lead to a reduction of social constraint towards misbehavior and influence of prevalent social norms expected by participants in that environment (Thompsen 1997, p. 301; O'Sullivan & Flanagin 2003, p. 71). The reduction of social cues in CMC encourages psychological states that lead to disinhibited and anti-normative behavior (Spears & Lea 1992, p. 37; Lea et al. 1992).

In the context of the Internet, Joinson (1998, p. 44) describes disinhibition as "behavior that is less inhibited than comparative behavior in real life". One example of disinhibited behavior is flaming (Lea et al. 1992). Flaming takes place in text-based forms of CMC, and is defined as hostile and aggressive interactions (Siegel et al. 1986, p. 161; O'Sullivan & Flanagin 2003, p. 69; Phillips 1996, p. 50). It is often characterized by harsh language, swearing and insults. The loss of social cues can lead to the institution of unruly and anti-hierarchical environments (Denegri-Knott 2003). It can also hinder the development of trust (Riddings et al. 2002, p. 275), which is in itself a key component in the building of social capital among participants of a community (Preece 2002, p. 37).

Another term associated with the reduction of social cues is deindividuation. Deindividuation refers to a psychological state where an individual becomes less self-aware (Postmes et al. 2001, p. 1244), and loses his sense of personal distinctiveness and identity (Reicher cited in Taylor & MacDonald 2002, p. 264). Deindividuation is argued to result in behavior that is compliant to the group, but it can also result in behavior that is emotional and irrational (Zimbardo cited in Hiltz et al. 1989, p. 220) or disinhibited (Siegel et al. 1986, p. 183). Such "depersonalization" of CMC (Kiesler et al. 1991, p. 342) can cause participants to become more reckless and assertive, and less likely to feel bound by societal norms that may have been established by the group. Tresca's (1998) quantitative study of anonymity and inflammatory Usenet postings revealed newsgroups where participants that were highly anonymous exhibited more inflammatory characteristics. Specifically, participants in these communities were more disposed to using expletives and emphasizing their arguments with

29

pointed notations, for example capital letters and exclamation marks (Tresca 1998). Many scholars note that anonymity encourages aggressive, hostile or dishonest behavior; including Smith (1999, p. 156), Utz (2000), Williams (2000, p. 100), Finn (2004, p. 470) and Suler (2004).

The chain of argument here so far seems to be this: when social cues are reduced, participants become more anonymous, and their inhibitions to bad behavior are lessened and they become less self-aware. Having said this, other studies propose that anonymity does not necessarily reduce self-awareness (Postmes et al. 2001, p. 1244). In fact, some scholars argue it may result in greater and not lesser self-awareness and possibly even normative behavior in online groups (Lea et al. 2001). In particular, the 'Social Identity Model of Deindividuation Effects' (Lea et al. 2001, p. 527) proposes that anonymity results in a shift of self-awareness from personal to group. According to Lea et al. (2001), anonymity actually leads to a reduction of "(inter)personal basis for social comparison, self-awareness, and self-presentation", and projects the group identity instead:

> Because anonymity removes interpersonal cues, it decreases attention to others, reduces concerns about being positively evaluated by others, and creates an impersonal, task-oriented focus for group interaction. (Lea et al. 2001, p. 528)

Furthermore, other scholars (Spears & Lea 1992; Walther 1997; Sassenberg & Boos 2003; Spears et al. 2002) note that the projection of identity—whether individual or group—depends also on the specific social context. In cases where personal identity is projected (Sassenberg & Boos 2003, p. 407), behavior will be individualistic and distinct. When a social or group identity is projected, behavior will be affected by group norms (Walther 1997). Thus, Postmes & Spears (2002, p. 1075) argue that stereotypical behavior should be more common online than less. However, the size of the player base in an MMORPG coupled with the fact that the player base itself is fragmented into smaller sized player communities makes it hard to say for certain if individual or group identity is projected. Still, the book will argue later that in some cases, players who are not normally inclined to cause misery on other players' experiences may still grief in order to fit into their player communities[30].

For other researchers, anonymity may not be a cause for bad behavior. Joinson (1998, p. 47) proposes this view when he discusses the causes of disinhibited behavior on the Internet. He cites an earlier study where he discovered that behavior on the World Wide Web continued to be

---

[30] See Chapter 5 – 'Griefer influenced'.

30

disinhibited even when participants were named. Hiltz et al. (1989, p. 227) in their study of behavior in computer conferences found that the relationship between their groups and disinhibition was inconclusive, although they recognized that the corporate structure in these groups could have influenced any depersonalization caused by the medium. Also, Taylor & MacDonald (2002) in their quantitative study of discussion groups did not find evidence suggesting that deindividuation was encouraging less inhibited behavior. Evidence in their study in fact suggested the converse: situations involving people who were less anonymous—for example they had provided information allowing personal identification—were more likely to result in inflammatory behavior (p. 270). Thus, questions are raised whether the Internet is really harmful to one's conduct (for example in Spears et al. 2002, p. 92), with some authors concluding that behavior in CMC environments is affected more by the context of the interaction, as opposed to the medium of that interaction (Kayany 1998, p. 1141).

Finally, anonymity in itself may not be wholly a bad thing. Suler (2002, p. 457) remarks that online people can exercise both negative and positive aspects of their psyches, and cites online romances as an example of a positive aspect. Anonymity has been argued to allow users to engage in sensitive speech without fear of retribution or retaliation (Johnson 1997, p. 63; Froomkin 1995). Anonymity has also been claimed to be the rescuer of personal freedom and liberty (Donath 1999, p. 53). People facing personal or sensitive problems can seek advice without fear that others will discover who they are. In the context of MUDs, Reid (1999, p. 111-112) argues that disinhibition has resulted in MUDs experiencing both more hostile and intimate behavior than would be normally accepted in the real-world. While she recognizes that disinhibition has led to instances of aggressive and abusive behavior, through the use of pseudonyms that offer feelings of safety, other users are encouraged to be more intimate and foster familiarity among themselves.

Dissociative anonymity

An extension of the issue of anonymity and bad behavior is whether a participant's behavior online when anonymous is really representative of that participant's real personality. Vrooman (2002, p. 53) for example draws a relation between identity and flaming, and argues that flaming is not dissimilar to other types of identity-centric performances. Flaming on Usenet in other words can be likened to a performance that attracts attention. Goffman (cited in Rasmussen 1997) notes the existence of "front stage" and "back stage" in reference to the motivations and conventions of conduct. This concept is useful in understanding why there is a difference in behavior when a

31

participant is put into an online environment. Front stage behavior occurs when the actor performs in ways that define the situation for the audience of that performance. Back stage behavior that is away from audiences occurs with the actor in a more natural and relaxed state. This duality is meaningful in attempting to characterize grief play, as Goffman's front stage behavior has a parallel in grief play: some players grief as they enjoy the attention, as the book will show in Chapter 5. Moreover, some griefers even disassociate their conduct in-game from their real-world behavior. For instance, the following appears on the Frequently Asked Questions of one MMORPG player site[31] where members post accounts of their grief play activities:

> Q: Are you guys really a bunch of racist, sexist, bastards?
>
> A: First of all, go read our legal agreement. What we say or do in-game or on the site has nothing to do with who we really are or what we really think.

This dissociation is similarly observed when griefers remark "it is just a game". Such a sentiment characterizes Huizinga's (1955, p. 8) observation that play should be distinguished from real-world activities, although this is not necessarily easy (Ito, 1997 p. 94; Dodig-Crnkovic & Larsson 2005, p. 2). Pham (2002) at *LA Times* interviewed one player who griefed in MMORPGs, but in real-life appeared to be a normal and well-adjusted family person. For this interviewee at least, the manner he plays is nothing like what he is in the real-world. Suler (2004) uses the term "dissociative anonymity" when explaining the disinhibition of participants to undertake disruptive or distressful action on others. He suggests that when people act out hostile feelings, they dissociate by convincing themselves that such behavior "aren't me at all".

Other scholars of CMC present contrasting viewpoints. Bromberg (1996, p. 146) and Turkle (1995) explain that participants can undertake actions online that will build their desired identity. Visual anonymity may even foster the expression of a true-self (McKenna et al. 2002, p. 10; Bargh et al. 2002, p. 35), with the Internet facilitating that very process (Bargh et al. 2002, p. 34-35). The anonymity possible allows participants to investigate and explore previously undiscovered aspects of one's self, even trying new ones (Turkle 1999, p. 290). Remarks made at *Wired News*[32] by one player of Electronic Art's *The Sims Online* certainly echoes this argument of identity play. This

---

[31] See http://www.darkwolves.biz/faq.html.

[32] See http://www.wired.com/news/culture/0,1284,59539,00.html.

self-styled 'mafia' player offered extortion, 'hits' and prostitution services to other players, and when interviewed remarked:

> Games give people the opportunity to either do something they've never had the ability to do before or allow them to do the stuff they are too afraid to do in real-life. ... This is as close to the real-life mafia that I'm going to be able to get.

However, interestingly, the same person adds later in that report that he was just role-playing, "like everyone else in the game".

These issues surrounding dissociative anonymity are closely tied to role-playing. Some grief motivations seem representative of a real-world person's character. For others, it is harder to tell. Still, such considerations may be interesting only in an academic sense. In practice, how game operators treat role-playing can be more straightforward. In the perception of the game operator, game rules dictate whether the activity is allowed or disallowed, regardless of any desire to role-play. These perceptions will be discussed in Chapter 4.

Administrative and user management of virtual communities

In relation to Porter's (2004) definition of the virtual community, an MMORPG is a virtual community comprising individuals around a shared interest. The shared interest in this case is online computer gaming. In Porter's typology, MMORPGs would be organization-sponsored and commercial virtual communities. This categorization of MMORPGs is important. It recognizes that communities in this category need to foster relationships between customer and employees and among individual customers as well.

One issue of many debates on the management of virtual communities is the role service providers have in managing the community, and whether these communities should be self-regulating. Roberts (1998, p. 361) argues that virtual communities should be self-regulating. CompuServe, an Internet service provider, certainly stated that it was not in its duty to monitor message traffic from its users (Branscomb 1996). Such a proclamation is not trivial in view of the inflammatory messages that can be posted online. As such, when CompuServe was served with litigation when defamation occurred, it was vindicated in court. In contrast, Branscomb notes that another service provider, Prodigy, became liable in a similar litigated case as it had claimed publisher status on all content that it had editorial control over. While the case was eventually dismissed, the judge in this instance noted that that since the service provider had claimed publisher status, it should be liable for message content that resided on their services (Branscomb 1996).

A virtual community can be administratively managed on the service provider level, or self-regulating by members of the community. Centralized and administrative management is not without risk for the service provider. Besides complications involving content management when claims of publisher status are made, the inequality of power between administration and users coupled with an administration's strategy of dealing with conflict can intensify or worsen user conflict (Smith 1999, p. 146). There is indeed a difference between the powers enjoyed by administrators and those of users (Denegri-Knott 2003; Wisebrod 1995; Grimmelmann 2005), and in the case of MMORPGs at least, the relationship between administration and users can be hostile or antagonistic (Scholder & Zimmerman 2003, p. 219). Still, Wisebrod (1995) argues that users themselves are not entirely powerless. They can leave the community and join another, which for commercial types of communities constitute concerns of business revenue generation.

Decentralized management mechanisms on the other hand are user-driven (Bruckman et al. 1994, p. 183). Typically, the service provider still provides tools for users to self-manage. Beyond this, decentralized mechanisms allow users to respond to conflict on their own. Lee (2005, p. 388) describes how users can respond to conflict in virtual communities. In his framework, users can be competitive-dominating and make use of aggressive responses, for example flaming, to resolve the conflict. Alternatively, users can be cooperative-integrating, which may involve apologizing or mediating the dispute. Phillips (1996, p. 50-57) also discusses a variety of strategies to counter problematic behavior on Usenet newsgroups. They include ostracism, education, and moderation. He adds that community members prefer to rely on peer-based rather than administrator-driven approaches (p. 59). Several researchers believe that communities where members moderate their own behavior tend to be particularly successful (for example Preece 2004, p. 59; Andrews 2004, p. 68; Ostrom cited in Kollock 1998). Key also to such self-management is the development of strong norms of participant etiquette (Preece 2004, p. 59).

There are also other tools that are useful in the management of virtual communities. Reputation systems can collect, distribute and aggregate feedback of users' historical behavior (Resnick et al. 2000, p. 46; Preece 2004, p. 60). Jensen et al. (2002, p. 448) describe reputation systems as a way of managing virtual communities. They cite several such systems, including ranking systems—

which track quantitative aspects of a user's behavior and generate a ranking based on it—and rating systems, which allow other users to rate each other's behavior.

Whether the regulation of the community comes from the service provider or from within its members, there are still tenets of regulation that hold true in both case. Regardless of where operational management is going to come from, someone has to set directions. The absence of leadership results in uninhibited behavior (Kiesler et al. 1991, p. 342). Also, Smith et al. (1998, p. 110) in their study of bad behavior in Usenet and the different types of reproaches note that the form and tone of reproaches can vary along with the different types of bad behavior on Usenet. Reproaches are less tolerant in cases where multiple offences had been committed. In the same way, the severity of the grief play act can affect the manner of response from either the player or the game operator.

Whilst research on online communities and online behavior have obvious relevance to this study, the need to investigate more general studies of misbehavior—in particular bullying and teasing— came about as a result of early data analysis. The next section looks at these two behavioral concepts.

Bullying and teasing

Bullying is behavior that is commonly seen as overbearing or intimidating (Land 2003, p. 148), and the intention behind the act is to cause distress (Randall 1997, p. 4). Typically, there is an absence of provocation from the victim (Land 2003, p. 148). Bullying also entails actions that are conducted repeatedly (Olweus 1993, p. 9; Einarsen 2000, p. 381). Several authors (Einarsen 2000, p. 384; Zapf & Einarsen 2001, p. 370; Salmivalli & Voeten 2004, p. 246) add that the targeted individual has difficulty defending himself, and victims tend to be passive or submissive (Smokowski & Kopasz 2005, p. 103). Bullying is thus characterized by a power imbalance between perpetrator and victim (Salin 2003, p. 1214; Scott et al. 2003, p. 106), and may be intended to establish social dominance (Crothers & Levinson 2004). Besag's (1989) definition includes many of these elements, and will be used for operational purposes:

> Bullying is a behavior which can be defined as the repeated attack—physical, psychological, social or verbal—by those in a position of power, which is formally or situationally defined, on those who are powerless to resist, with the intention of causing distress for their own gain or gratification. (p. 4)

35

Other studies have classified bullying into different types: direct bullying—relatively visible attacks on the victim—and indirect bullying—acts which intend to socially exclude or isolate the victim (Olweus 1993, p. 10; Zapf & Einarsen 2001, p. 370). Bullying can also be physical—for example hitting or pushing—or verbal—for example threatening or taunting (Ma et al. 2001, p. 249). Finally, bullying contributes towards a cycle of violence. Elementary school children who bully continue to do so upon reaching high school and adulthood, and in turn model the same behavior to their children who also become bullies as well (Colvin et al. 1998, p. 296).

Teasing has also been described and characterized in different ways. Shapiro et al. (1991) defines teasing as:

> A personal communication, directed by an agent toward a target, that includes three
> components: aggression, humor, and ambiguity... (p. 460)

Teasing is intentional provocation, always targeted (Keltner et al. 2001, p. 235) and with an attendant audience (Pawluk 1989, p. 161). There are also prosocial and constructive instances of teasing (Keltner et al. 2001, p. 232). It can be used to control undesirable behavior or to express affections in male-male friendship relationships (Mills & Babrow 2003, p. 276). It may also be a form of humor that in an ideal situation all parties can enjoy (Shapiro et al. 1991, p. 460). However, teasing can also be a form of annoyance that is hurtful or irritating (Bollmer et al. 2003, p. 558). Several authors, including Tragesser & Lippman (2005, p. 264), Kowalski (2000, p. 231) and Driscoll (cited in Alberts et al. 1996, p. 337) echo this duality of teasing—that it has both positive and negative connotations. The tease can be aggressive and intended to hurt another person's feelings, or a harmless joke played on others for good-natured fun.

In studies of children who tease, it was revealed that motivations included wanting to look cool (Kowalski 2000, p. 232). The actor may also be intending to demonstrate status and superiority (Tragesser & Lippman 2005, p. 265), or to establish social dominance within a group (Shapiro et al. 1991, p. 464). The act is always intended to elicit a response from the target (Keltner et al. 2001, p. 236). Other causes include retaliation as the children had been teased themselves, had a dislike for the target, or because they were in a bad mood and wanted themselves to feel better (Shapiro et al. 1991, p. 463). Palmer (cited in Alberts et al. 1996, p. 339) notes that a victim's response to a tease is instrumental in determining if the tease is successful. Many of these motivations can be related to grief play, and will be discussed in Chapter 5.

Teasing and bullying can be differentiated based on the intent of the perpetrator (Landau et al. 2001, p. 330; Scott et al. 2003, p. 106). In bullying, the intent is often more hostile. Teasing is more playful and less aggressive, and thus more acceptable to recipients when compared to bullying (Land 2003, p. 151). Acts of bullying and teasing can also be expedited using CMC tools. Amy Harmon (2004) in an article for *The New York Times* reports that computer technology now allows bullies to pursue their victims from the school yard back to their homes. Tools like e-mail, Internet messaging, and web sites postings can be used to continually harass individuals. This 'cyber-bullying' differs from schoolyard bullying in its use of these modern technologies, but is still similar in its intent (Keith & Martin 2005, p. 224).

The tragedy of the commons

The idea that some types of grief play are driven by selfish intentions without regard for the needs of the collective emerged early on in data collection. One such model depicting the social dilemma of individual interests versus the collective good is "the tragedy of the commons," the "commons" referring to an area of land that is intended for cattle crazing. Hardin (1968, p. 1244) describes a scenario where herders each undertake individualistic decisions when deciding if they should put more cattle onto a limited area for their cattle to graze. Each herder stands to increase his personal gains by adding one more cattle to his herd. The negative consequence of this is over-use of the common area, the pasture in this case. However, the herder feels since the overgrazing effect of his adding one cattle will be shared by all herders, the personal cost to him seems lower. The problem arises when every herder decides to make the same decision by adding more cattle to their herds, because in doing so, the common area will be damaged, and every herder will suffer the consequences of it.

Since Hardin's (1968) paper, "the tragedy of the commons" has been used to depict scenarios where degradation of the environment happens when a resource in limited supply is used by many individuals (Ostrom 1990, p. 2). While this model is more commonly associated with the overuse of natural resources of planet Earth, Kollock & Smith (1996) relates this tragedy to Usenet. They note that an individual who sees the large amount of readily available resources in online newsgroups may feel that it would not matter too much if he 'free-rode'. The individual does this by taking from the pool of information but not contributing to it. For example, he asks questions but does not answer any. When a sufficiently large number of people do the same thing, the pool of knowledge contained in the Usenet newsgroup diminishes. Grudin (1994, p. 96) contextualizes similar behavior to information systems, where groupware does not get used properly if every user 'freeloads' and does not contribute.

Hardin's (1968) Tragedy seems pertinent to a study of grief play. Specifically, the limited natural resources in Hardin's environment are similar to the scarcity of game resources in a virtual world. This scarcity is an intentional aspect of game design (Grimmelmann 2005). The acquisition of these resources is competitive, as it increases the value of the resource for players. However, players in an MMORPG may engage in behavior to acquire these resources and further their own advancement without care for the rest, and in so doing cause disruption. They may feel that the effects of their behavior are not enough to affect the collective good. But if every player in the game engages in this type of player behavior, everyone suffers. Hardin's Tragedy will be discussed again in Chapter 5.

That the study of grief play involves several bodies of knowledge—on computer medicated communication, virtual communities and its management, anonymity and identity, bad behavior, bullying, teasing, and social models on the scarcity of resources—is testament both to the complexity of the subject and its status as a new area of research. The lack of scholarly understanding on the subject demanded careful consideration of the research methodology to be employed, which is detailed in the next chapter.

CHAPTER 3: RESEARCH DESIGN

The Literature review chapter surveyed the areas of knowledge related to grief play. This chapter presents the research methodology of this study, and explains the reasoning behind choosing grounded theory as its primary approach. Data for the study consists primarily of observations and perceptions from players and also developers. Two methods of collection were employed to gather data from these sources: semi-structured interviews, and investigation of discussion postings. Since data gathering work was conducted online, further considerations were taken to ensure that data collected was accurately representative of a participant's perception, and also that participant identity would be protected.

Research methodology - grounded theory

A qualitative method of research was chosen for this study. There were two reasons for this. Firstly, data exists as first-hand observations of players and commentaries from game developers. Both are expressed as text. A qualitative method of research accepts that these observations are subjective. Secondly, little research had been conducted so far into grief play. Hence, the study was intended to discover and explore perceptions of both developer and player participants on grief play.

Grounded theory (Glaser & Strauss 1967; Glaser 1992) is a method of theory generation that is used in qualitative research. It is so-called as it demands that the researcher allows theories to emerge from data. No prior conceptions of a theory or hypothesis (Charmaz 1994a p. 68) should be made prior to formal research.

The choice of research method was in consideration of the differing perceptions of grief play, one of which was if grief play constituted 'problematic' behavior. According to The American Heritage Dictionary, a problem can be a question to be solved, a situation that presents difficulty, or a misgiving or complaint. Grief play is seen as a harmful type of behavior by both developers and players subject to its effects. Evidence of these perceptions comes in two forms: the discussion postings[33] made by players who are affected by grief play across MMORPGs, and commentaries from developers as they attempt to manage grief play through game mechanisms. With reference to the literal meaning of a problem stated above, initial consideration of grief play from anecdotal evidence revealed that it includes all of these elements: that it is a situation that needs resolution, that it poses challenges to game design, and that players express negative sentiments about it. In this sense, there was an early basis for grief play to be regarded as problematic behavior.

Having said this, the study did not preconceive that grief play constitutes problematic behavior. There were two reasons for this. Firstly, this study of grief play is the first substantial foray into the player behavior. Hence, I had to keep an open mind until data could conclusively show one finding or another. Secondly, discussion postings purporting incidents that were claimed to be grief play still frequently saw debate, and anecdotal evidence also revealed that some players enjoyed the challenging circumstances posed by grief play. In view of this, there is a countering basis against preconceiving grief play as problematic behavior. Rather, grief play at the onset would be treated merely as player behavior to be first understood and explored before conclusions on whether it is problematic or not are drawn.

Grounded theory is particularly suited to investigations of new areas of knowledge, or to gain new perceptions into a familiar area (Stern 1994, p. 116). In a sense, this study of grief play in the context of MMORPGs can be considered explorative, and a journey into 'uncharted waters'. Operationally, grounded theory itself encompasses several aspects (Glaser & Strauss 1967; Taylor & Bogdan 1984; Strauss & Corbin 1994; Charmaz 1994b; Dey 1999). They include:

1. An identification of a problem scenario or subject area to study.

2. Theoretical sensitivity: familiarity with many theories without exhibiting a preference to one of them until theory emerges.

---

[33] It is difficult to say for certain if players who expressed their perceptions in discussion forums were a fair representation of the player base. The persons posting into the discussion forums may had been a vocal group of players. Whether their observations and perceptions only constitute that of a vocal minority and that the perceptions offered were not shared by players at large could not be ascertained from the methods used in the research. Having said this, this study is not intended to be representative of general perceptions—a quantitative type of study would be more suited for that. Nevertheless, commentaries on the types of players who post in discussion forums and how they may differ from other players have been made, including one at MUD-Dev: see
http://comments.gmane.org/gmane.comp.games.mud.devel/2146 posting made by Damion Schubert, an MMORPG developer, on 15 August 2005.

3. Theoretical sampling: the analyst collects data, then codes and analyses it in order to determine where data should be next collected to investigate the emerging theory.

4. Constant comparative generation and analysis of data: including the generation of categories, their properties, and relationships between categories.

In the method, theoretical saturation is reached when new categories, properties and relationships no longer emerge. Data collection stops at this juncture. The integrated categories then form a main storyline (Glaser & Strauss 1967). Analysis continues around this storyline, and writing stops when the appropriate theory has emerged (Dey 1999, p. 9).

That grief play was studied from an explorative point of view did not mean I approached the subject field without prior knowledge. I have been actively participating in MMORPGs since 1997, and spent between 30 to 40 hours a week across several games in the course of the study. Many of the contexts, biases and terms of reference used by participants of MMORPGs are familiar to myself. In grounded theory, if the researcher has been exposed to the subject, he can have "hunches" (Charmaz 1994a p. 69-70) on where interest areas may lie in. As a result of my exposure, an initial conceptual framework was created in April 2003 to identify potential interest areas. This framework was included in my research proposal and used as a discussion tool to illustrate grief play in relation to other aspects of an MMORPG:

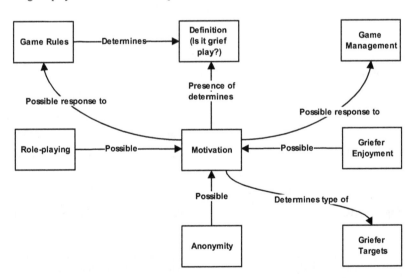

Figure 1: Initial conceptual framework of grief play (April 2003)

41

This conceptual framework was discarded upon commencement of data collection.

Data collection

MMORPGs are created by game developers, published and managed by game operators, and participated in by paying subscribers. Jakobsson & Taylor (2003, p. 89) in their study of social networks[34] in *EverQuest* player communities argue that research involving MMORPGs requires taking the primary actors as participants. In this study, both players and developers were considered primary sources for data collection. A note on developers is in order here: the perceptions gathered from developers were considered to be representative of game operation. The category 'developers' itself is somewhat of a generalization: several developer respondents were discharging fairly managerial responsibilities in MMORPG operation and development, and many have worked in different areas in several games even, including design, testing, and customer service. Hence, the term 'developers' as used in this study denote a group of respondents who are familiar with the design and operation of MMORPGs as opposed to the only responsibility implied by the term.

The two methods of data collection employed in the study are as follows:

- Interviews with developers and players (D1)
- Investigation of discussion postings from players (D2)

Thomsen et al. (1998) also maintain that ethnographic approaches are important for researchers of virtual communities. They argue that through sustained participation over a period of time, researchers can understand, and become a part of the world he is studying. While I was an active participant of MMORPGs throughout the study and continue to be now that the study is reaching its end, it became apparent early on that observation work alone was not efficient or adequate if used as the primary means of data collection. While I was familiar with the context of grief play, too much time would have been expended to uncover the areas of interest if only this method of data collection was used. Simply put, the game world in an MMORPG is too large for a single player to be everywhere, all the time. This is not withstanding the fact that there are many MMORPGs with differing rule sets. An act of grief play in one game could be perceived differently in another, which

---

[34] Kautz et al. (1997, p. 64) describe a social network as a graph comprising nodes that denote individuals, with edges between nodes denoting direct relationships that exist between that pair of individuals. One could envision that a graphical representation showing the network relationships between all players of an MMORPG to be very large indeed.

made it necessary to study multiple MMORPGs. Moreover, the ability to witness grief play first-hand was limited by the in-game prowess of the characters I played. For example, an incident of grief play taking place in one part of the game world may well be over when traversed to by my character. If grief play is recognized as a subjective experience (for example participants disagree on what it entails), it requires direct involvement from the players who perpetrate it, or are victimized by it. My exposure to MMORPGs allowed for the identification of interest areas early on and lent itself to better understanding of many contexts expressed by respondents. There are also a few instances in this book where data from an incident came from first hand observation, particularly in the games which I spent the most time in, namely *Ultima Online*, *EverQuest*, *EverQuest 2*, *Dark Age of Camelot*, and *Star Wars Galaxies*. Beyond this however, observation was not directly employed as a distinct method of data collection.

It is also important to keep in mind that the study has been qualitative and interpretivistic. It is intended to discover through exploration the spectrum of perceptions about grief play. Information pertaining to how *representative*, for example in percentile figures, is a perception of grief play to players and developers would indeed be valuable. However, a quantitative and positivistic type of study would be better suited to achieve this.

D1: interviews with developers and players

Sorrell & Redmond (1995) emphasizes the importance of interviewing in qualitative research: the skilled interviewer is the research instrument itself, and "uses responses of the participant to guide data collection, probing for further information as needed for depth and clarity." (p. 1118) Thomsen et al. (1998) explain that the 'meanings' associated by participants of virtual communities to their experiences can be teased out with interviews, with online interviewing itself a fundamental tool of virtual community research (Preece & Maloney-Krichmar 2005). Online interviewing was chosen as MMORPG players are spread around the world. Given both time and financial constraints, it was unfeasible to conduct face-to-face interviewing. Under these constraints, online interviewing was the practical means of gathering data. Moreover, the context of the MMORPG is that it resides on the Internet; it is reasonable for interviews to be conducted online, since the respondents themselves would be more comfortable in familiar territory (Hammersley & Atkinson, cited in Henderson & Gilding 2004, p. 494).

87 respondents comprising developers and players were interviewed by email from August 2003 to September 2005. Making use of contact points in the game development industry and also mailing

lists, developer respondents were identified, selectively approached, and invited to participate. 17 developers participated in the study. Developers that were interviewed worked on not just one but across several MMORPGs.

70 players—some who have griefed others—were interviewed. A degree of purposive sampling was employed (Bogdan & Biklen 1992, pp. 71-72), in that some players were identified and selectively approached after expressing a particular sentiment on grief play in public discussion forums. Other players responded through a public call for participation that was posted on web sites.

For both groups of respondents, two to three questions were asked in each email. An average of 24 questions were answered per respondent. In some cases, the number of questions eventually answered reached more than 45. New questions were only posed upon the receipt of answers from the last email. In order to minimize the risk of respondent fatigue, a period of at least two days normally elapsed between emails. The exceptions were respondents who requested the interviewing be accelerated.

Interview sessions were also semi-structured, with structure denoting the degree of control that the interviewer maintains over the session (Nunkoosing 2005, p. 700). While a general set of interest areas were identified for both groups of respondents, the interview remained sensitive to comments and alternative viewpoints offered by respondents. On many occasions, analysis of a remark or story led to the emergence of a new interest area. Questions were then asked to further investigate this new area (Wimpenny & Gass 2000, p. 1490). In this sense, there was a constant re-creation of the interview (Nunkoosing 2005, p. 704), with each subsequent interview with a new respondent at least subtly different from the last one. Also, to expedite theoretical sampling, as categories emerged from data analysis of these areas, selected respondents were interviewed again after their sessions had been completed. In some cases, additional data was gathered in 2005 from respondents who had completed their initial sessions in 2003. In all cases, the degree of interaction I had with the respondent was high. Each reply was interpreted, and the meaning 'sent' back for clarification and further elaboration (Kvale 1996, p. 189; Hall & Callery 2001, p. 260). Given varying perceptions of grief play, grief play was not referred to as a 'problem' on the onset of each session in order to avoid potential influences on the perceptions of the interviewee.

Lastly, researchers tend to develop preferred interviews for use (Järvinen 2000, p. 374), and this may be the result of selected interviewees providing richer insights or perceptions of higher quality. In the interviews for this study, the length and quality of replies varied—some respondents wrote sentences for each question, others wrote pages[35]. The developer respondents were able to reflect upon their experiences across a range of MMORPGs. In many cases, they presented a point of view that compared game mechanisms in one MMORPG to another. The same comparative element between MMORPGs was less common among player respondents. This was not the result of the player respondent being familiar with just one MMORPG. In many cases, the player had participated across several MMORPGs. Rather, that replies were occasionally centered on a specific MMORPG was because of their having been approached through MMORPG-specific web sites. Having said this, several respondents were still able to relate their experiences across games. For both developers and players, while the study is sensitive to remarks and comments made by all respondents, there are indeed instances in this work of particular respondents getting referenced more often than others as a result of the quality of data provided.

Considerations

There are several considerations in the general conduct of online interviews that necessitate further elaboration. These are the truthfulness of responses, differences in power between interviewee and interviewer, and the potential difficulties in getting respondents to talk about experiences that may be emotional for them.

The first consideration was whether respondents were telling the truth or fabricating responses. It is indeed harder to validate the responses an interviewee makes online compared to an interviewee in the physical world. Henderson and Gilding (2004) posit that anonymity on the Internet "potentially compromises the data" (p. 494). On the other hand, Taylor (1999, p. 443) while recognizing the potential difficulties posed by anonymity on the Internet argues that such issues are not specific to research and data gathering that is conducted online. Other researchers (for example Capurro & Pingel 2002, p. 191) argue that face-to-face communication does not necessarily mean there is "a higher degree of moral authenticity"—participants may lie face-to-face but tell the truth in a chat room. An example of this dilemma is in whether online interview participants when stating that

---

[35] The interview transcript for one respondent at the end of the session was more than 15,000 words long. Stories related by respondents or in discussion postings in many other cases were equally substantial. In the interest of keeping this work succinct and readable, as a general rule, quotations as opposed to the entire inclusion of a story are used.

they are of legal age to give consent are really of that age. Flicker et al. (2004, p. 127) in their commentary on ethics remark that in reality, most youths participate in online activities without parental supervision. In their study, they relied on the basis of 'good faith' and accepted as truth the information that was provided by their participants (p. 128).

Ultimately, there are things from the interviewee that the researcher must accept as truth, as is also in the physical world. The argument to accept things 'as they are' is made the more important when one considers that this research was conducted in a qualitative fashion—it recognizes that participant perceptions are subjective. Like Flicker et al.'s (2004) study, this project relied on the basis of good faith that the comments expressed in each interview were honest representations of that person's perceptions.

Nonetheless, the research design attempted to minimize the risk of fabricated responses through its respondent selection process and question design. Firstly, some player respondents were solicited through their postings in the discussion forums. As mentioned above, a player would first offer an opinion or relate an incident to a public discussion area. I would then make contact and inquire if the player would be receptive to further querying. The responses in the interview were then matched to the standpoints and perceptions expressed in the discussion forum. Secondly, questions were included to verify a particular response or standpoint expressed by a respondent to an earlier question. When they were not congruous, questions seeking clarification were asked.

The second consideration lies in the differences of power between the interviewer and interviewee. The interviewer is the researcher, and expert in methodological aspects of the session (Nunkoosing 2005, p. 699). The interviewee is the provider of that knowledge. Interestingly, in an online interview, the inquirer could be at a disadvantage in this play of power. The interview's identity and affiliation is known to the interviewee, but the interviewee can remain anonymous. This concern was evident in my mind as I interviewed players. Fortunately, with the exception of one respondent who was condescending at one point (but whose attitude became more amiable after I explained again the purposes and importance of my research), the majority of respondents were obligingly and patient with my queries. The difference in power was even less of an issue where developer respondents were concerned. Unlike player respondents, I was aware of the names and organization affiliations of developer respondents in the study. Many of them are also active participants of MMORPG research or development communities, and their expert knowledge in the domain well known.

The third consideration lies in the context of grief play and its relationships to bullying. Ma et al. (2001, p. 263) note that there is a disadvantage when interviews are used in researching bullying. They note that victims fear shame and retaliation from the bullies, and hence are hesitant in disclosing their experiences. This was not a problem in this study. When a public call was made inviting player participants as interviewees, many came forward wanting to share their experiences. The interviewees solicited via their postings in the discussion forums were equally forthcoming in their sharing of experiences. This could have been the result of several factors. Firstly, players of MMORPGs are mostly older[36] than the victims of school bullying studied in the literature review. Respondents were able to provide reflective accounts of their experiences. Secondly, the anonymity in the game that protects griefers also protects their victims. Player respondents in this study were not required to reveal their real-world identities nor did I seek personal information on each respondent, although some willingly supplied it without my asking. Some of the player respondents even requested that they be fully identified.

D2: investigation of discussion postings from players

One advantage in the use of discussion postings lies in the volume of available data. There are hundreds of discussion forums for MMORPGs, and a huge number of postings exist across many topics of interest. For example, a discussion forum for *EverQuest 2* at http://eqiiforums.station.sony.com already comprises more than one million postings since the game was publicly released in November 2004.

Some sites cover MMORPGs in general. An example of one such site is http://www.mmorpg.com. Others are specific to one MMORPG, for example http://eq.stratics.com for *EverQuest*, and http://uo.stratics.com for *Ultima Online*. Some sites are independent of the game operator, for example rec.games.computer.ultima.online. Other sites are owned by the game operator. For example http://eqiiforums.station.sony.com is a discussion forum for *EverQuest 2*, and is owned by Sony Online Entertainment. In all, about 7,400 discussion postings on grief play were examined to supplement interview work.

There were two benefits of using discussion postings as a source of data in this study. Firstly, it identified players who were exhibiting strong sentiments on grief play. These players were

---

[36] For instance, Yee (2001) notes that the average age of an *EverQuest* player is 25.6 years.

approached privately and asked if they would consent to interviewing and further investigation of the experiences they had shared in the discussion forum. Secondly, discussion postings were instrumental in the validation of a particular idea or perception that had been expressed in the interviews. In many instances, discussion forums were revisited several times to gather data on new areas of interest that were emerging from the interviews.

The use of discussion postings posed challenges as well. Firstly, it was well beyond the realm of practicality to investigate every posting to see if grief play was discussed. As a result, initial sampling was selective. Postings were sampled based on a search for the keywords 'abuse', 'harass', or 'grief'. Although the keyword range was gradually expanded in light of theoretical sampling, the consequences of using a key word search meant that several postings on grief play that did not contain any of these keywords were missed in the selection. Secondly, occasionally, a discussion thread would imply that fuller details of an incident had been shared privately among individual parties. I was not privy to such interactions. Thirdly, an incident could span across several threads. It was difficult to trace a poster's perceptions *across* postings. While it was possible to accumulate data and perceptions that were consolidated in a single thread of discussion, it was much harder to use or validate incidents that span across multiple threads. Fourthly, the amount of noise in a discussion posting was high. Frequently, postings that contained little usable data were made. Examples of these included inflammatory postings that criticized a particular person's posting manner as opposed to the discussion of the incident.

Ethical issues

Bassett & O'Riordan (2002, p. 233) note that with the Internet increasingly becoming the medium and also the object of research, there is concern over ethics in Internet research. Of particular interest is the use of data from public discussion forums. For example, to what degree is data in these places public or private? Proponents of the view that data is public argue that it is accessible publicly to any person who wants to view them (Bakardjieva & Feenberg 2001, p. 234; Flicker et al. 2004, p. 130; Salem et al. 1997, p. 202). Other researchers (for example King 1996, p. 123) have noted that there is a perception of privacy among participants in a discussion forum even when these forums are public for all to view and participate if they so wish. Bromseth (2002, p. 34) further points out that postings are often archived in these forums. Search engines make it possible to accurately associate a quotation from a posting to the poster. Waskul & Douglas (1996, p. 131) describe these forums as "publicly private" and "privately public"—or more simply put, these forums are neither totally public, nor totally private.

Bakardjieva & Feenberg (2001, p. 234) posit that insofar as methodological considerations are concerned, the researcher should refrain from making his presence visible to participants in the discussion forum. A researcher who actively identifies his role and intention to observe and investigate in a public area can change the behavior of that area's participants. This can destroy the accuracy of data gathered (Bromseth 2002, p. 54). Lastly, the study of grief play is of interest to game developers, players who have been affected by it, and scholars investigating social behavior in virtual worlds. In this sense, it could be argued that the study belongs to the public domain of interest.

Still, some guidelines to the use of discussion postings were necessary, and in particular guidelines to the gathering of consent from participants of discussion forums. Bruckman's (2002) Ethical Guidelines for Research Online has been cited in other treatments of the subject, and she argues that the need for consent can be waived if the postings are publicly accessible and archived, and that the topic is not too sensitive, among other guidelines.

For public areas, for example Usenet newsgroups, Bruckman (2002) suggests that such public material does not require informed consent for use. Moreover, email addresses in public discussion forums are often changed, or altogether made inaccessible for public viewing. Still, other researchers provide contrasting arguments. Schrum (1997, p. 121) argues that the identity of participants in the community should always be respected, and these identities hidden unless permission has been granted to reveal them. King (1996, p. 120) adds that research should be published in such ways that the participants in Internet communities cannot be identified. In essence, identities of participants and communities should be protected, with the origins of each data source hidden where appropriate.

Having said this, there is a strong case of arguing that data surrounding grief play is more public than private. There are several reasons. Firstly, griefers do not usually hide their acts. Some post accounts of their exploits on the World Wide Web. Secondly, many incidents of grief play take place publicly in the game world. Lastly, victims of grief play are often frustrated enough to complain about these acts via public channels, for example chat or discussion forums.

Still, to err on the side of caution, ethical considerations were implemented for the two data collection methods used, and approval was attained by the supervising institution.

Ethics in interviews with developers and players

My identity as researcher and the characteristics of the study were made known. Respondents were queried on their consent to participate and how their data would be used through an information sheet explaining the specifications of the study, and informed that they had to be of legal age to give consent to participate. In the study, several participants without my prompting readily offered their full names, stating that they had nothing to fear. A few even asked if they could be cited as a resource. Nevertheless, all data sources are identified using a neutral identifier that bears no relation to the participant's identity.

Ethics in investigation of discussion postings from players

There are both private and public discussion forums. The following considerations prevailed: firstly, only public discussion forums were investigated. Secondly, the intention to observe and investigate was not announced in these public forums, nor was informed consent obtained. However, players are not identified in this work, nor their posting names revealed. With the sole exception of public game play announcements made by game operators in discussion forums, no player quotations from these forums are used in this work, and all material from these sources are paraphrased. The discussion forum where a posting comes from is hidden through the use of a neutral identifier. This, in essence, removed any association between a data point and its original discussion forum source. In all cases, only the MMORPG concerned is cited to provide a general context for the source, given the importance of the type of rule sets in the discussion of grief play.

Limitations in data collection

Aside from the limitations specific to both methods of data collection mentioned earlier, there were other constraints present in data collection. Firstly, invitations for interview respondents made to grief play-centric web sites did not result in many players consenting to participate. These web sites are good resources to study grief play, and representation from players there would have meant better representation of griefers. Invitations sent to griefers from other MMORPG web sites were comparatively more successful, and several agreed to participate. Moreover, the study's intention is to better understand grief play, and perceptions from griefers are just one of many representations from involved participants. The value of understanding player perceptions—from victim or observant points of view—of grief play is equally integral to the study. Many players have either been griefed before and had first-hand exposure to the circumstances of that incident, or have an impression or understanding based on their witnessing of the incidents. Likewise, perceptions from developers in game design provided alternative points of view, as they are themselves conscious of griefer motivations and design mechanisms to manage their behavior.

The study is also time-limited, with the games chosen as sites of study limited to those that are available in market release up till May 2005. As new MMORPGs are released, new types of grief play will emerge, possibly in response to grief play management mechanisms in the newer MMORPGs. Hence, while the study may be an accurate representation of grief play as it is currently understood, grief play needs to be continually studied as new games become available.

Choice of games in study

Wikipedia[37] lists more than one hundred MMORPGs either published or in development. It would have been impossible for a single researcher to study every one of these games. As a result, the choice of games was limited and kept in mind three considerations. Firstly, many players play more than one MMORPG at a time. Also, many would have played a number of MMORPGs prior to the one(s) they are currently participating in. Hence, the selection of data from players of one game does not mean their perceptions would be limited to just that game. Secondly, grief play takes place in games with large numbers of participants. The sites of discussion postings data collection centered on reasonably popular or large MMORPGs, with the subscription numbers at http://www.mmogchart.com employed to assist in selection. Thirdly, the language medium of research limited the selection of games to those populated by English-speaking participants. For example, the majority of *Lineage*'s several million players are in South Korea, Taiwan, Japan and Hong Kong (Olavsrud 2002 for *Asia.internet.com news*). While several of the interview respondents played *Lineage* and were able to relate perceptions in view of their experiences there, discussion forums centered on this game itself were not selected as sites for data collection.

---

[37] See http://en.wikipedia.org/wiki/List_of_MMORPGs.

The MMORPGs that were reasonably represented in terms of the relative amount of data gathered from include the following, with subscription numbers[38] at the time of writing (August 2005) remarked against the title name:

1. Blizzard Entertainment's *World of Warcraft* (WoW), 2,000,000[39] subscribers.

2. CCP Games' *EVE Online* (EveO), 57,929 subscribers.

3. Electronic Art's *The Sims Online* (TSO), 35,500 subscribers.

4. Electronic Art's *Ultima Online* (UO), 157,000 subscribers.

5. Funcom's *Anarchy Online* (AO), 23,000 subscribers.

6. Microsoft's *Asheron's Call* (AC), 37,000 subscribers.

7. Mythic Entertainment's *Dark Age of Camelot* (DAoC), 175,000 subscribers.

8. NCsoft's *City of Heroes* (CoH), 140,481 subscribers.

9. Sony Online Entertainment's *EverQuest* (EQ), 454,000 subscribers.

10. Sony Online Entertainment's *EverQuest 2* (EQ2), 278,000 subscribers.

11. Sony Online Entertainment's *Star Wars Galaxies* (SWG), 255,000 subscribers.

12. Ubisoft's *Shadowbane* (SB), 20,000 subscribers.

In the study, many data points were generalized by respondents and not made specific to a game. However, in instances where the data point was made specific to the game, indications specifying the game are made in the book. For example, the reporting of a player perception of a particular game mechanic or rule will include an indicator of the game concerned if such information was mentioned in the interview. In the case of discussion postings, the identifier reveals the game to which the posting was sourced from. For example, an identifier [CoH-002] refers to a data source from a discussion forum centered on *City of Heroes*. The exceptions are the [GP-XXX] identifiers. These denote data sources from griefer web sites, which are kept anonymous in this work.

---

[38] See http://www.mmogchart.com.

[39] This number has increased to five million as of December 2005 (Blizzard 2005b).

Data analysis and results

One advantage shared by both data collection methods is that data transcripts are automatically generated in the data collection process. The transcripts were textual, and imported into the qualitative research tool, QSR NVivo[40]. The tool allowed key text to be directly extracted from each transcripts, and coded into 'nodes', or organized units representing ideas, themes and initial categories that were emerging from data. These nodes were the basis for the creation of the 'final' categories used in this study.

Of the two methods of data collection used, interviewing provided the most useful data. Three cycles of interviewing were conducted, with the first cycle of interviewing involving 30 respondents beginning in September 2003. In qualitative research, data is analyzed and collected hand-in-hand (Taylor & Bogdan 1984, p. 128), and Constats (1992, p. 257) notes the importance of allowing categories to be generated from the data origins. This first cycle revealed a large number of emerging ideas and themes (Taylor & Bogdan 1984, p. 131), which upon coding initially generated 23 nodes. Investigation of discussion postings began in January 2004 after the first set of nodes was identified, and continued throughout the study until the cessation of data collection. The second cycle of interviewing started in July 2004, and resulted in three additional nodes. In both interviewing and investigation of postings, data collection proceeded with an interest in validation for the emerging categories and exploration of further ideas. At the end of September 2004, theoretical saturation had been reached when no new nodes were surfacing. A third limited cycle of interviewing was conducted in March 2005 with a select group of developer respondents, which did not result in new nodes. Data collection formally ended in October 2005.

By September 2004, coding in NVivo had resulted in the identification of 26 nodes. They are as follows:

---

[40] See http://www.qsrinternational.com.

Table 2: NVivo nodes

NVivo nodes				
Anonymity	Competition	Grief play definition	Game balance	Game management
Game rules	Greed play	Grief effects	Snowballing	Grief styles
Grief types	Intention	Motivations	Natural selection	Resistance
Player expectations	Player judiciary	Player justice	Player response	Punishment
Role-playing	Targets	Griefing benefits	Griefer organization	Power imposition
Spamming				

The five topics of interest in this study are: investigating what grief play means, motivations of grief players, impacts of grief play, player expectations (of grief play management), and grief play management. Upon conclusion of selective coding (Neuman 2003, p. 444) and in light of the topics of interest, the 26 nodes were refined to 17 'final' categories. These categories were in turn further analyzed to create relationships among them. These final 'related' categories were then represented as a conceptual framework, which was in turn used as a guiding framework for further analysis. The table below lists the 17 categories, each enumerated in reference to Figure 2.

Table 3: Final categories

Final categories				
Rules (1)	Intention (2)	Implicit grief play (3)	Explicit grief play (4)	Game influenced motivations (5)
Player influenced motivation (6)	Griefer influenced motivation (7)	Motivation from self (8)	Impacts on players (9)	Impacts on game operator (10)
Expectations of game management (11)	Expectations of game design (12)	Expectations of game masters (13)	Player-driven management (14)	Game operator-driven management (15)
Anonymity (16)	Role-playing (17)			

The 17 categories as organized around the five topics of interest are as follows:

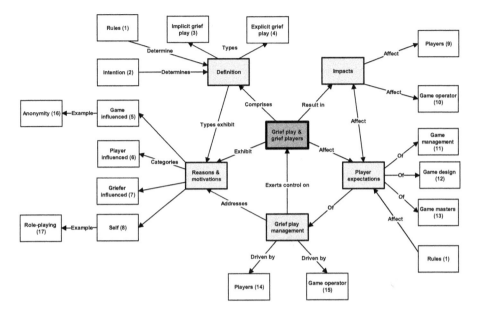

Figure 2: Conceptual framework of grief play

In this framework, grief play and griefers are interrelated to the 17 identified categories, and grouped into the five topics. Each relationship is tagged with a descriptor. For example:

- 'Grief play and grief players' *exhibit* 'reasons and motivations' for their behavior.

- The presence of 'grief play and grief players' *affect* 'player expectations'.

- 'Player expectations' can *affect* the 'impacts' felt by players, and vice versa.

- 'Grief play management' *exerts control on* 'grief play and grief players'.

- 'Rules' and 'intention' *determine* how grief play is 'defined' by players and developers.

It is useful to keep in mind this framework as one reads through this book and examines each of the five topics of interest in this study.

To begin the study of grief play, grief play as a play style needs to be understood first. Chapter 4 next explores player and developer perceptions of grief play.

CHAPTER 4: DEFINING GRIEF PLAY

Discussion postings reveal that many players differ on their perceptions of what grief play is. Debate often occurs when an incident is reported in discussion forums, with posters disputing whether a reported incident should be considered grief play.

The first objective of this research is to better understand what grief play is. This chapter has two operationalized objectives[41]:

1. To explore perceptions of grief play.

2. To investigate types of grief play activities.

Grief play as defined in published sources will be investigated, and then compared to participant definitions. Next, characteristics in an incident that may exemplify it as grief play will be explored. The study will reveal that while many players' definitions of grief play are similar to those found in published sources, what characterizes the act can be more variable. Some areas of contention are whether grief play is allowed by rules, and whether there needs to be a deliberate intention to disrupt for an activity to be considered grief play.

Grief play

At this moment, there is little scholarly work on grief play. Definitions of grief play or a griefer are limited to a handful of published research articles, books and news articles. In journalistic media, Becker (2004) at CNET News.com writes that griefers are an "irradicable set of players who want nothing more than to murder, loot and otherwise frustrate the heck out of everyone else", and reports of one such player who "liked to torture new players". Pham (2002) in his own coverage of grief play writes that a griefer is "someone who plays to make others cry. They stalk, hurl insults, extort, form gangs, kill and loot." Varney (2005, p. 35-37) in *The Escapist*[42] magazine compares

---

[41] The material from this chapter was partially presented in two papers I wrote in 2004. The citation details are as follows: Foo, C Y & Koivisto, E M I 2004, 'Defining grief play in MMORPGs: player and developer perceptions', in *SIGCHI International Conference on Advances in computer entertainment technology*, Singapore, pp. 245-250; and Foo, C Y 2004, 'Redefefining grief play", in *Other Players-conference on multiplayer phenomena*, Copenhagen.

[42] *The Escapist* is a magazine that covers gaming and gaming culture, with each issue centred on a gaming theme. Issue 19, published on 15 November 2005, covers grief play specifically. Some of the articles in this issue are mentioned in this work.

griefers to equivalents in real-world societies, including vandals of web sites, disease carriers, and thrill killers.

The academic sources are more definitional by comparison, with Lin & Sun's (2005) and Mulligan & Patrovsky's (2003) definitions of griefers quite similar. Citing the latter, they note that a griefer is:

> A player who derives his/her enjoyment not from playing the game, but from performing actions that detract from the enjoyment of the game by other players. (p. 475)

These definitions suggest that griefers cause difficulties for other players, and they do so intentionally. For the purposes of this chapter, Mulligan & Patrovsky's (2003) definition of a *griefer* will be used to illustrate a working definition of grief *play*. According to this definition, there are three important elements of grief play:

1. Grief play is intentional.

2. It causes other players to enjoy the game less.

3. The griefer enjoys the act.

The definition used by Mulligan & Patrovsky (2003) describes 'classic' grief play. Here, the griefer enjoys ruining the play experience of others. It is worthwhile to note too that the enjoyment derived comes from having caused disruption to other players. Whether the griefer also enjoys the *type* of grief play as a play activity would be incidental. For example, according to this definition:

- A player who kills another player only because he enjoys PvP would not be considered grief play.

- A player kills another player, knowing fully well his victim would not like it. He nonetheless does it still because he enjoys the reaction of distress from his victim. Such an act would be considered 'classic' grief play.

Keeping in mind that an objective of the study is to explore perceptions of grief play, data gathering recognized that each respondent may have their own definition of the term. Hence, for each respondent, an initial question on how they would define grief play was asked, and their definition used as a basis for the remainder of each session. Table 4 presents some examples of their responses and comparison towards the three elements noted above. The selection in this table is not exhaustive, but it represents a reasonable view of the range of responses offered. The presence of the three elements—noted as '1', '2', and '3'—are denoted by a tick against each respondent's reply.

Table 4: Respondents' perception of grief play

Respondent	Definition	1	2	3
R2	"…harassing people for the 'sheer joy of doing it'."	√	√	√
R6	"Repeated antisocial acts on other players that result in temporary satisfaction for the abuser and upsetting their victims play experience."	√	√	√
R7	"…as behavior of an individual… (whose) only objective of which is to damage gaming experience of other(s) human players."	√	√	
R10	"Grief play is something that is done intentionally and repeatedly to cause another player to have a bad time in a game (emotionally affected). It may or may not benefit the griefer, but most always causes enjoyment for the griefer."	√	√	√
R15	"Doing something specifically to ruin another person's play experience."	√	√	
R19	"When a fellow gamer decides that it is fun to create problems in the gaming environment at the expense of other gamers."	√	√	√
R20	"Grief play is (a play style) whose purpose … is to ruin other player's playing experience in a way or another."	√	√	
R21	"Grief play is defined as any player that is purposefully inhibiting or negatively impacting another player's gaming experience through taunting, killing, "kill-stealing" or luring."	√	√	
R25	"A type of play that [sic] sole purpose is to ruin other people's fun in a manner that was not meant to be in-game."	√	√	
R28	"A player going out of their way to upset another player, or disrupt another's game play."	√	√	
R30	"Play in a game with the intention of annoying, disrupting, and otherwise ruining the game play experience of the community."	√	√	
R43	"Play designed to boost one's own ego through the domination, control, harassment, or unhappiness of others through inherently unfair acts."	√	√	√
R51	"Grief play is the total of the actions from players outside the acceptable behavior which knowingly spoil the gaming experience for others and are the result of deliberate actions."	√	√	
R54	"Game behavior designed to impede the enjoyment of other people playing the game and stop them from accomplishing what they want to, or provoke negative attention towards yourself."	√	√	
R57	"Any instance whereby a player's actions are intended for the sole purpose of disrupting the game for others and being a nuisance making the experience painfully untenable for other players."	√	√	
R61	"Grief play is when one or more players intentionally do certain actions or behaviors that cause someone to feel angry, upset, distressed, uncomfortable or bullied."	√	√	

Phrases like "(whose) only objective", "done intentionally", "doing something specifically", "purposefully", and "designed to" show respondent perceptions: that grief play for them is not accidental but intentional. Interestingly, the same data revealed in some instances the absence of the 'enjoyment' element. At first, the absence of this element in some replies seemed coincidental.

However, observations soon surfaced to challenge this belief. As the interviews progressed, I found that some players regarded several activities to be grief play even when the perpetrators did not seem to 'enjoy' causing disruption for its sake. Moreover, a few players who stated that grief play was always 'intentional' on the session's onset seemed less sure whether this was a mandatory characteristic when they related incidents where they were inconvenienced.

Both of these observations reveal that while there is familiarity among players on the meaning of grief play and its characteristics, there is disagreement whether an act of grief play must be enjoyable or intentional on the part of the perpetrator. Mulligan & Patrovsky's (2003) definition pertains to activities where griefers have enjoyed causing distress to other players. That not every player believed that grief play is immediately enjoyable to the perpetrator, whether it is through the type of grief play or the very act of having caused other players to enjoy the game less, is a result of some grief play activities that stem from greed first and not from a sadistic desire to cause misery. This will be discussed in a later section in this chapter[43]. The debate on intention also has its own discussion in a later section.

There are two additional perspectives of this definition worth noting. Firstly, some players ([R23], [R78], [R86]) remarked that if the victim possesses the skill or ability to retaliate or defend themselves, then the activity should not be considered grief play. Besag's (1989, p. 4) definition of bullying notes that the individual has difficulty in defending himself or herself, as does Salmivalli & Voeten's (2004, p. 246). This is consistent with players' ([R78], [R23]) remarks that the victims cannot retaliate or are defenseless. Many players particularly regarded acts involving defenseless victims to be grief play. In contrast, the perception that the victims *must* be defenseless for an act to be grief play was not shared by all respondents. The statement "if a player can retaliate against the griefer, then it is no longer griefing" was posed to other players, and they replied whether an act is grief play or not should be independent of the ability to respond.

The second perspective of note came through one player [R66]'s remark that an act should be especially considered grief play if it involves little or no skill on the part of the perpetrator. Some types of grief play—for instance newbie-killing—indeed do not require substantial skill (though this is not to say the griefers are not skilful). Paraphrasing his perception, an act is grief play when

---

[43] See also Chapter 5 – 'Motivations interrelated'.

it requires little or no skill. This perception is noteworthy as it poses a question on the converse: whether a play activity involving skill should *not* be considered grief play. Some types of grief play are expedited by the exploitation of buggy game code. Alternatively, they may be expedited by game design itself (for example newbies are considered legitimate targets under PvP game rules). In both circumstances, griefers did not need much skill to commit their acts. However, other types of grief play involve meticulous planning. For example, the Trinsic incident involved a band of griefers who were aware of how the event was organized and knew exactly what to do to cause disruption. In some cases, griefers engaging in PvP types of grief play not only possess superior equipment and more advanced characters, they demonstrate skill and teamwork. In these cases, skill on the part of griefers was evident, but victims continued to believe they had been griefed.

In any case, data analysis revealed two issues surrounding what grief play meant to respondents. They are rules, and intention. The next section discusses both of these issues.

Rules

To further the discussion, a reiteration of the taxonomy of rules used in this study is necessary. They are:

1. 'Law of code' or what has been written into program code.

2. Rules found in the ROC accompanying MMORPG titles, which are referred to as 'game rules' in this study.

3. Implicit rules which are the loosely defined, social rules of 'fair-play' and etiquette expected by players.

Many MMORPGs identify specific play activities and disallow them. In some cases, they are punishable offences in their ROCs, regardless of whether the act had been intending to disrupt. For example, player blocking[44] is disallowed in *EverQuest* (Sony Online Entertainment Inc. 2004a), and its ROC does not distinguish whether the act was purposeful with the intention to disrupt or not. Such distinguishing is important in other games however. For example, at one point, player blocking was allowed in *Ultima Online*'s game rules (Electronic Arts Inc. 2003b). *Ultima Online*'s player harassment policy recognized this activity as a legitimate game mechanic. However, it had this caveat: "While an action may cause others distress, it is not considered harassment until it is

---

[44] Or physically obstructing another player's movement in the game.

determined by OSI/EA[45] that it was done to intentionally cause distress or to offend other players." (Electronic Arts Inc. 2003a) This is evidence that some game operators believe there must be a deliberate intention to disrupt for an act to be grief play, and that such determination has to be made by their game masters.

While one should be mindful that MMORPGs make use of different game rules (Grimmelmann 2004, p. 167), in the above case of *Ultima Online*, an act of player blocking is always discomforting to the victim. Moreover, while the occasional physical obstruction of passage through the game world may be accidental, if persistent it is almost certainly intentional. There seems to be a difference between official rules informing players on how the game *should* be played and how it is *actually* played, and this is noted by Jakobsson & Taylor (2003, p. 89). It does not help that one rule in the game disallows such behavior on the basis of intention to disrupt, but on the other hand recognizes it as a legitimate game mechanic in its player harassment policy. This polar characteristic can also be illustrated by a description of grief play made by Steven B. Davis, CEO of IT GlobalSecure Inc. He remarks that grief play is:

> … An act, action, or communication that is technically legal under the rules of the game (as implemented and enforced in software), but is disruptive to the game experience of others. Such activities may be prohibited by Terms of Service… (Davis 2005)

This description shows the interplay of grief play with game rules. According to Davis' definition, grief play is allowed under Law of code but disallowed by game rules. Using his definition as a basis, player blocking in *EverQuest* for the example above would be grief play.

With reference to the example of player blocking: firstly, the game rule of *EverQuest* suggests there need not be an explicit intention to disrupt for a play style to be considered punishable. Secondly, the game rule of *Ultima Online* suggests there needs to be explicit intention to disrupt for a play style to be considered punishable (but at the same time recognizes some of these play styles as legitimate).

For this instance of player blocking, one could conclude that the rule in *EverQuest* is less open to ambiguity in comparison to *Ultima Online*. In *EverQuest*'s case, if the disallowed activity has been committed, there is no consideration of the intention behind that activity. In *Ultima Online*'s case,

---

[45] OSI, or Origin Systems, Inc, the developers of *Ultima Online*. EA stands for Electronic Arts, its game operator.

the assessment is based on the presence of a deliberate intention to disrupt—which is not easy to ascertain[46]. What is also noteworthy is that the ROCs here do not mention that these activities are grief play. The game rules merely state whether an activity is allowed or disallowed, and under what circumstances if it is allowed. That these activities are considered grief play here is only in light of the operational definition of grief play used: that the activities are disruptive, intentional, and enjoyable to the perpetrator for having caused disruption. Having said that, going by the example of player blocking above, when games can identify a specific play activity and state clearly if it is permitted or not without needing to explain mitigating circumstances (for example if it was intended to disrupt), the course of response is clear. The trouble begins when such play activities are not identified by the game operator. In the absence of explicit rules identifying the permissibility of specific play activities, when these activities take place, there is vigorous disagreement among players on its permissibility.

Consider two further illustrations. Investigation of discussion postings revealed several threads of considerable length with posters debating if an act constitutes grief play even when the intention to disrupt is clear, and if such acts are allowed by game rules. Firstly: in order to help player groups establish community identity in *Star Wars Galaxies*, player groups are allowed to establish cities of their own. Players are also allowed to choose their affiliation, either as a member of 'The Empire', or 'The Rebel Alliance'. In one case, a player of The Rebel Alliance purposefully put his own establishment into a player city owned by a group in the opposing affiliation (The Empire), and quite literally at its door step [SWG-006a]. The city's player inhabitants viewed this as an obstruction and eye sore, and were displeased. However, responses to the discussion thread were not all sympathetic. Many players believed that the act may have been intentional to upset the victims, but this player had not engaged in any code exploitation nor broken any game rules. Moreover, being of opposing player affiliation, he had reasonable cause in putting down an obstruction—he was, after all, their 'enemy' in the game. This player himself posted into the thread, and after enjoying the attention he got, removed the offending obstruction. He remarked that some people had no sense of humor, adding that this was just a video game. In this incident, the act was purposeful, enjoyable to the perpetrator and disruptive to the victims. It meets the three criteria listed in Mulligan & Patrovsky's definition (2003). However, it was not against game rules, and

---

[46] See 'The catch all statement' section in this chapter.

from poster responses, some regarded it as legitimate (even if discourteous) role-playing behavior. Thus, even if an act qualifies as grief play according to literature, some players believe that no response on the game operator's part is required since no game rules have been broken.

The second illustration comes from *World of Warcraft*, a game in which PvP is an integral and acceptable play style. In a play area known as "Gadgetzan", players were able to get onto an advantageous spot: a rooftop. They were then able to attack other players with impunity, occasionally sometimes even enlisting NPC[47] guards (who were very powerful) to kill their victims quickly. Their victims were often unable to defend themselves. This play style was known in the game as "rooftop griefing". For a while, players who petitioned for game master intervention were advised that no action would be taken against these griefers as no game rules had been broken[48]. While no game rules at that juncture had indeed been broken, discussion postings revealed that many players believed they had been griefed [WoW-001]. The characteristics of note here are the inability of players to defend themselves, and that they were killed by these acts—a circumstance that always provokes reactions when coupled with the belief that unfair tactics had been used.

To summarize, firstly, the incident in *Star Wars Galaxies* suggested that even when no game rules had been broken, players felt grief play had taken place, since there had been an explicit intention to disrupt, and the act was enjoyable to the perpetrator. Secondly, the incident in *World of Warcraft* suggested that even when no game rules had been broken, players felt grief play had taken place as they were powerless to react and unfair tactics had been employed.

Clearly, there is disagreement among players on what makes an incident grief play, and when it should become actionable on the part of the game operator. Also, when there are no specific rules governing the activity, other game rules governing general conduct may not be helpful in expediting any determination. Even if there is a general game rule that players should exhibit good, courteous and harmonious behavior, perceptions vary on what constitutes such behavior when the very environment encourages conflict. What is clear however is that whether or not game rules were broken, for those afflicted, implicit rules were not adhered to.

---

[47] Non-player, or computer controlled, characters. See Chapter 1 – 'Key terms'

[48] Shortly after the use of this tactic became widespread, a policy was announced disallowing such tactics.

The issues introduced by the examples above can be distilled into the following. Firstly, players themselves internally disagree on when an activity is grief play, and secondly their perceptions differ from the game operator. In this study, these issues were operationalized into two questions:

1. Who decides if players have been intentionally griefed?

2. How do player perceptions of grief play differ from the game operator?

As it is, the debate on these two questions lies in the realm of game rules and implicit rules. Law of code is not involved in what is and when an activity becomes grief play. Whether an activity is grief play or not is a moot consideration when Law of code is broken. In these cases, the game operator will respond with punitive measures against offenders, and players will regard these activities as cheating and exploitative. Whether the act is grief play (and player experiences disrupted) or not, and whether there was intention to disrupt is no longer relevant in the eyes of the game operator.

Player perceptions

Who decides if players have been intentionally griefed? Sage (2003, p. 93) posits that the people who can determine intention the most accurately are those involved. This does not mean that the game master responding to the petition cannot make a reasonable resolution to the incident[49]—they do enjoy the vantage point of a neutral person, and can likely access historical evidence that may aid their decision making. Furthermore, there is no rule requiring game masters to see the incident from the players' point of view even if players expect it. However, insofar as the process of determining intention is concerned, game masters responding to a grief play petition do not determine intention any better than the people involved.

To further explore this question, there was evidence gathered during the study suggesting that grief play can be compared to teasing and bullying. For bullying, consider these three illustrations. Firstly, one player [R69] remarked:

> I liken it (grief play) to be very similar to the "big schoolyard bully" mentality—someone who has a position of power, or perceived power (either through their ability to cause trouble or through the other person's inability to stop them in any way), and is getting a kick out of feeling powerful by griefing others.

---

[49] Despite this, there is still player dissatisfaction with game master resolutions. See Chapter 7 – 'Game masters'.

Secondly, another player [R8]—himself a griefer—when asked why people grief shared a similar bullying element in his response:

> Grief play can stem from a person wanting to take on a bully role. This bullying role would be physical or oral attacks upon another player.

Thirdly, a player who was bullied in the real-world became a bully in the game [R67].

For teasing, consider two illustrations. Firstly, one player [R61] of *Ultima Online* related the following incident:

> Instead of helping this player who might not have known about the hazards of that kind of 'between character transfer', and instead of helping him by keeping the ribs safe from someone stealing them, and then returning them to the player with tips on how to prevent someone from stealing their goods, Joe made a conscious decision to take those ribs, knowing that someone would be returning to get them. He also made a conscious decision to goad, taunt and tease the player who knew full well that Joe had his ribs.

The second incident is that cited above from *Star Wars Galaxies* [SWG-006a]: the perpetrator who placed the obstruction in the player city demonstrated teasing characteristics.

From the five illustrations above, it seems there is some relation between grief play to bullying and teasing, and that there may be similar dynamics in the relationship between perpetrator and victim. Furthermore, the motivations in teasing and factors resulting in grief play can be similar. For example, Shapiro et al. (1991, p. 464) observe that teasing may occur as a result of the teaser desiring to demonstrate social status among his peers. There is evidence to suggest a similar motivation in grief play[50].

It is also useful to consider these behavioral concepts when addressing the question of who decides if grief play has occurred. While Mulligan & Patrovsky's (2003) definition and data earlier on emphasizes the issue of intent on the part of the perpetrator, Palmer (cited in Alberts et al. 1996, p. 339) argue that whether a successful tease has occurred depends on the victim's response. If the victim is hurt, teasing has occurred regardless of the actor's intent. Furthermore, people react differently to the same tease (Kowalski 2000, p. 232). It cannot be assumed that all victims of teasing will respond similarly and can shrug off the behavior. In the context of games, a certain behavior may be considered 'bad' depending on the victim's interpretation of that behavior (Davis

---

[50] Bullying and teasing in relation to grief play are further discussed in Chapter 5.

2002). If cues from teasing are to be taken, teasing suggests that whether an act is grief play or not needs to take into account victim perceptions. Bullying is differentiated from teasing primarily on the level of hostility, and is similar to teasing in the regard that victim perceptions are involved.

Having seen what behavioral concepts indicate, data showed an array of perceptions. Firstly, some players I spoke to believed game masters should make the determination on whether grief play has occurred. In general, players have differing ideas on what grief play is. As such, they feel that the standards on what is grief play and unacceptable behavior should be set and enforced by an impartial body, for example a game employee [R76], even if game masters face difficulties in determining intention.

Secondly, other players believed implicit rules should be used. One player [R69] remarked that while it is ideal for personal perception to be the determinant, each player has their own interpretation and standards that they expect others to follow. As such, it may be more feasible to base determination on general consensus in order to achieve a more uniform application of rules. This sentiment was echoed by another player [R60]—that many individuals have "odd misconceptions" about what grief play is. He added that mechanisms put in place to deter or prevent grief play should be a reflection on what society at large feels is acceptable. This is, in other words, implicit rules. While there may be players that do not comply with a general set of implicit rules because they have very individualistic styles of play, the majority of players seem to keep looking back to what they believe is general consensus of the collective, and there is indeed broad consensus on some rules of play (for example, that players should not monopolize game areas). This underlines again the significance of implicit rules in any discussion of grief play.

Thirdly and finally, some players believed that the perception of the victim should be considered. I found two reasons that could create this belief. Firstly, when persistent griefing against a targeted person does occur, there may be a context for it. One player [R46] remarked:

> Complaints from the victim shouldn't criminalize the griefer after one or two incidents, but should be used as a compilation to who's the suspect's history of griefing over time, so that it doesn't turn out to be a conspiracy by a disgruntled clan or PA[51] to get back at a player.

---

[51] Or player association. See Chapter 1 – 'Key terms'.

When these situations of persistent and targeted grief play happen, surely the perceptions of the victim need to be considered. If nothing else, it is necessary to properly understand the context of such acts. Secondly, in many cases, whether the perception of the victim should be considered or not may be a moot point—because the victim *will* believe he has been griefed when he reports an incident. When that perception exists, he will request attention from the game operator and demand a resolution.

Interestingly, few respondents believed that the perpetrator's standards of behavior should be directly taken when considering if grief play has occurred, particularly if he attempts to defend his actions as 'fair play' or legitimate play. This does not mean that the perpetrator's point of view on the incident is disregarded. Rather, between the perpetrator's and the victim's standards of behavior, that the latter is the party afflicted adds weight if one had to choose between the two standards.

In essence, there is no clear answer to the question. Participants have differing perceptions, which again points to the subjectivity of grief play as an MMORPG activity. Perhaps it is simply enough to conclude here that some participants are inclined to rely on general consensus of implicit rules, others (particularly game operators, as we will see later on) on game master determination based on Law of code and game rules, and yet others on victim perceptions. What could be useful, however, is to keep in mind that there is no reason *not* to consider all three angles of perspective. Consideration need not be mutually exclusive even if perceptions are contrasting, and that each perception carries more weight to its associated party (other players, game operator, and victims). In any determination of grief play, none of the three angles of perspective should be discounted.

Having investigated the first question, the next section looks at how player perceptions of grief play differ from the game operator's. In order to do this, a discussion of the game's general rules of good behavior is first necessary.

The catch all statement

With the prevalence of anonymity and the reduction of social cues existent in an online environment, it can be difficult to determine the real intention behind a perpetrated activity. Many respondents echo this perception: that it is not easy to determine in a virtual world if an act is deliberately intending to disrupt. There may be differing viewpoints between the perpetrator and victim. As a result, game masters frequently get involved as arbiters in incident resolution even if they themselves will find it difficult to determine intention.

One player of *Ultima Online* [R63] when queried about the issue of intention in a disruptive incident said that:

> The problem is no one is qualified to determine true intent. … The key here is EA allows her GMs (game masters) to make this determination. … Unfortunately, what really happened (in my incident) doesn't matter as much as what people saw happened. Even what people saw happened doesn't matter at all. The only thing that matters is what is written in the GM rulebook. Rule: runner brings monsters to another player then invis (or makes himself invisible) himself is bannable. GM don't care you ran for your dear life and finally get a chance to invis yourself to get a breather.

This incident will be referred to as the 'invis' incident. In this case, the player believed there were circumstances that justified an activity. He had not intended to disrupt, but he was still punished. In his perception, players in the vicinity were unable to decipher intention, as was the game master. What complicates matters is that the intent of a player cannot be determined by his actions alone (Sage 2003, p. 92). There may be context that can only be understood if one saw what happened before the incident. In many cases, as the arbitrating party, game masters can only make best guesses of a player's intent in order to resolve an incident. This will often be through the consideration of evidence from surrounding circumstances and also from a historical record of that player's past behavior, but not necessarily evidence that occurred immediately before the incident.

Given the problems of determining intention, and also that the amount of grief play in a game is affected by the permissibility of the environment, it becomes necessary for the game operator to institute rules stating the behavior they want in their games. If the prerogative is to keep rule enforcement simple, then rule making should not take into account the intention of the perpetrator. Rather, they should be predicated on whether the activity has been committed—and if it has been, punitive measures are meted out. Intention to disrupt becomes moot since the decision making process is binary: has the activity been committed or not. Having said this, in practice, it is difficult to institute a complete set of rules that cover every possible activity in an MMORPG. An activity allowed by Law of code may be used in a fashion that was not realized in game design[52]. This is not

---

[52] Or "emergent game play". Emergent game play refers to play styles that were not initially predicted or intended by the game developer. A discussion of such play styles are in Chapter 7.

counting the many permutations when different activities are put together. Two separate activities may be allowed by Law of code and game rules, but when engaged together in sequence may result in unintended behavior that goes against the spirit of the game (Smith 2004, p. 4). Even if it was somehow possible to state in the ROC every rule of play and its permutation with other rules, it would be too difficult for players to retain such awareness of every rule during play.

Many game operators deal with the above issues by doing two things: they still identify selected activities and disallow them in game rules. They also institute more general statements of conduct that disallow players from engaging in bad behavior to cover every other activity they cannot list. In many cases, this behavior would include the disruption of play experiences of other players in the game. For example, the ROC in *Ultima Online* (Electronic Arts Inc. 2003c) states that:

> You may not victimize, harass, threaten, or cause another player unwanted distress or discomfort, as determined by Support Staff.

The component regarding conduct in *Ultima Online*'s ROC is "… unwanted distress or discomfort". The EULA in *Dark Age of Camelot* has a more general statement (Mythic Entertainment Inc. 2001) disallowing players from engaging in disruptive activity:

> Player may not engage in any conduct or communication while using the DAoC Services which is unlawful or which restricts or inhibits any other Player from using or enjoying these Services.

These general statements demanding good behavior are known among developers as 'catch all' statements.

Even with these statements, game operator determination of whether players have played in legitimate fashion seems to lie in more specific game rules that allow or disallow particular activities. This is because while the catch all statements can serve the purpose of reminding players that they may not play in ways that are disruptive to others, functionally, it seems limited in utility. Firstly, they are so broad that many activities that make up game play could become disallowed under such rules. Secondly, the catch all statements carry caveats. Consider that the policy in *Dark Age of Camelot* (Mythic Entertainment Inc. 2001) adds this:

> … Anything considered a valid play style in DAoC is not considered harassment.

and this caveat:

> The key to determining whether the mechanic is being misused or abused is to determine 'intent'. ... While an action may cause others distress, it is not considered harassment until it is determined by DAoC CS[53] Staff that it was done to intentionally cause distress or to offend other players.

The use of the catch all statement is still saddled with the need to determine disruptive intention in the activity, as observed in the case of *Dark Age of Camelot* above. While game operators do recognize the importance of determining an intention to disrupt, practically, it can be difficult. Game masters respond under the pressure of time, and frequently well after the incident has occurred. Too often, game masters face the volume of petitions that are lodged every night when tens of thousands of players are playing the game. They become hard pressed to make quick decisions that may or may not be accurate assessments of what really happened in an incident[54]. Game masters have rule sets put before them to follow, as one developer explained [R88]. With reference to the incident cited by the player in the 'invis' incident [R68], it is easier to resolve an alleged grief play incident by considering if specific game rules—for example a rule like "You may not train players under any circumstance"—have been broken. This is as opposed to using a catch all statement—for example a rule like "You may not play in ways that disrupt others" which is difficult to enforce since it covers so many legitimate play activities that impose on each other. Adding the caveat that deliberate intention to disrupt must be demonstrated in the catch all statement will not help either, given the difficulties involving that determination. Moreover, if the game operator relies more often on the catch all statement than specific rules, it creates precedence and loses its effect. By its nature, the catch all statement is broad. If overused, players may begin to make liberal use of the statement to demand attention on any activity they find disruptive. A statement like "Anything considered a valid play style ... is not considered harassment" will send players scrambling to the ROC to scrutinize if the act has been listed as a legitimate play style. And even if that act is allowed in the ROC, many will argue that mitigating circumstances make it a disallowed play style.

In essence, the catch all statement is more effective when game operators build a case to ban players when they cannot be caught breaking a specific rule. Outside this, the statement is limited in use. In many cases, game masters still make use of specific game rules when ruling on incidents.

---

[53] Or customer service.

[54] See Chapter 7 – 'Game masters'.

However, the presence of catch all statements in games hint that game operators may be conceding two things: that there are disruptive activities that are unintentional but still need to be managed in order to keep players happy, and that it is difficult to state the permissibility of every activity in the game.

Having explained the existence of rules governing behavior and how they are applied, the next section now addresses the question: how do player and game operator perceptions of grief play differ.

Player and game operator perceptions of grief play

To begin, the difference in perceptions can be illustrated by one developer's remark [R1]:

> Players themselves often define 'griefing' as anything that interferes with their enjoyment of game play. This is regardless of any rules or policies that may allow such behavior.

Grimmelmann (2004, p. 168) posits that griefing is behavior that "bothers most players of the game in question", although he also notes that different games possess different rule sets.

In order to better understand the issue of intent, two scenarios were posed to some interview respondents. Respondents were then asked to comment on these scenarios and if they considered them to be instances of grief play. The two scenarios were as follow:

> A player with vendors somehow succeeds in cornering an important resource needed by players and is normally sold on NPC vendors, so that it no longer becomes available for sale on NPCs. Players can only buy the resource at increased prices, and the seller does this for the purpose of making large profits.

> A player persistently camps a high-level mob for an item he wants. But because his character isn't advanced enough, this mob kills the player, and proceeds to kill other neighboring players. The others are unhappy and feel their gaming is being affected, but this player refuses to leave the area and continues to fight the high-level mob, as he wants that item.

The two scenarios were designed to show a relative lack of explicit intent to disrupt another player's gaming experience. They were drawn from my experience as a player in *Ultima Online* and *EverQuest* for the first and second scenarios respectively.

In answering the question, one developer [R1] remarked that an intended game mechanic would not be considered a grief tactic. Another developer [R3] remarked that the player may have responded to in-game incentives to earn profit and had found means to do so that was unexpected. Moreover, not all disruptive behavior among players should be regarded as grief play. There has to be a demonstration of willful disruptive behavior that serves no other purpose, as a third developer explained [R88].

The above remarks came from developer and not player respondents. If the responses of developer respondents are representative of the game operator, it hints that from the point of view of the game operation, of particular concern is if disallowed tactics have been employed and game rules been broken. Since game rules had not been broken in the scenarios and the intention to disrupt is not explicit, developers were not inclined to believe grief play had taken place. It corroborates the earlier discussion of game rules: that game operators view disruptive activity on the presence of intention to harass or disrupt and if their rules have been broken. Their perceptions are summarized in the table below:

Table 5: Game operator perceptions of grief play

Activity distressing other players	Game rules not broken	Game rules broken
Unclear intention to disrupt	Not griefing. The game operator does not usually respond. If they do, it will be to arbitrate a settlement among players.	Whether activity is griefing is irrelevant; the game operator will respond with punitive measures.
Explicit intention to disrupt	Likely considered griefing, particularly in non-PvP circumstances; the game operator responds with punitive measures.	

On the other hand, some players are concerned with implicit rules in addition to game rules, and if the perpetrator has broken acceptable norms of conduct in the game. For instance, one player [R29] believed that resource hoarding—which is rarely against game rules— in order to manipulate the game economy of an MMORPG is grief play. With reference to scenario 2, several respondents remarked that while the perpetrator did not specifically intend to disrupt, he was aware that his actions posed potential harm to surrounding players, and his behavior was repeated. While some players did not feel this was grief play, others did. Of the latter, one believed that such behavior is selfish [R19] and breaks implicit rules that no player should be allowed to monopolize an area, and that players should share. Another player [R15] remarked that if a player knowingly and with full realization of the likely consequences of his actions continues with the action that has already harmed others, it would be grief play to him.

There are other examples showing how allowed activities are still perceived as grief play. Some MMORPGs allow PvP and hence player-killing within that premise. In some instances, player-killing may have been conducted in the context of player factions, since players who pledge allegiance to a faction are expected to violently engage players in opposing factions. Even then, as noted in Chapter 1, if the game allows PvP, player-killing in some forms is tantamount to harassment and abuse for some players. While PvP should not be equated to grief play, players are more personally affected when they are beaten by fellow players than by constructs controlled by the game's artificial intelligence, for example mobs in PvE. The association between PvP and abusive play is also alluded to by Bartle (2004), who remarks that the degree of PvP allowed in a game world is dependent on several factors, including the tolerance level for abuse displayed by players, and the level of support customer service staff can handle (p. 409). Data corroborates this through perceptions from players that revealed an association between player-killing and grief play: that the most violent activities that can occur among players are of the PvP and combative kind, and they always involve player death. One example would be newbie-killing. An implicit rule that some players expect every PvP participant to abide by is that defenseless or vulnerable targets should be left alone. There is also an element of consent in the debate: that even in a PvP-centric game, there are some situations where players in general feel they should not be attacked—which in other words implies that they did not consent to engage in PvP, no matter what the rules said.

In essence, there are at least two circumstances where player-killing becomes grief play. They concern the issues of fair-play as expected by implicit rules, and of consent. Firstly, players expect PvP to be fair. When it is not, for example because the victim is particularly vulnerable, players will believe they have been griefed. Secondly, players want to agree wholeheartedly to engage in violent activities against each other before they expect to be inflicted with such violence. In some cases, their consent is pegged to their character status—for example, if they had already been killed a few times. On this issue of consent, Bartle (2004, p. 412) notes that there are two levels of "consentuality" in games: by principle when players accept that something *may* happen to them, and by fact when players accept that something *will* happen. When players engage in PvP, they are—or should be—accepting the latter[55]. As it is, some players still feel griefed even if they have given or implied such consent.

---

[55] The issues of consent and fair-play will be further discussed in Chapters 7 and 8 respectively.

So, keeping in mind the issues of fair-play and consent, even if PvP is part of the game and by extension player-killing, a PvP act may be perceived as grief play under any of the following circumstances:

1. The victim's death offered little or no benefit to the player (outside faction or affiliation).

2. Verbal abuse or other antisocial behavior accompanied the act.

3. The victim was killed multiple times.

4. 'Unfair' tactics were used or loopholes were exploited.

The criteria above pertain to PvP, but some of its characterizations can also apply to non-PvP forms of grief play. One player [R24] of *Ultima Online* related this story:

> Some punk kid came along one day and ran inside my house as I was coming out. He stood in the doorway, holding the door open and called to passers by "come on in and take anything you want for free!" I had no recourse at that time for getting rid of him, closing my door or keep anyone from coming in and taking my stuff (there was no way to lock stuff down. I killed him three times (trashing my reputation) and he just rezzed (or resurrected) himself back in my house and continued the harassment.

In this case, aside from the catch all statement in the ROC and the fact that the perpetrator had been persistent, no other game rules had been broken. There was no verbal abuse on the victim, nor had game exploits been engaged or mechanisms used in an unintended way by game design. However, this did not stop the player from feeling griefed: the act had been repeated many times.

It is thus possible to adopt the list of four criteria for PvP-centric grief play to create a more general set of criteria that exemplifies when an activity becomes grief play for a player. A disruptive but allowable play activity may be perceived to be grief play when accompanied by any of the following circumstances:

1. The act offered little or no benefit to the player.

2. Verbal abuse or other antisocial behavior accompanied the act.

3. The act is repeated even when players have signaled they are discontented with the perpetrator, or have found the act disruptive.

4. 'Unfair' tactics were used or loopholes were exploited.

Criteria 2 and 3 in particular do not always involve an explicit intention to disrupt. For example, an accidental 'train' at the edge of a zone resulting in the deaths of several players may or may not be considered grief play. But if the act—accidental and non-intentional as it is—is accompanied by the perpetrator saying "you newbies suck—you should have known better to stand clear so stop complaining" or other visible antisocial behavior, it can result in players believing they have been griefed.

The perceptions of players are summarized in the table below.

Table 6: Player perceptions of grief play

Activity distressing other players	Game rules not broken	Game rules broken
Unclear intention to disrupt	May be considered griefing if social rules of fair-play and etiquette expected by players were broken. It does not matter if game rules were not broken.	
Explicit intention to disrupt	Very likely considered griefing if social rules of fair-play and etiquette expected by players were broken. It does not matter if game rules were not broken.	

Both Table 5 and Table 6 suggest that there are differences in perception on when an activity becomes grief play. To answer the question in the previous section "How do player perceptions of grief play differ from the game operator", this study posits that for:

1. *Game operators*: game rules need to be broken (regardless if the activity had been intending to disrupt) or there is clear intention to disrupt for an act to be considered grief play.

2. *Players*: some will feel griefed if implicit—and not game—rules have been broken. This can happen even if the intention to disrupt is unclear.

There is a strong element of 'expectations' in the second position. Specifically, when the circumstances of a game—for example if it involves non-consensual PvP—have been suitably made known to players, implicit rules are formed through the development of expectations. If players are cognizant of the conditions the game environment demands, they are less likely to view a disruptive incident as grief play and more likely to treat it as acceptable game play. However, whether every player agrees or even understands those expectations cannot be assumed as fact. The issue of expectations merits a substantial discussion, which is presented in Chapter 7.

In summary, while the requirement of an explicit intention to disrupt for an act to be grief play in Mulligan & Patrovsky's (2003) definition is consistent with game operator perception, it is not to all players. When coupled with the fact that often, whether grief play has occurred can be predicated on the victim's perception, it suggests a need to reconsider the 'classical' definition of grief play; that in some cases, there may not be an explicit intention to disrupt for players to feel they have been griefed.

Redefining grief play

The argument to distinguish between grief play that is intentional and non-intentional is further supported by the different types of players who may grief. There are several studies of player motivations and types. Among them is Bartle (1996), who identifies four player types (in MUDs), two of which are 'achievers' and 'killers'. Achievers consider the virtual world foremost as a game and want to reach goals, whereas killers like dominating other people. Yee (2002) also identifies five player motivations, two of which are 'achievement' and 'grief'. Achievement is the desire to be 'powerful' in the game, for example in terms of character prowess, possessions or wealth. Grief is the desire to use other players for one's own advantage. Finally, Fullerton et al. (2004, p. 90) identify 'the achiever' and 'the competitor'. The achiever plays to accomplish tasks, and the competitor plays to beat other players[56].

While the two types or motivations in each of the three models are not identical fits with each other, the three models are still similar enough to suggest the existence of two distinct types of players. The first type is Bartle's (1996) killer, Yee's (2002) grief motivation and Fullerton et al.'s (2004, p. 90) competitors. These players play to exert strong and dominating influence or power, and do so consciously. In Bartle's (1996) and Yee's (2002) models at least, these players could engage in intentional grief play.

The second type: Bartle's (1996) achievers, players belonging to Yee's (2002) achievement, and Fullerton et al.'s (2004) achievers play with the express purpose of accomplishing objectives, whether it is status, advancement, or wealth. Keeping in mind this book's position in the last section—that grief play as perceived by players may not always be with the explicit intention to disrupt—a disruptive activity without explicit intention can be motivated by greed and the desire to accumulate in-game wealth. Alternatively, the player may want to progress in character advancement or acquire a powerful item regardless of any harm or inconvenience inflicted on

---

[56] These models will be discussed further in Chapter 5.

others. Consider two incidents that illustrate this type of activity. The first comes from *Dark Age of Camelot*:

> This player came along and asked to join us but we told him the spot was reserved. ... He was about 6 levels lower than all of us and wouldn't be able to help the group much and would only leech our xp (experience gained), so we politely declined. He got offended and started shooting at the mobs we were killing, boasting about the damage he was doing. We nicely asked him to stop leeching and kill-stealing because he was hurting our xp gain, but he acted like a spoilt brat and continued leeching. [R18]

The second incident comes from *Ultima Online*. In this case, a group of three players were in a dungeon fighting mobs. However, another player persistently attacked the same mob they were about to engage or already engaging. When one of the three players asked the perpetrator to stop, the latter replied by calling them newbies, adding that he had no time for the three to attain loot rewards from the mobs. He then continued kill-stealing [UO-007].

In the first incident, a player in a group is said to be 'leeching' if he cannot contribute effectively when fighting mobs. Nevertheless, he wants to remain (in the group) in order to benefit from the resulting experience and reward gain upon the mob's defeat. In the second incident, the player was not demonstrating a clear intention to disrupt. Rather, that his actions were disruptive was coincidental to his desire to defeat the targeted mob and obtain its rewards for himself. Replies to the discussion thread were divided over whether this was grief play. But in both incidents, that the perpetrators responded with retorts resulted in the victims believing they had been griefed. In both cases, aside from catch all statements, no game rules had been broken nor was there a clear intention to grief even though player experiences had been disrupted. These examples of players desiring to achieve goals above other considerations are consistent with the achiever player types and motivations described by Bartle (1996), Yee (2002) and Fullerton et al. (2004). These players could be seen to be engaging in non-intentional grief play.

Two kinds of grief play now seem demonstrable:

1. An act which is clearly intending to disrupt player experiences, with the actor deriving enjoyment from having been disruptive. This type of grief play is consistent with that exhibited by Mulligan & Patrovsky's (2003) griefer, and could be considered 'classic' griefing.

2. An act which is not clearly intending to disrupt, even though it still is disruptive. If the perpetrator is the sole beneficiary and repeats the act, regardless of the harm or distress he may be causing other players, the act may be stemming from greed.

77

With this in mind, this work defines grief play as:

> Play styles that disrupt another player's gaming experience, usually with deliberate intention to. When the act is not specifically intended to disrupt and yet the perpetrator is the sole beneficiary, it is greed play, a subtle form of grief play.

This expanded definition recognizes that while intention to disrupt is evident in some forms of grief play, in other cases, it is not, even though gaming experiences have been affected.

The differentiation on intention can be contextualized into two 'types' of grief play. Grief play can be 'explicit' or clear demonstrations of activities intending to disrupt, with the actor enjoying the very act of disruption. On the extreme end of this type, explicit grief play would be the type of grief play that meets all three of Mulligan & Patrovsky's (2003) criteria. Grief play can also be 'implicit', ambiguous or less clear demonstrations of deliberately disruptive activity. In many cases, implicit types of grief play would be greed play. Also, game rules may or may not disallow implicit greed play. For example, a clearly stated game rule may demand that players cannot monopolize a play area. However, even if the play activity is allowed, as the discussion has shown, some players will still regard it as grief play and demand game master resolution.

The next section presents a taxonomy of grief play activities, after which each category of grief play will be characterized as an implicit or explicit form.

A taxonomy of grief play

Data analysis resulted in a large number of activities that players perceived as grief play. This section presents a taxonomy of the 19 grief play activities observed in data. In this taxonomy, grief play activities are organized into four categories: harassment, power imposition, scamming, and greed play.

1. *Harassment*: the griefer disturbs, irritates, or impedes the activities of another player.

2. *Power imposition*: the griefer acts with the purpose of demonstrating he is 'better' than others.

3. *Scamming*: the griefer cheats or swindles another player of items, money or information.

4. *Greed play*: the griefer acts solely for his own benefit and while the purpose is not necessarily to disrupt, it still causes annoyance and disturbance to other players.

The table below presents the four grief play categories, with each activity known as a 'subtype'[57] in this work.

Table 7: A taxonomy of grief play—categories and subtypes

Categories	Subtypes
Harassment	1.1 Slurs 1.2 Intentional spamming 1.3 Spatial intrusion 1.4 Event disruption 1.5 Stalking 1.6 Eavesdropping 1.7 Threatening
Power imposition	2.1 Use of loopholes 2.2 Rez-killing 2.3 Newbie-killing 2.4 Training 2.5 Player blocking
Scamming	3.1 Trade scamming 3.2 Promise breaking 3.3 Identity deception
Greed play	4.1 Ninja-looting 4.2 Kill-stealing 4.3 Area monopolizing 4.4 Item farming

A brief recap on game exploitation is appropriate here. While perceptions among players and developers differ on when an activity becomes grief play, exploitation of game design in PvE[58] settings is always seen with disdain by players and disallowed by the game operator altogether. Consider an example where a player who is blocking another player's path with the intention of getting him killed by mobs. The game operator can treat this as a punishable offence if the ROC has already disallowed such activity. The incident becomes murkier if both Law of code and the ROC do not disallow such behavior. This could be an emergent play style, and game design had not anticipated the activity to be engaged in this way. While the game operator can determine in some

---

[57] At this juncture, it is helpful to refresh ourselves on three terms used to describe grief play. Grief play "types" refer to implicit or explicit grief play. Grief play "categories" refer to harassment, power imposition, scamming, and greed play. Grief play "subtypes" refer to the 19 grief play activities covered in this section.

[58] Or player versus environment; see Chapter 1 – 'Key terms'. Rules in PvP tend to be more tolerant of how game mechanisms are used by players.

instances that such activities are not exploitative for a PvE setting, more often than not when it is used to disrupt other players' experience, they will be determined as such. Exploitation of game design may also be used to expedite implicit types of grief play. In these cases, the exploiter's intent may be to benefit from the deficiencies of game design and not to grief, even if the effects of that exploitation may indirectly affect the gaming experience of other players. In all cases, if third party programs have *also* been used to exploit, then it is *always* considered punishable offences by game operators, regardless of whether the game is PvE or PvP-centric.

The next section presents a discussion of each grief play subtype.

Harassment

Game rules for MMORPGs frequently state that harassment is strictly disallowed, while other games like *Shadowbane* state in their ROC that players can resolve issues of harassment on their own (for example by attacking their griefers). Harassment normally breaks game rules and implicit rules but not usually Law of code. This is because many forms of harassment are verbal or emotive in nature. As such, any form of player to player communication could be used to harass.

In harassment, the griefer's intention may be to cause emotional distress on the victim. Aside from the enjoyment of seeing the victim suffer, the griefer does not normally benefit from the act. Also, where Kowalski (2000, p. 232) in his study of teasing notes that people react differently to the same tease, players also react to harassment in different ways. Some players become distressed, others shrug it off. In some cases, harassment may be perceived even in the absence of an intention to be abusive. This can happen if the griefer does not know his behavior upsets other players. For example the usage of a term in his speech or in his character name may be racially offensive to another player, but he is unaware of this. Regardless, if the player has been asked to stop using this term but does not do so, he may be seen by others as griefing, regardless of his intent.

1.1 Slurs. Of harassment types, shouting slurs or other disparaging remarks is a common way of harassing other players. In one case, members of one player community that engaged in PvP with another community spammed racial slurs. This went on until a game master arrived and upon witnessing the scene, removed the guilty parties from the area [R70]. Slurs are often easy for the game operator to prosecute as all chat messages are logged in game servers. Moreover, players can also log these utterances and post them as their 'proof' as they demand responses from the game operator.

80

1.2 Intentional spamming. The player may also intentionally spam a chat channel repeatedly with messages of low relevance, utility or just for fun. As one player [R68] of *Ultima Online* related:

> People on UO will come up to you and spam "OWNED NEWBIE LOL!!" or something like that, and then when you reply with <insert offensive term here> they page on you for harassment and try to get you banned.

In other occasions, griefers may also emote in an offensive way. For example, the griefer may emote a so-called 'virtual rape' of a victim.

1.3 Spatial intrusion. Spatial intrusion occurs when a player repeatedly violates the space perceived to be private to another player. For example, a griefer can enter a player-owned house or establishment and become a nuisance by spamming slurs. An example has been cited earlier by one player [R24] in *Ultima Online,* where a griefer sneaked into his home and held the door open, beckoning passer-bys to come into the house and take whatever they wanted for free.

Game design improvements in many MMORPGs since then allow the owners of player establishments to eject other players selectively, or disallow all other players beside themselves from entering their properties unless specific permission is granted.

1.4 Event disruption. Event disruption occurs when an activity organized by players is purposefully interrupted by other players. The Trinsic incident is an example of event disruption. Griefers can either disrupt events directly by spamming chat messages that violate the spirit of the event, or engage in destructive action to hinder or upset its arrangement or organization. Not all event disruptions—like some other types of grief play—involve explicitly abusive behavior. In one case in *World of Warcraft,* a particularly difficult mob known as Lord Kazzak could only be defeated by a raid group comprising a large number of high-level characters. In order to make the encounter more challenging, game design gave Kazzak an interesting ability: if any one of the attackers was killed in the fight with him, the mob would have a large amount of its 'health' replenished, essentially eliminating a good part of whatever progress the raid group had made towards beating him. As such, the attackers would have to play with great skill to defeat the mob. As it turned out, griefers began situating very low-level characters near such fights as and when they were organized. When the timing was appropriate, one griefer would rush headlong like a suicide bomber, get killed by Kazzak, and restore its health. This had the effect of turning the whole encounter around to the players' disadvantage [WoW-003e]. While such tactics could have been expedited by poor encounter design, no game rules had been broken[59]. Moreover, the player rushing headlong did not need to make any abusive utterances for him to create the necessary impact.

One player of the same game remarked that the game could not be working as intended if a low-level player was able to grief an entire raid group of high-level players. In this case, event disruption had occurred in the perception of players, with several remarking similar sentiments: that it should not be possible for one person to grief or disrupt an organized raid event [WoW-003c]. This was made the more evident by the use of a very low-level character to disrupt—low-level characters have little to lose in character death or reputation from the act of griefing, compared to high-level characters.

1.5 Stalking, 1.6 Eavesdropping, 1.7 Threatening. In addition, because many of the play activities in MMORPGs are modeled after the real-world, other types of non-verbal harassment that are possible in real-life are possible in the game as well. Some examples include stalking, threatening and eavesdropping. A grief play who persistently intrudes into the perceived space of another player may be stalking this victim. In another case in *Dark Age of Camelot*, one player community was coordinating a server-wide raid on an enemy faction. As these things go, the planning was in secret so that the opposing players could not discover what was coming. Just before the event, a player—who belonged to the faction planning the event—posted details of those plans in a public forum. The event failed as a result, and this griefer was labeled a spy and traitor by players on the server [R18]. This is an example of eavesdropping. Some grief players may threaten other players, and this can happen where there is disparity of prowess levels[60].

Power imposition

Besag (1989, p. 4) notes that bullying takes place between a person in power against someone who is powerless to resist. The demonstration of power—for example by a player who shows off the better equipment he possesses—in itself is not normally perceived by players as grief play. However, when power is demonstrated through imposition, i.e. acts *against* a player, it may be

---

[59] This rule was later changed through a "Lord Kazzak Griefing Policy". This policy treated as grief play a similar faction player committing this act.

[60] See Chapter 8 – 'Might is right'.

perceived as grief play. For example, several demonstrable forms of power imposition are centered on player-killing. As described in an earlier section, ROCs in PvP-centric games may not regard the ambush, unexpected or repeated killing of players as grief play. Moreover, player-killing may be motivated by a desire other than to impose power over the victim—for example because the game by design encourages consensual player-killing in the form of player faction conflict. However, as noted before, players employ implicit rules when determining if a PvP act is grief play, with actual circumstances surrounding the incident influencing that determination. A player [R23] of *Ultima Online* related the following:

> A friend and I were in his house just talking when we were approached by another player. He lived just next door and we chatting with him for a bit. He invited us over to see his house and we agreed, as he seemed like a nice guy. Being very trusting, we kept all of our amour and items on us. Once close to his house he turned around and attacked us. My friend fell first and then I fell next. He looted our things and refused to resurrect us. When we finally did get resurrected, we went back to my friend's house only to be killed again. We were killed by him 4 times that night, without any reason.

In this case, the respondent's character was killed repeatedly, and without good reason (to the respondent). In addition, there were other incidents where player characters were killed when in helpless states. A player who has just been killed by a mob is typically temporarily weakened when revived. New or inexperienced players are also vulnerable. Verbal abuse often accompanies these acts too. When players are killed under these circumstances, the difference in power levels from attacker to victim may lead the victims to believe they were killed as a demonstration of power.

2.1 Use of loopholes. The use of loopholes to cause the death of another player's character or to gain advantage in PvP will often lead the victim to conclude he has been griefed, since the perpetrators had 'unnatural' advantages that the victims did not have or use. For example, at one point in *Star Wars Galaxies*, faction-based players were ambushing opposing faction players. The attackers would then escape into player-owned houses to rest and recuperate in safety as the opposing players could not enter these houses to continue the fight [R21]. This is an example of players creating play tactics that are emergent game play[61], and there were perceptions that the fights had not been fair. When the tactic became prevalent, changes were made to code making it impossible for the use of such a loophole.

---

[61] See Chapter 7 – 'Game management'.

2.2 Rez-killing, 2.3 Newbie-killing. Regardless of what is allowed by Law of code, player-killing may be considered grief play depending on specific circumstances. The following was stated in an earlier section, and is reiterated again: a PvP act may be perceived to be grief play if any of the following circumstances are true:

1. The victim's death offered little or no benefit to the player (outside faction or affiliation).

2. Verbal abuse or other antisocial behavior accompanied the act.

3. The victim was killed multiple times.

4. 'Unfair' tactics were used or loopholes were exploited.

In relation to the circumstances listed above, rez-killing and newbie-killing may be perceived as grief play since there is little benefit from the action [R84]. Moreover, rez-killing occurs when the griefer kills his victim after the victim has been 'resurrected', and possibly does so repeatedly. The following incident was related by a player [R46] of *Star Wars Galaxies*:

> The bounty hunter[62] profession has the ability to hunt Jedi and kill them for profit. A group of bounty hunters simply surrounded my friend and killed him. That would have been acceptable, but they constantly 'camped' the nearest respawn[63] point and used an exploit to continue killing my friend. Nobody could do anything about it, and even when confronted, the bounty hunters simply replied something along the lines of "he's a Jedi, he brought it upon himself."

A similar incident occurred in *EverQuest*. One high-level player on the PvP server fell asleep on his keyboard while playing. Over the course of the next several hours, he was attacked and resurrected repeatedly without his knowledge. This continued until his friends arrived at the scene to stop the attackers. As a result of penalties accrued from death, the player suffered a large loss of advancement that had taken about 200 hours of play time to reach [R54].

In both cases, when players were killed, they respawned in weakened states, either without possession of equipment, or with diminished character prowess. Their defenseless states were taken advantage of by their attackers, who killed these players repeatedly (circumstance 3 in the list

---

[62] The role of the bounty hunter in PvP games has been suggested as a possible way of encouraging players to combat and control player-killers (Rogers 2003, p. 465). This will be further discussed in Chapter 8 – 'The city-state government'.

[63] See Chapter 1 – 'Key terms'.

above) even though there was no benefit to gain in such repetition (circumstance 1). Some griefers will even camp at respawn locations to repeatedly attack all recently killed players who respawn there [R84].

Newbie-killing, as the name suggests, refers to the killing of new and frequently inexperienced players of the game. In one case in Near Death Studios' *Meridian 59*, an early PvP MMORPG, newbies were targeted specifically even though they were never rich nor carried any items worth winning upon their defeats [R68]. In newbie-killing, the large difference in character prowess levels between attacker and victim means that apart from the possible enjoyment of seeing the victim killed, there is usually little other benefit to be gained. This is because newbies frequently own little equipment that the attacker will want or need.

For both rez and newbie-killing, the victims have to suffer some degree of loss, for example equipment degradation, upon each death. Player-killers may kill to inflict such loss on their victims, and they do so to demonstrate their power. In the case of *Shadowbane*, rez-killing awards no experience or loot[64]. Moreover, in the game, there is no strategic benefit through these killings since the respawn point can be random [R84]. Hence, even though the game is oriented around PvP, such actions would be perceived as grief play.

As it is, newbie-killing and rez-killing may be against implicit rules, but rarely against game rules. Law of code may however accord vulnerable players some temporary protection. For example, game design may protect new players from player attack until they reach some designated level of advancement, after which the game regards these players as experienced enough to fend for themselves.

2.4 Training, 2.5 Player blocking. Subtle ways of imposing power include training and player blocking. Training is defined, for example in *Star Wars Galaxies'* ROC (Sony Online Entertainment Inc. 2004b), as "pulling/leading a hostile NPC or creature along behind you and attempting to get it to attack another player who does not desire that engagement." One *EverQuest* player [R55] related the following story of training:

---

[64] Other PvP games do allow the looting of players killed by their attackers. The design intent in this is that allowing player corpses to be looted gives a legitimate basis for players to engage in PvP, since there is reward for the risks they take (Sage 2003, p. 91).

> A troll shadow knight had come to us in the Dreadlands with a mob hitting on him. He just stood there, hoping for help, saying nothing. We didn't help him because someone in our group was coming back with a pull. So he runs out, collects three more mobs then runs behind our group and feigns death. The mobs attack us and many of us die.

In the above example, the abilities of a character class expedite training. The example here concerns an ability called 'feign death'. This ability is also possessed by players playing 'monk' characters in *EverQuest 2*. One player [EQ2-007] related an incident where a monk trained a mob onto a group using this skill, resulting in the deaths of several group members. The player remarked that the perpetrator's attitude was smug, leading him to conclude that the action had been deliberate.

Trains of mobs can also create graphical lag on a player's computer, as its graphics processor has to work harder to render images of numerous characters and objects. Unless the player is making use of computer equipment capable of handling the additional processing load, it can result in lowered game performance. In one case, a group of players camping a room in *EverQuest 2* encountered another group which wanted the mob that was spawning in this room [EQ2-003]. The player in the posting related that the second group next pulled mobs from surrounding areas, fighting them right next to his group. He called this 'lag' training.

Having said this, not all trains are intentional. In *EverQuest*, a player seeking to escape from a mob in a high-level dungeon could accidentally lead a mob attacking him and other mobs to nearby players. This creates an unintentional train. However, if this action is carried out repeatedly, players are likely to regard it as grief play. Game rules often regard only intentional training as grief play.

Player blocking refers to the obstruction of another player's path of movement. When players are chased by mobs and their movement is obstructed, they may get killed. For both intentional training and player blocking to get players killed, the griefer feels powerful for having caused the deaths of other players.

Training and player blocking may be rendered impossible by Law of code. When no such code exists, they may or may not be prohibited by game rules. Both play styles are, however, commonly perceived as grief play by implicit rules.

Scamming

A scam commonly refers to a fraudulent business scheme or a swindle. In games that support player theft—for example in some play areas of *Ultima Online*—game rules do not consider thievery to be grief play. In other games, scamming poses analytical challenges, and there is disagreement on whether scamming is grief play. The root of this lies in the context an MMORPG operates in—that it is a role-playing game after all, and some players want to role-play unsavory characters alongside others who role-play morally upright characters. In this study, the following scenario was posed to respondents:

> A player's character is a thief, and this is visibly tagged on this character for all to see. What if this person scams another player, but when queried by the game master, he insists he was role-playing in a manner consistent to that of a thief?

Assuming that the game has not explicitly disallowed the role-playing of a scammer, player respondents were divided over whether such a scenario constitutes grief play. Jakobsson & Taylor (2003, p. 81) note that in-character and out-of-character spaces can be hard to distinguish. The perceptions from data certainly revealed debate on what is really legitimate role-play. Some players believed that player transactions should operate on caveat emptor ("let the purchaser beware"). One player [R25] explained "This is not grief play, but 'smart play' on the part of the thief and 'dumb play' on the part of the buyer." Rossignol (2005, p. 20) for *The Escapist* writes of an instance in *EVE Online* where griefers scammed a player community of in-game money, the amount of which was the equivalent of USD1,000 in real-world cash. No game rules had been broken in the incident. On the other hand, other players interviewed in this study believed that there are some actions in a game that must occur 'out of character'. Player sales and transactions are in this exception list. There is a perception that the bartering of items among players is always made on good faith, and such transactions do not occur in role-play mode [R16].

The developers interviewed say that the above role-playing scenario is tricky. If the game by design supports a play style that rewards 'achiever' players (for example in Bartle 1996) for getting ahead, can players who turn dishonest really be called griefers? On the other hand, a player who claims he is role-playing is more likely attempting to get away with bad behavior than demonstrating true role-playing on his part. This observation was echoed by several players.

Role-playing or not, players may not get much help from game mechanisms if they are to watch out for themselves. It is not easy to create mechanisms that can determine another player's trustworthiness. There are reputation systems built into some games that allow players to have an idea on each other's play dispositions, but they are not foolproof[65]. The ROCs of some games, for example *EverQuest* (Sony Online Entertainment Inc. 2004a) and *Star Wars Galaxies* (Sony Online Entertainment Inc. 2004b), side-step the problem of role-playing by clarifying their positions explicitly: their ROCs specifically disallow fraud, and add that role-playing does not excuse such behavior.

3.1 Trade scamming. Trade scamming—or the engagement of fraudulent transactions against other players—is considered grief play when it is exploitative of poorly designed trading systems. It was possible in some early MMORPGs to cheat players by surreptitiously moving items in and out of the trade windows that facilitate item transactions between players. Several players of *Ultima Online* posted how they were scammed before trading mechanisms were improved. It can still occur in more recent games, as one player [R39] of *The Sims Online* related:

> I was defrauded out of §100,000[66] by a player who offered me a rare pet for sale, which turned out to be a normal pet worth around §6,000 in the game. He showed me the rare pet in his house, but then swapped the pet carriers around without me noticing when trading the pet between the players. When I got home and released the pet, realizing that I had been conned, I contacted the person immediately who laughed at me then put me on ignore. There is nothing I can do to get my money back.

Many current MMORPGs use 'secure' trade windows for player trading. These require players to give explicit consent for item and money exchanges before the transaction is complete. Consent is required again if the terms of transaction are modified in any way.

3.2 Promise breaking. Secure trade systems are less effective in preventing scams from promise breaking. This occurs when a player promises to do something, for example render a service, in exchange for payment. However, upon the receipt of payment, the player does not fulfill his promise. Alternatively, a player may promise to deliver a service or exchange an item outside the trade window, but refuses to do so upon receipt of payment. One player [R22] of *Ultima Online* shared his experience of promise breaking that occurred between servers:

---

[65] See Chapter 8 – 'Reputation'

[66] § is short for Simolean, the currency used in *The Sims Online*.

I went to a trade board, posted that I wished to make a cross shard transfer of one mil gold. I received an ICQ[67] from another player, stating he wished to play Pacific and would be willing to do the transfer. ... So, we did my shard first. I met him at the bank, gave him a mil in checks. ... I had to log out of the game. ... When I did get back in, he was nowhere to be found. I messaged him, got no response. It took me all of an hour to realize I had just lost a million gold, and that really really [sic] devastated me. He had put me on ignore ICQ or deleted me.

Customer service did not reimburse the losses incurred in both of these cases.

3.3 Identity deception. Identity deception happens when a player attempts to pass himself off as another player. On some Internet communities, identity deception is common (Donath 1999, p. 44). Like scamming, some players believe that the context of an MMORPG requires that identity deception be treated as role-playing rather than grief play. For example, a player could attempt to portray himself of the opposite gender, different age, or other personality traits. The player may be intending to be consistent with the type of character role-played. When it can become grief play is if the impersonation is intended to abuse or scam while disguised as someone else, as opposed to a player deceiving to play a joke on his regular companions. In *Ultima Online* for instance, there were cases of griefers who joined player communities, and bid their time for an opportunity to kill other members of their communities. These griefers did not hide the fact that they enjoyed causing such destruction [R69]. Such infiltration and effort to gain trust and confidence before causing mayhem is an example of identity deception.

Interestingly, ROCs do not usually explicitly disallow the impersonation of another player's character. The impersonation of another player's character is not easily accomplished to begin with in most games. Some games allow a player to alter his character's physical appearance to resemble the targeted victim in visible appearance, or even allow a player to choose a name that is similar to the victim's.

Greed play

The player's motive in greed play is to benefit, regardless if the action annoys the other players around him. The unsportsmanlike behavior described by Salen & Zimmerman (2004, p. 269) is similar to greed play—the player will do anything to win. He follows the operational rules of a game, but violates the spirit of the game and its implicit rules.

---

[67] The Internet messaging tool at http://www.icq.com.

Discussion in the earlier section has revealed that players do not all agree that greed play constitutes grief play since there is an absence of a deliberate intention to disrupt. Often, the intention is to get ahead and if the game encourages the competitive play cited by Vorderer et al. (2003), one could argue that it seems unreasonable to blame players for selfish play. For example, the most 'powerful' items in the game are attained as rewards for the most fiercely contested mobs. In the case of *EVE Online*, Rossignol (2005, p. 18) writes in *The Escapist* about how the malevolent methods players use to get money from each other are emphasized as part of the game. Moreover, a greed play subtype allowed in one MMORPG may be disallowed in another even if the motivation to gain despite causing annoyance is the same. The mechanics for greed play may differ from game to game, but the underlying issue of whether greed play is grief play remains.

In general, however, players seem more forgiving when greed play is merely inconveniencing them, even if they still get upset. An example would be the hoarding of resources or the competition for a contested mob. On the other hand, players are less forgiving and more likely to consider greed play to be grief play when the act poses direct risk or causes harm to their characters.

4.1 Ninja-looting. One form of greed play is ninja-looting. The term 'ninja' is a reference to the mercenary agents in feudal Japan who were trained for secret operations, and known for their speed of movement. Ninja-looting is commonly defined (for example in Mulligan & Patrovsky 2003, p. 479) as the taking of items that had been rightly earned by or awarded to another player, using the speed or stealthy tactics of such ninjas in feudal Japan.

Ninja-looting can occur in three situations. Firstly, the griefer did not participate in the fight against the mob. This kind of ninja-looting can be prevented in code, as looting rights can be awarded only to the player or group who succeeds in administering the most damage to the mob, since it is reasonable to assume that the party who did the most work deserves the reward. However, this may encourage griefers to 'kill-steal' (see below) and then loot the mob immediately after the battle. If no such quantifiably-based damage rules in code exist, it can encourage players in the vicinity to all 'have a go' at a mob when it appears since they each have some chance of getting looting rights.

Secondly, the griefer participated as part of the group but had trivial contribution. This kind of ninja-looting is harder to prevent through game design. While looting rights can be awarded by Law of code only to the player or group who collectively renders the most damage to the mob, it is harder to code a mechanism that will fairly determine looting rights based on contribution. This is because players playing support or utility classes—for example healers—are less likely to administer direct damage to the mob. In these cases, players of these classes may be disadvantaged.

Some MMORPGs allow looting rights to be managed in a less arbitrary fashion. For example in *EverQuest 2*, settings can allow only the group leader to loot every item first and distribute them fairly later. This resolves the third kind of ninja-looting: the griefer is part of the group but someone else has already been assigned to loot the mob. However, it assumes that the group leader can be trusted. Games with clearly laid out ninja-looting rules include *EverQuest*, which disallows it in its ROC (Sony Online Entertainment Inc. 2004a).

4.2 Kill-stealing. Kill-stealing occurs when a player attacks a mob that is already engaged in a fight with another player or team, with the intention of 'stealing' the items or rewards that would come about from the defeat of that mob. The story cited by a player of *Dark Age of Camelot* [R18] in an earlier section where a player who was refused admission into a group is an example of kill-stealing.

Like ninja-looting, kill-stealing as a form of greed play is recognized as disruptive and annoying behavior. Still, perception is divided over whether it is explicit grief play, since kill-stealing (and ninja-looting) does not normally lead to player deaths. Moreover, if the mob carries an item that many players want, some will believe they are justified in engaging in competitive behavior for it. An example of this is the competition for contested mobs in *EverQuest* and *EverQuest 2*. Another example was observed in *Star Wars Galaxies*. For a short period of time in this game, fierce competition for an item known as the "holocron" resulted in large groups of players camping known spots spawning mobs that carried the item. When the mob appeared, surrounding players abandoned any prior arrangements of turn taking, and all attacked the mob simultaneously in a wild frenzy, each hoping to do the most damage and gain the required looting rights. Such competitive behavior corroborates Davis' (2002) observation that competition in online games can lead to bad behavior.

Kill-stealing may also be perceived as grief play when the perpetrator is much more powerful in relation to the mob's ability and the already engaged player or group's collective abilities. For example, a group of low-level characters fight a mob, and midway a highly powered character appears and engages the same mob, killing it quickly. Whether this mob will grant this highly powered character any worthwhile loot becomes a moot issue. Rather, that there is a large difference between the prowess levels of this high-level character and the mob causes surrounding players to perceive that grief play has occurred, since this player has defeated the mob with little risk or effort involved. Kill-stealing when there is nothing to gain may also be a form of power imposition.

4.3 Area monopolizing. Area monopolizing takes place when a player or a group gains exclusive access to a public area. Typically, the player or group intends to be the sole occupants to an area where a mob or resource appears. Area monopolizing is most commonly associated with a group camping an area. Camping is allowed by game rules, but players are occasionally reminded by ROCs that they cannot monopolize an area. For example, *EverQuest*'s 'play nice' rules (Sony Online Entertainment Inc. 2004a) states that:

> You may not disrupt the normal playability of a zone or area.
>
> Zone/Area Disruption is defined as any activity designed to harm or inconvenience a number of groups rather than a specific player or group of players. This includes, but is not limited to:
>
> - Monopolizing most or all of the kills in an area.

Implicit rules, however, expect a new group arriving at an already camped area to state their intention, for example to camp the same area, through chat messages. When it is considered grief play by some players is if the new group situates itself in close proximity without first explicitly stating their intention to fight the same mob appearing in that area. This can happen if the new group mingles with the incumbent group. The incumbent group will perceive this as an intrusion into their private space. When the mob does appear, chaos and kill-stealing can result if both groups have not made arrangements to take turns. Typically, the incumbent group will feel griefed by the new group.

Like other types of grief play, in these cases, there may not have been a deliberate intention to disrupt play experiences of others. However, some players will be annoyed and feel that this is not fair-play ("we were here first"). This is even if game rules demand that players share.

4.4 Item farming. Related to area monopolizing is item farming. Item farming occurs when a player continuously camps an area with a mob spawning an item. He does so with the sole purpose of acquiring as many of these items in as short a time as possible. Of the four types of greed play

92

explained here, item farming is least likely an activity with the explicit intention to distress other players. It is typically stemming from greed, and therefore may be greed play. Other players believe that this constitutes unfair-play if it is a high-level player 'farming' the weaker mob. One player of *EverQuest 2* [EQ2-014] reported 'farmers' who were monopolizing a mob and depriving other players who needed this mob to progress along in their quests. He added that any player who monopolizes an area in the game is griefing, regardless of whether the intention of the perpetrator is to obstruct another player's quest progression or not. Like area monopolizing, the difference in prowess levels and the ability to administer damage (and thus winning looting rights) can intensify the perception that this is griefing. This is because these players believe they have no reasonable chance of contesting and defeating the same mob in the presence of the high-level character, i.e. unfair tactics had been employed.

Some forms of greed play can be managed by Law of code. For example, to counter ninja-looting, games can be designed to award looting rights to the first group that engages a mob. Similarly, to counter item farming, games can be designed such that encounters involving mobs that offer little or no challenge to a player will not reward the player with items when the mob is defeated.

Discussion

The argument to distinguish between implicit and explicit grief types was presented in an earlier section. Powers (2003, p. 197) notes that bad behavior in online RPGs can run from "low-end" (for example being a new and clueless player to the game) to "high-end" (for example hate speech). Powers' differentiation is loosely comparable to implicit (low-end) and explicit (high-end) grief play types. However, implicit and explicit types of grief play are differentiated not on the amount of disruption caused, but on the presence of a clear intention to disrupt. The former is an important distinction: an act can be widely disruptive, but it can still be implicit grief play if it was not specifically intending to disrupt. One example of this would be unintentional training, which can lead to many player character deaths. The qualitative and interpretivistic methods adopted in this study could not determine with certainty how many players perceived a grief play subtype to be implicit or explicit. Nevertheless, the study was still interested in investigating player perceptions of when they would consider an activity implicit or explicit grief play. In some cases, respondents were asked to cite examples. In other cases, scenarios were posed to respondents. Through an analysis of each response, it was possible to say with confidence if that subtype was implicit or explicit to that respondent. These results were then correlated with discussion postings to suggest a very general position on each grief play subtype.

The subtypes of grief play that were often considered implicit were those centered on the acquisition of rewards and resources in the game, and those considered explicit were when abuse, harassment or power imposition was evident. For instance, many considered newbie-killing to be a demonstration of explicit grief play. However, ninja-looting, kill-stealing, area monopolizing, and item farming were generally considered less clear demonstrations—all grief play subtypes that fall under the greed play category.

The table below proposes the following placement of each grief play category:

Table 8: Implicit and explicit grief play

	Grief play categories
Implicit grief play	Greed play
Explicit grief play	Harassment, Power imposition, Scamming

It was explained in an earlier section that greed play stems from a player's desire to selfishly gain without regard to other players, even if there is no deliberate intention to be disruptive. Area monopolization is a good example that illustrates this. Specifically, while there may be game rules that state players may not monopolize an area of mobs or resources, these rules can be difficult to enforce. This is because any given situation can have mitigating circumstances where players expect the influence of implicit rules, no matter what game rules say. For example, a game area with an attractive reward or important mob can be difficult to reach. In *EverQuest*, it may be necessary for players to 'clear' a path through a dungeon to reach the area, and this path could be filled with dangerous mobs to defeat. A player group could expend hours of effort just to get to this area. When they do get there, the players will believe they have worked hard to get to this area, and have exclusive 'rights' to it. They will be unwilling to give up these rights or share the area. A subsequent party of players that follows the first group closely will not have to clear the same path. However, when they arrive in the area, they will often face resistance from the first group that cleared the path and got there first. While the second group can petition for a game master to arbitrate, either resolution—that both groups must share the area, or one group is to leave the area—would be dissatisfactory to at least one party. This again points to the issue of differing rules used as a basis for perceptions: that game rules may demand players play the game in some way, but implicit rules may influence players perceptions on how incidents like these should be played out. As Jakobsson & Taylor (2003, p. 89) note, official rules telling players how the game should be played does not mean players will actually play it that way.

In the case of area monopolization, many players of games like *EverQuest* with similar play activities manage these situations by ignoring game rules and instead employ implicit rules when multiple groups converge in an area. The implicit rule can be this: unless the area is large enough to support multiple groups, an area that is already camped by a group should not be challenged by subsequent groups. For example in *EverQuest*, upon reaching a new play zone, players are expected to call for a 'camp check' in the public chat channel. Groups that are already situated at occupied areas of the play zone will respond by replying in the public chat channel. If a group still contests an occupied area, the implicit rule of not contesting an already occupied camp spot would be considered broken by players. Still, these instances while seemingly selfish are still ambiguous in that not every player believes selfish behavior should be actionable on the part of the game operator. In the case of kill-stealing, many will regard the behavior as selfish. However, the perpetrator may believe otherwise and that he is an 'achiever'. In any case, implicit grief play is characterized by the absence of a deliberate intention to disrupt and that the victims are usually inconvenienced rather than have suffered character death or item loss.

The other three grief play categories are considered explicit grief play as they are characterized by a usually clear intention to disrupt through abuse, harassment and power imposition, and that the victims of explicit grief play typically suffer either direct loss or distress, or have been greatly inconvenienced. These kind of losses could include (repeated) player deaths or items through fraudulent transactions. The players may be agitated through harassment or verbal abuse. In some cases of explicit grief play, game masters are able to respond determinedly if the grief play subtype breaks specific game rules. For example, there could be specific rules disallowing fraudulent transactions, or specific types of verbal harassment. In the case of the latter, a player who is harassing another player by hurling racial abuse could be punished.

Lin & Sun (2005) in their study of grief play cite a list of grief play behaviors, and a few behaviors in their list were not mentioned as grief play by the respondents in my study. For instance, one such behavior is "New-Taiwan-Dollar worriers", which Lin & Sun (2005) regard as players making use of real-world currency to purchase in-game currency. Such practices can affect the game world's economy, and were briefly discussed in the eBay section of Chapter 1. However, none of the respondents in my study mentioned such activities as grief play. To be fair, in Lin & Sun's (2005) work, they note that this particular subtype of grief play was mentioned just once in their interviews with players.

That grief play can be implicit or explicit will be revisited in the next chapter when factors that result in players griefing are correlated to the grief play type exhibited.

Conclusion

This chapter has shown several things. Firstly, there is contention over what constitutes grief play. There is a large amount of discussion postings that frequently debate if a reported incident was grief play or not. Just a small portion of these discussion postings was gathered to supplement interview work. For some players, grief play activity is an unavoidable type of conflict that makes up part of normal game play. Other players are unhappy, and express dissatisfaction with the game operator on their resolution of grief play incidents. This lack of consensus stems from differing perceptions of when an activity becomes grief play. Game operators will base their assessment on game rules, while players tend towards implicit rules. Game operators seem reluctant to use implicit rules as an important, let alone sole, element in determining if grief play has taken place. This is not without reason; expectations of player etiquette can be arbitrary, and not all players comply with implicit rules. Other players feel they have been griefed as long as their enjoyment has been affected in some way and their personal (and not necessarily common) expectations of what is 'fair' impugned upon. Moreover, as the game matures in content, expectations of player etiquette can change. Some players do become more tolerant of bad behavior and also experienced in how to respond to grief play.

In essence, game operators and players employ different types of rules when determining if grief play has occurred. This, coupled with the absence of intention in some types of disruptive activity, led to grief play being divided into implicit and explicit types. This distinguishing was also supported by the two player types/motivations that may disrupt player enjoyment in different ways. These player types/motivations will be further discussed in the next chapter.

The existing definition of grief play was also expanded upon. MMORPG literature has defined grief play as intentional activities where the player disrupts the gaming experience of other players. As the chapter has shown, disruptive activities may not always be intentional, nor can intent be easily determined online in the absence of visual cues. With these difficulties in mind, the existing definition of grief play was refined. A new term, greed play, was proposed, and the study has posited that greed play is a type of implicit grief play.

Finally, as above, implicit rules are affected by player expectations, for example what players believe is fair-play. In one sense, if player expectations are managed, players may become less likely to view certain acts as grief play. Given the very large player bodies in MMORPGs, it can be difficult to create games that meet the expectations of every participant. The expectations of players on grief play management will be revisited in Chapter 7. For the moment, the next chapter investigates the second research objective: what motivates players to engage in grief play.

CHAPTER 5: GRIEF PLAYER MOTIVATIONS

The last chapter has explored the meaning of grief play, the issue of intention, and the interplay between grief play and rules. It revealed that while literature has defined grief play, perceptions of what is grief play differ among participants. It showed that the catch all statement in the ROC can disallow players from playing in ways that disrupt the enjoyment of others. However, in practice, game operators often take action against griefers only when their intention to disrupt is explicitly demonstrated, or they have engaged in activities that are specifically disallowed.

The second objective of this research is to investigate what motivates player to engage in grief play. This chapter has two operationalized objectives[68]:

1. To explore factors that can cause players to grief.

2. To investigate if these factors are interrelated with each other, and to grief play subtypes.

Before an understanding can be reached on why players grief, we need to discuss why people play computer games to begin with. Two types of models will be used in this discussion: player types, and player motivations. Grief play has also been observed to bear some relation to bullying and teasing. Hence, motivations in both of these two behavioral concepts will be included in the discussion.

Existing models of player motivations and types

Bartle (2004, pp.128-129) notes that people play games because it is "fun". Hunicke et al.'s (2004) taxonomy even lists specific types of fun, for example "narrative" when the game is played as drama, or "discovery" when the game is played as territory to be explored. In practice, these reasons commonly take the form of a goal or an objective to reach. For example, a player who plays to discover has the goal of exploring territory. In order to expedite this process of play, there needs to be in the play session goals or objectives to reach and attain. Occasionally, some of these goals are provided in the game. Single-player computer games often have end goals. For instance, the end goal in *Quake* could be to get past every level, reach the deepest level in the game and beat the hard encounter there. When this objective is reached, the game is considered 'completed'. The

---

[68] The material from this chapter was partially presented in a paper I wrote in 2004. The citation details are as follows: Foo, C Y & Koivisto E M I 2004, 'Grief player motivations", in *Other Players-conference on multiplayer phenomena*, Copenhagen.

pay-off is, commonly, a well-rendered end-game video sequence that gets played back on the screen, after which the game ends.

In comparison, there are some game systems in MMORPGs with similar elements of finality. For example, players are allowed to advance up to a limit each time (with this limit usually raised whenever new content is added), and there is a theoretically finite size to the game world. However, beyond this, the end goals in MMORPGs are usually less well defined (Lastowka & Hunter 2004; Cornett 2004, p. 703). There are no 'victory' or end game screens in the MMORPG. An MMORPG game world is large and its included content so voluminous that few players are able to exhaust all game content. Moreover, the game world continues to exist and get maintained by the game operator even after players have reached the highest attainable level of advancement. In the absence of well-defined end goals provided in a game, players create their own goals and objectives. This makes understanding the motivations of players to play games even the more important.

To motivate, according to The American Heritage Dictionary of the English Language, is to "provide with an incentive", "move to action" or "impel". The discussion in this section covers seven models of player types and motivations. Each of the seven models relates to one of three facets in an MMORPG: that it is a computer game, a role-playing game, and a game involving large numbers of participants. Each of these three facets characterizes a differing dimension of the MMORPG: that it is a computer game driven by technology, a role-playing game that allows players to develop their characters in ways that are determined by the roles chosen, and a multi-player game where interaction exists with other players.

The table below shows the three facets. As each facet traverses down, the one preceding it continues to hold true. Hence, Hallford & Hallford's (2001) model refers to *both* 'a role-playing game' and 'a computer game'. Bartle's (1996) model refers to all three facets.

Table 9: Player models and facets

	Facet	Model
1.	A computer game	Lazzaro (2004), Rouse (2005), Fullerton et al. (2004)
2.	A computer game, and a role-playing game	Hallford & Hallford (2001)
3.	A computer game, a role-playing game, and involving large numbers of players	Bartle (1996), Yee (2002), Rozak (2005)

Some of these models are called player 'types' while others are called 'motivations'. For example, Bartle (1996), Fullerton et al. (2004), and Hallford & Hallford (2001) present player types. Yee (2002), Lazaaro (2004), Rouse (2005) and Rozak (2005) present player motivations. However, there are close relationships between each player type and its motivator to justify a joint exploration to understand why people play games. Examples can illustrate this close relationship. Players in Bartle's 'achiever' type are motivated by their desire to reach the goals and objectives they set for themselves. Players in Hallford & Hallford's 'fragmaster' type are motivated by their desire to deal with goals and objectives using violent mechanisms, for example combat.

Lazzaro's model

Lazzaro's (2004) study of player motivations at XEODesign involved 34 adult players of games—PC, console, handheld, and online games, including MMORPGs. Three types of data were collected in her study. They were video recordings of player activity, player responses to questionnaires, and verbal and non-verbal emotional cues during play. Through her analysis of the data gathered, Lazzaro's resultant model comprises:

1. *Internal experience key*: emotions are created during play, and players enjoy these changes in their "internal states." Games are therapeutic in this motivation.

2. *Hard fun: the challenge and strategy key:* the player plays to overcome obstacles and challenges.

3. *Easy fun: the immersion key*: the player plays to immerse himself through exploration in the game world and 'living' in it.

4. *Other players: the social experience key:* players play to socialize with friends and to observe other people.

Rouse's model

Rouse (2005, p. 2) in his book "*Game Design: Theory and Practice*" poses the question "Why do players play?" His list comprises eight reasons, among which he notes that players want:

1. *A challenge*: players can even, subconsciously, apply lessons learnt through game play to other aspects of their life.

2. *To socialize*: players spend a large amount of their time in online games interacting with friends. The activities in the game are merely the backdrop where players engage in while interacting.

3. *Bragging rights*: some players may not have much to brag about in the real-world. However, winning high scores that are visible for other subsequent players to see or let them tell other players how quickly they have beaten the most difficult parts of a game gives them a sense of satisfaction.

4. *An emotional experience*: Rouse (2005) lists a range of emotions that players may be seeking after when they play games. These include an adrenaline rush when they play action type of games, and satisfaction from having successfully created and managed a large city in city-building type of games.

5. *To explore*: players may be motivated by their desire to investigate and discover not just new areas and environments in the game, but also new ways to manipulate game mechanics.

Rouse's reasons pertain to computer games in general, and he adds that multi-player games can change some of these reasons (p. 238). For example, there is greater potential for bragging rights for players since there are now other people to brag to, which can lead to a more emotional experience as well. Moreover, he notes that the success of multi-player games can be attributed to satisfying all the 'wants' players may have in playing games (p. 239).

Fullerton et al.'s model

Fullerton et al. (2004) in their book "*Game Design: Theory & Practice*" state that there are at least 10 player types: *competitor, explorer, collector, achiever, joker, artist, director, storyteller, performer*, and *craftsman*. Of these player types, Fullerton et al. (p. 90) notes the following:

1. The *competitor* plays the game to beat other players.

2. The *achiever* "plays for varying levels of achievement."

3. The *joker* does not take the game seriously.

4. The *performer* is a player who likes to "put on a show for other players".

5. The *director* likes to be in control and direct the play.

Interestingly, Fullerton et al. recognize that the joker has the potential to be annoying to other players around him. However, at the same time, players in this type can make the game more social and less competitive (p. 90).

Hallford & Hallford's model

Hallford & Hallford (2001, p. 21-29) in their book "*Swords & Circuitry: A Designer's Guide to Computer Role-Playing Games*" identify six player types. They are:

1. *The fragmaster*: players who want game objectives that can be resolved mainly through violent confrontation. The combat system in the game is critical for these players.

2. *The problem solver*: players who want to make creative use of game mechanics, rules and strategy to solve puzzles and riddles in the game.

3. *The treasure hound*: players who want rewards to be readily available as part of the game. These rewards could be in the form of items for them to investigate, hoard or barter—or in-game money for them to purchase the services and goods they need to advance in the game.

4. *The story chaser*: players who immerse themselves in the narrative and story-telling elements of the game.

5. *The navel gazer*: players who are motivated by character advancement, and their accessing of new abilities and skills as their characters progress.

6. *The tourist*: players who want to explore, discover and interact with new environments.

Hallford & Hallford (p. 29) note that these player types are not mutually exclusive: the reasons for players to participate in games could span across several types in their list.

Bartle's model

Bartle's (1996) model is centered on MUDs and created via an analysis of replies from MUD players engaging in a debate on "what do people want out of a MUD?" (Bartle 2004, p. 130). His model continues to be widely studied by MMORPG researchers. It comprises four player types differentiated on degrees of player-to-player and player-to-game interactions. The four types are:

1. *Achievers*: who play primarily to achieve goals and 'beat' the game. Achievers prefer to act on the game world.

2. *Socializers*: who play primarily to interact with other players. They do this either by maintaining their real-world persona, or as role-players.

3. *Explorers*: who play primarily to discover and interact with the game world.

4. *Killers*: who play primarily to dominate other players.

Yee's model

Yee's (2002) study, on the other hand, is survey-based and quantitative. By analyzing the responses from the thousands of players who participated in his survey, he created his own model of player motivations, comprising:

1. *Relationship*: the desire to make friends with others in the game.

2. *Immersion*: the desire to deeply engage with the MMORPG game world and its fantastic constructs.

3. *Grief*: the desire to use other players for one's own advantage.

4. *Leadership*: the desire to exert authority and direction on other players.

5. *Achievement*: the desire to be powerful (for example in terms of character advancement) within the game.

Yee's study is extensive and has involved 6,700 respondents. However, the questions he asked were based on his own observations of possible player motivations, and this may have limited the discovery of other possible motivations. Yee also notes that his data did not validate the existence of "exploration" as a motivation, although it appears in five of the seven models discussed here.

Rozak's model

Lastly, Mike Rozak, an MMORPG researcher who writes commentaries on various aspects of MMORPG design, has his own list of reasons why players play a multi-player game rather than a single-player game. His list is included in this discussion because it takes a different angle from the other six models cited here. Rozak's model emphasizes differentiating game features based on the different reasons players have for participating in multi-player games. Selected motivations in his list include the following: *hang out with friends, role-playing, be part of a group, rank/competition, griefer*, and *leader*.

Upon analysis, it was realized that many of the player types and motivations in the seven models described above are interrelated. For example Bartle's killer player type is related to Yee's grief motivation in that some griefers player-kill in an abusive fashion. In some cases, it is identical to each other. For example Bartle's socializer is identical to Yee's relationship. In some cases, similarity exists even if the models cover differing aspects of the MMORPG. For example, Lazzaro's other players is similar to Bartle's socializer and Yee's relationship, and her hard fun motivation is closely related to Bartle's achiever.

The table below categorizes these player types and motivations across models. Several of these turn out to be motivations explaining why players grief, as the book will show later.

Table 10: Related player motivations and types categorization

Motivation /Type	Category 1	Category 2	Category 3	Category 4	Category 5	Category 6
Lazzaro	Hard fun	Other players	Easy fun		Easy fun	
Rouse	A challenge	To socialize	To explore			
Fullerton et al.	Achiever	Joker	Explorer	Competitor	Storyteller	Director
Hallford & Hallford	Treasure hound, Navel gazer		Tourist	Fragmaster	Story chaser	
Bartle	Achiever	Socialize	Explorer	Killer		
Yee	Achieve-ment	Relation-ship		Grief	Immersion	Leadership
Rozak	Rank/Compe tition	Hang out with friends; Be part of a group; Meet new people		Griefer	Role playing	Leader

In some cases, it is not possible to properly categorize selected types and motivations together even if there is some implicit relation between them. For example, players who grief (Yee 2002) may brag about their successes over victims. But this does not mean that players who play for bragging rights (Rouse 2005) are griefers. Players in single-player games can brag about high scores. In multi-player games, they can brag about becoming the first to attain a level of character advancement, and this may have nothing to do with grief play. Hence, Yee's griefers are not categorized with Rouse's bragging rights players. In other cases, there are player motivations or types which are too dissimilar to be categorized with any other. These include Fullerton et al.'s artist, or Rouse's an emotional experience.

Keeping in mind again that there are few well-defined end goals in an MMORPG, the internalized goals and objectives that players have become the more important in explaining why they play games. Also, Chapter 4 has noted that some players grief because they desire to achieve goals above other considerations, and other players grief as a way of demonstrating power. Hence, in the context of this study, of particular interest in

Table 10 above are categories 1 and 4. Category 1 denotes players who enjoy competition, challenges, and achieving. They play to meet goals and objectives set in the game, whether it comes in the form of character advancement, recognition, or rewards. Category 4 denotes players who enjoy imposing on others, either in strongly competitive or abusive fashions. They enjoy confrontational type of game activities as well.

Chapter 4 has also explained that there is some similarity between grief play and the concepts of bullying and teasing. The next section investigates these two concepts.

Motivations in bullying and teasing

Much of the bullying and teasing literature reviewed for this study concerns school children, while other literature concerns the workplace. Hence, not all aspects of these two concepts can be imported into this study. For example Fox & Boulton (2005, p. 324) note that victims of school bullying were perceived to possess lesser social skills than non-victims. These characteristics marked them out as targets. There is no evidence that victims of grief play are chosen on the basis of their social skills. The attributes between a workplace and an online game are also different. There is the immediate issue of online anonymity for instance. Moreover, all users of the MMORPG are paying subscribers for the same service, which in turn brings about certain expectations and perceived responsibilities of the game operator on their part as service provider[69]. Finally, MMORPG players tend to be older than those studied in school bullying. The range of approaches to manage bullying in schools include those suggested by Colvin et al. (1998, p. 307), for example teaching social skills to victims to improve their relationships to peers and problem-solving and anger management skills to the bullies themselves, and intervention strategies which include the engagement of psychologists or social workers (Smokowski & Kopasz 2005, p. 106). These management approaches are not quite appropriate in the context of managing bad behavior among adult participants that can make up a subscription-based online game. As it was, early data collection showed that the similar aspects between grief play and teasing/bullying lied primarily in its definitional aspects, and selected characterizations and motivations. This section explains some of the motivations of teasing and bullying to see if they are comparable to why players grief.

---

[69] See Chapter 7.

For bullying, Land (2003, p. 157) cites reasons that include the actor's desire to dominate and the actor's previous bad experiences, for instance with domestic violence. The target's attributes and actor's jealousy towards the target are also mentioned as bullying and teasing motivations. Bullying is also a process of establishing and maintaining social dominance (Crothers & Levinson 2004). Salmivalli & Voeten (2004, p. 246) also posit in their study of bullying that personality factors for boys and group context for girls are 'predictors' of such behavior. Anger has also been cited as a predictor for bullying behavior, with more intense bullying associated with higher levels of anger (Bosworth et al. 1999, p. 345).

Land's (2003, p. 157) study presents some motivations for teasing. These include positive peer status, and fun or play for the actor. Likewise, Shapiro et al.'s (1991, p. 463) study of teasing motivations among school children reveal motivators like reciprocation, jealousy, and that the actors were merely playing and joking. Some subjects also said that they tease when they dislike the target, or when they are in bad mood. The level of aggression in the actor's personality can also affect the desire to tease. Shapiro et al. observe that teasing can be used to demonstrate the pecking order in the group, with the teased children in the lower levels of that hierarchy. Teasing can be a way of demonstrating superiority and status (Tragesser & Lippman 2005, p. 265).

Antisocial behavior that occurs online is also related to grief play. Suler's (1997; 2004)[70] work is reviewed here: while his work is not specific to bullying and teasing, it is still illuminating to help understand the motivations of people who perpetrate such behavior online. Some motivations for bad behavior cited by Suler include anonymity. Some participants also misbehave as a form of protest, some to spite. Yet others misbehave as a way of gaining reputation and notoriety. Some participants even reason their behavior by telling themselves their behavior do not represent their real personalities[71]. Some of his findings are echoed by Davis (2002). Davis' quantitative study asked respondents to select reasons they thought were the causes of bad behavior that occur online, and two of the causes that respondents cited are "anonymity online," and "misbehavers crave attention."

---

[70] Suler's extensive article on managing deviant behavior in virtual communities is found at http://www.rider.edu/~suler/psycyber/badboys.html. A condensed version is published as: Suler, J R and Phillips, W 1998, 'The bad boys of cyberspace: deviant behavior in multimedia chat communities', *CyberPsychology and Behavior*, vol. 1 no. 3, pp. 275-294.

[71] See Chapter 2 – 'Dissociative anonymity'.

Having looked at player types and motivations, and also motivations in teasing, bullying and bad behavior online, the next section presents the factors that can cause players to grief.

Grief player motivations

In the study, 16 factors that can cause a player to grief were identified in data. Upon analysis, these factors seemed to fall into three distinct aspects within MMORPGs (game, player, and griefer) and one aspect outside it (self). The factors have been categorized into four types:

1. *Game influenced*: factors oriented around the game world and its operation.

2. *Player influenced*: factors oriented around other non-griefing players in the game.

3. *Griefer influenced*: factors oriented around other griefers in the game.

4. *Self*: factors oriented around the griefer's personality and his desire to immerse in character.

Factors can be either a 'reason' or a 'motivation' to grief. Both are circumstances that result in a player griefing—the distinction lies in whether or not the factor is a compelling and driving force. A reason for griefing is a circumstance where a player engages in grief activity as a consequence. Typically, this circumstance would not be a compelling push. Rather, it would be a premise or a game setting that ferments (provides fertile ground) or facilitates (makes possible) such behavior. A motivation for griefing, on the other hand, is a driving force that compels or stimulates a player going out of his way to grief.

The descriptors for these two types of factors may lead one to believe that there is little difference between a reason and a motivation. However, whether a factor is a reason or a motivation can lead to differing perceptions of whether an incident is seen as grief play. A later section will show which of these factors are reasons and which are motivations. However, for the moment and to aid in readability, all factors will be called 'motivations' from this point onwards.

The 16 grief player motivations identified in this study are as follows.

Table 11: Grief player motivations

Type	Motivations
Game influenced	1.1 Anonymity 1.2 Boredom 1.3 Greed 1.4 Protest 1.5 Testing 1.6 Game premise
Player influenced	2.1 Spite 2.2 Victim vulnerability 2.3 Revenge
Griefer influenced	3.1 Ritualization and group identity 3.2 Reputation
Self	4.1 Bad mood 4.2 Wanting to feel powerful 4.3 Attention 4.4 Enjoyment 4.5 Role-playing

Some of these motivations do not fall exclusively into single types. For instance, 'attention' is categorized as a motivation stemming from self. Even then, an audience is necessary for getting attention, which suggests that attention could also be placed in the player influenced category. Other motivations are closely related. For instance, 'reputation' is related to attention. In this section, best fits have been applied for each motivation. In other instances, closely related motivators have been grouped as a single motivation. Some griefers also treat grief play as a metagame[72] [R84]. For example, that some griefers disrupt the game service through the use of exploits to damage the virtual world's economy is its own metagame [R35]. In these cases, their activities involve behavior that has nothing to do with playing the game in the way it was designed for.

Game rules and Law of code in the game can also affect a player's propensity to grief. Specifically, it can be easy to grief because of how a game is designed. If the game is not restrictive on the types

---

[72] The term metagaming appeared a few times in data where respondents remarked upon how some players perceive grief play. Metagaming, again, refers to the existence of a game system within another game.

of activity players can inflict on each other, then players are more likely to grief. Game rules also require enforcement by game masters. Persistent griefers are attracted to games with lax policies where they are likely able to get away with breaking rules [R34].

Furthermore, a player's propensity to grief can be affected by whether social cost is suffered as a consequence of the act. Some griefers do get identified by their victims or witnesses in public discussion forums and may be shunned. However, player bases in MMORPGs are large enough for players to be relatively invisible and unknown. A well-known griefer may not be invited into player groups and communities, or may even be expelled from existing player communities. But with so many players in a game, there will be player communities that are not aware he is a griefer. A player community itself may be fringe with its own members demonstrating grief play behavior. These communities will be too happy to invite the griefer into its ranks. Moreover, a player who gains a reputation for griefing can simply not log on. Over a period of time, people will forget his actions. Alternatively, he can simply play another character in the game on another server, or if the game allows multiple characters per server, on the same server and potentially with his victims who may not know he was their griefer. Increasing the social cost suffered by griefers is one way of managing grief play, and will be discussed in Chapter 8.

Lastly, this study is concerned with grief play as related to the game environment, with attention paid on aspects that can be addressed by game design. While some players believed that a player may grief because of psychological reasons like mental illness— Joinson & Dietz-Uhler (2002, p. 279) note that psychiatric illness could be a possible reason for persons engaging in attention seeking and deception online—circumstances which require deep psychoanalysis of a person's temperament or mental state have not been included in this work.

Game influenced

1.1 Anonymity. Deindividuation theory states that anonymity and the reduction of self-awareness can lead to uninhibited behavior (Festinger et al. cited in Thompsen 1997, p. 300). Current subscription levels for the larger MMORPGs run into hundreds of thousands of players. The large numbers of participants facilitate anonymity. Some griefers act because they are protected by this layer of anonymity.

This anonymity, ironically, protects victims as well. As a rule, griefers do not target specific individuals. Griefers may instead pick on players who play in a certain way—for example, newbies,

109

players who role-play, or players in some opposing faction or player community. Other than this, there is no evidence to suggest that griefers will usually go out of their way to target a specific individual all the time, unless there is some existing context between the griefer and victim for targeted and repeated attacks to occur.

A more substantial discussion of anonymity in light of the existing literature on whether it encourages bad behavior will be presented in a later section of this chapter.

1.2 Boredom. While a griefer can be bored with an MMORPG right from the onset, one commonly cited motivation for players to grief is boredom with current game content after playing for a period of time. For one player of *Ultima Online*, the game was quickly losing his interest and he intended to go back to griefing just for fun [R28]. A self-professed griefer in *World of Warcraft* [WoW-005b] similarly remarked that there was nothing else to do in the game other than to grief someone. As a result, he was going to continue targeting newbies.

Still, not all bored players become hard-core griefers. Boredom can instead result in fringe players turning opportunistic and indulging in a little grief play [73]. One player remarked:

> My play style is such that I would normally not go out of my way to grief, but if an opportunity presents itself, I would never ignore it. ... Likewise, if an opportunity presented itself for me to scam someone of their possessions, I would do it in a heartbeat. [R10]

1.3 Greed. A player's desire to benefit, regardless of the annoyance that it may cause other players, is a common motivation for grief play. Behavior driven by greed may be exhibited by achievers (Bartle 1996). Grief play subtypes like kill-stealing and area monopolizing are often motivated by the desire to progress in character advancement or wealth above other considerations, particularly implicit rules of player etiquette and expectations of fairness. On this, a relationship between acts of greed and Hardin's (1968) "the tragedy of the commons" can be drawn. Specifically, players who monopolize areas with the use of macro programs may believe that the effects of their action are too limited to affect the rest of the player body. In one case, one game area known as "Feerrott" in *EverQuest 2* contained numerous resources for players to acquire, either for resale to other players or for their characters to practice their crafting skills on. At one stage, a small number of players making use of third party programs were able to automate the acquisition of these resources, even

---

[73] Some respondents in Lin & Sun's (2005) study remark that every player may grief. Both researchers even cite occasional and unconscious griefers as a type of griefer.

though the use of such programs is disallowed in *EverQuest 2*. Initially, the effects of just these few players acquiring resources through these programs were trivial. This was until the macro program usage became widespread with more players using the same programs. The area quickly became barren of resources, upsetting the rest of the players who were attempting to acquire the same resources without using these programs to automate the process. This situation is similar to the exhaustion of commons when enough participants each undertake the same decision to benefit.

Finally, as Chapter 4 has noted, there is disagreement whether an activity motivated by greed really constitutes grief play. This is because the intention to disrupt another's gaming experience may not be particularly evident or even present. The perpetrators could have merely been competitive in their acquisition of resources or items for their character to advance (Davis 2002). Still, if the activity inconveniences players in some considerable way or if their characters are put at risk, it can intensify victim perception that they have been griefed.

1.4 Protest. Lin & Sun (2005) note that some players grief as a way of rebelling against game rules. Similarly, some players will grief as a show of dissatisfaction with game rules or its management. Genender (2005, p. 29-30) in an article for *The Escapist* writes about an incident in eGenesis' *A Tale in the Desert* where a pair of players disgruntled with the game operation took to griefing other players. In *Ultima Online*, rampant player-killing and griefer problems were among the reasons for the game world getting split into the Trammel and Felucca 'aspects'. This split was, ostensibly, to separate player-killers—many of them griefers—from other players who did not want to participate in PvP (Koivisto 2003). Some players became dissatisfied with the division, with some feeling that players in Trammel—the non-PvP part of the game world—were given preferential treatment. As a result, some players specifically targeted and griefed players from this aspect. One griefer [R12] added:

> At one time I took pleasure in causing grief to Trammel players but eventually I realized that it is a waste of time and that the grief and anger should of (have) been directed at OSI instead of the players.

Another player [UO-009] when hypothesizing why players grief remarked that OSI has 'griefed' grief players, so they do the same on other players. There was even one occasion where a group of players became so upset with the game operator that they organized a protest event inside the game [R35]. They got many players to show up in the same area as drunken characters. This substantially increased the network traffic load, and the server slowed to a crawl as a result.

Occasionally, these proclamations of protest can come from a sizable group of griefers. One guild comprising hundreds of players in *Ultima Online* had a war cry that stated their express intention: to "destroy" Electronic Arts and *Ultima Online* because they felt the game company had been lax in dealing with players who had cheated, hacked, or exploited. They were eventually banned en masse for bad behavior [R65].

1.5 Testing. Related to protest is testing. In the context of online environments, that some activities can elicit censure from establishments is "sufficient to attract the defiant, or the irresistibly curious", as Grabosky (2001, p. 244) remarks. MMORPGs are complex game software, and can contain many bugs and loopholes. Some, but not all, of these get rectified through ongoing code maintenance. At one stage in *Ultima Online*, griefers were able to flood the game server with extraneous on-screen messages. This resulted in surrounding players experiencing large amounts of lag, occasionally crashing their game clients altogether. The existence of web sites that publicize existing game exploits, often to players who subscribe to these services, suggest that some players— griefers included—continually stretch the game and its rules to see how far they can go. In this sense, some griefers are motivated by a desire to challenge or 'test' the game system. One developer [R34] remarked that griefers are attracted to new games, as they can test the boundaries and stretch rules. They can do this for any reason, including as a sign of protest (against game operation), or as a demonstration of technological mastery (for example in Bromberg 1996, p. 149). In other instances, griefers test players as they are curious to see how their victims react to different kinds of grief play [R20][74].

1.6 Game premise. Davis (2002) notes that some forms of bad behavior may be considered acceptable and part of the game. In the absence of specifically stated game rules or Law of code that disallow a game mechanic, the onus of restraint is placed on players (Powers 2003, p. 197). Whether players are restrained from exhibiting bad behavior is in turn influenced by game rules governing conduct, implicit rules, and their individual expectations of what should be permissible behavior. Some players grief because they believe their play styles are tolerated or expected in the game premise. They feel that if their play styles are allowed by Law of code, their actions cannot be considered grief play [TSO-005]. This can happen if the griefer is new to the game as he may

---

[74] It is interesting to note that in the testing of games prior to publication, players may be encouraged to grief the system (Myers 2005). Myers notes that this type of play helps designers as it exposes the game system still under development to large-scale stress testing. This impact of griefing is discussed further in Chapter 6.

assume "this is how the game is played", or if the game encourages violent interaction among players, for example PvP, as a legitimate play style. Some players even tell themselves that "it is just a game", and that milder or implicit types of grief play, such as kill-stealing, should not be taken seriously [CoH-014].

The line between legitimate game play and abusive play can be thin. Dismembering and cutting players into pieces may still be acceptable under some conditions, but when accompanied with other circumstances, for example verbal abuse and repetition of the act[75], it rarely is for players. One developer has noted that an intended game mechanic cannot be considered a griefing tactic, even if distressing to other players [R1]. The issue then becomes whether a game mechanic has been used 'as intended', and Chapter 4 has argued that developer and player perceptions can be different on this.

One interesting case of a large body of griefers getting banned who in turn protested that they had not broken rules concerned a guild[76] in *Ultima Online*. Players who were affiliated to this guild were banned in 1999. In the guild's own statement that was made public on their web site, they declared that they (the banned players) had done nothing wrong. They had merely chosen to use their game time to hunt and kill other players, and that player-killing was not in any violation of game rules in *Ultima Online* [UO-013] since PvP was an acceptable game style in the game. Their statement even claimed that they killed close to 10,000 players in their 18 months of playing. However, few players in the follow-up postings of subsequent discussion threads believed that this was their only reason for engaging in PvP. As it was, victims had posted into the discussion forums reports of how they had been killed by members of this guild in particularly violent ways. Moreover, the guild posted on their web site pictures and narratives of how they cheerfully killed their victims and how their actions were facilitated through the use of third party programs or code exploitation. In some instances, they emoted rape messages on their victims when they lay dead, and defended these rape messages as role-playing. In response to victims who complained against these alleged acts of virtual raping, they stated that the emotes were victory chants that they uttered after winning a PvP encounter [UO-013]. While it could be argued that this guild did believe they

---

[75] See Chapter 4 – 'Player and game operator perceptions of grief play'.

[76] For reasons of sensitivity, the name of this guild has been kept anonymous, even though the incident was widely discussed in Usenet.

were playing within the rules, they were also clearly enjoying this play style despite the outcries of their victims. This was evidence to other players that they had gone beyond the limits of acceptable behavior. In the final analysis, the game operator decided that they would rather lose the subscriptions of the players associated with the guild than the accounts of the many more players who had been attacked.

I note that the game premise in itself is not normally a 'motivation' in the sense of it being a compelling reason driving players to grief. Rather, it affects the expectations that players have on what is permissible conduct, which is in itself dependent on existent game rules and if and how they are enforced, two aspects of rules cited by Sternberg (2001). Depending on the permissibility of the game environment, players may or may not find it easy to grief. Game rules and premise can affect player expectations for both the players who grief—including the griefing guild cited above—and those on the receiving end. Player expectations is the subject of discussion in Chapter 7.

Player influenced

2.1 Spite. With reference to the Lord Kazzak encounter in *World of Warcraft* cited in Chapter 4, there was a related incident. One player observed that groups that failed to defeat the mob remained in the area. When it came to his own guild's turn, these groups tried to sabotage his guild's attempt—apparently out of malice because they were angry they had not been successful in defeating Kazzak themselves [WoW-003e]. These players employed the same tactics of suicidal rushing, and were doing so to spite other players.

Occasionally, the spite demonstrated is more specific towards player segments. Some griefers are motivated by the desire to 'put down' certain types of players. One PvP player [R10] who was an opportunistic griefer claimed that role-players resented PvP players after they were player-killed, and called them "immature little brats". He added that "I just get my kicks making them (role-players) feel miserable and hearing them keep saying those things to themselves. Honestly, I couldn't care if they don't change, because it's more fun for me." In another case, a griefer [R12] remarked that Trammel players were initially targeted because griefers felt that they were cowardly by 'fleeing' to the safer havens of Trammel. When asked for reasons why these players were targeted, the same respondent cited anger, hatred, and jealousy as possible motivators.

114

2.2 Victim vulnerability. A vulnerable victim may motivate a player to grief. Newbies are particularly popular targets ([R16], [GP-017]). They are susceptible to griefing as they are unfamiliar with the game and often trusting of other players. Evidence from discussion postings also revealed frequent mentioning of newbies getting targeted, as were players who had just been killed and had respawned. Also, while spite towards role-players is a possible motivation for grief play, they can be targeted also because they are vulnerable. Role-players often cannot defend themselves well as their emphasis as players is to enjoy an immersive experience rather than advance their characters in the same way Bartle's (1996) achievers would. This occasionally results in their characters becoming less 'powerful' when compared to other players.

2.3 Revenge. Some players are not normally griefers, but they grief because they have been griefed first. For instance, a player who has been scammed may grief his scammer by spamming messages against him in the public chat channel. Tito (2005, p. 26) for *The Escapist* cites a griefer of *World of Warcraft* who engaged in rez-killing. When interviewed by the author, this griefer cited revenge as a motivator. In another case in *City of Heroes*, an argument occurred between two players, with one player getting called names. The latter subsequently logged on his more powerful character to rez-kill the other player [CoH-013]. Grief play can 'snowball' this way. Snowballing is an impact of grief play, and will be further discussed in Chapter 6.

Griefer influenced

3.1 Ritualization and group identity. Like gangs in the real-world, well-organized grief player communities have behavioral codes that members adhere to. One developer [R5] cited instances where player groups exhibited distinctive identity by demonstrating behavior that some would consider grief play. In one case in *Ultima Online*, a player group staked out a commonly used path of travel, and waited for players possessing specific types of equipment. When these players passed by, they were ambushed. The targeted victims wore plate mail amour[77], and when killed by this group were told never to return to the area while wearing this equipment. The victims felt griefed, because apart from their possession of a fairly common type of equipment, in their perception, they had been singled out for attack. As it was, the griefer group had marked out a geographical location, and decided that this was their territory and players passing by must abide by their rules. Such an activity was their distinctive identity.

---

[77] A defensive type of equipment acquired and worn by player characters.

Griefer groups may also have rituals or 'rites of passage' for entry into their community. For instance, entry requisites could demand that new entrants must have been warned for bad behavior at least once by customer service representatives, or have killed a stipulated number of newbies. Some self-styled "mafia" groups in *The Sims Online* required their new recruits to conduct attack operations as a qualification for membership or rewards [R48]. Such groups were also identified by Wadhams (2003) when he reported on griefers in the same game for *Baltimore Sun*. In these cases, the motivation has stemmed from a desire to establish group identity[78] as opposed to a deliberate intent to disrupt gaming experiences.

Related to the ritualization and group identity motivation is peer pressure. One griefer [R12] remarked that some inductees into player groups may be influenced by others to play in a certain way. He added that there were some well-known griefers who did not start out that way. Rather they just got involved in player communities who happened to griefed. In order for them to remain in that community, they would also have had to grief. Players can also be influenced by strong leaders in their respective communities. In these cases guild griefing may result [R43].

3.2 Reputation. Postings on web sites that relate the exploits of griefers, for example at http://www.darkwolves.biz[79], suggest that griefers are unabashed about their play styles. In fact, they may feel pride in being proficient in grief play. One griefer [GP-017] bragged to others in a discussion forum that he would PK any newbie he comes across, as these players are 'easier' kills for him. He would go out of his way to grief, exploit any game weakness he can find, and 'gank[80]' other players. For others, getting punished for grief play only adds to their reputation. Getting banned is a reward for persistent griefers and a "badge of honor" to attain [R2].

Self

4.1 Bad mood. Some griefers act out negative emotions sparked from the real-world. For instance, one player griefed because "his dog took a crap on his rug." [R12] Another griefer [GP-017]

---

[78] Axelsson & Regan (2002) provide an interesting argument about this. In their quantitative study of player attitudes towards bad behavior in relation to the communities they belong to in *Asheron's Call*, the authors suggest that most players demonstrate a moral attitude regardless of the communities they are in. According to their report, players are more disposed towards behaving well among people they are familiar with. Their study however was centred on communities in general as opposed to grief player communities and the attitudes of its members remarked here.

[79] Some of these web sites come and go quickly. Early on in the study, two griefer web sites visited were http://galad.griefgaming.com and http://www.pk-hq.com, but by October 2005, both sites were no longer running.

[80] In MMORPGs, the term 'gank' refers to PvP attacks where the player-killer is much more powerful than his victim.

remarked that he usually PKed only when he was in a bad mood. When that mood struck, he would PK anything he saw, even when his chances of winning the encounter were low.

4.2 Wanting to feel powerful. The desire to feel powerful over victims is a motivator. Newbie-killing and rez-killing have been described in Chapter 4 as examples of power imposition. Several respondents ([R18], [R24]) believed that players grief in the game because they have no power in the real-world. It was not possible in this study to validate if griefers indeed lacked power in the real-world, since it would have required griefers to provide personal background and information. Journalistic media however does provide some information on this. Pham (2002) at *LA Times* interviewed one player who griefed in the game, but in real-life was a normal and well-adjusted family person. Whether griefers have power in the real-world or not, what seems clear at least is that griefers like feeling powerful. One griefer remarked that he would actually help another player depending on his mood. For him, choosing not to kill another player gives him more power than if he had killed him [GP-017]. Pham's (2002) interviewee himself remarked: "There's nothing sweeter than when you kill someone and they spout insults at you for hours. That's when you know you got him." Finally, rez-killers and newbie-killers do not want or need the rewards from killing vulnerable players. That there may be loot rewards would be incidental. Rather, they engage in these acts and other grief play—for example verbally harassment or kill-stealing—just to rile players up emotionally [R61].

4.3 Attention. Just as the need for an audience is important in teasing, some griefers like attention as well ([CoH-003], [TSO-001], [SWG-006]). Griefers who are motivated in this way will post accounts of their acts in public platforms, including discussion forums or web sites. On some occasions, incidents stemming from attention seeking can be related to 'protest'. Griefers may be attempting to attract the attention of developers, for instance because they believe a certain aspect of the game has not received adequate attention. Players in different segments, including griefers and role-players, do compete for attention from developers, or for prominence in the game. They just go about doing it differently. Role-players hold in-game events and invite game masters to participate in. Griefers on the other hand attempt to get attention by publicly playing in disruptive fashions. One developer [R33] described such attention-seeking in the following way:

> It's kind of like saying "Look, no police show up when I shoot someone, so I'm going to shoot people until it is a big enough problem that police start showing up on time."

4.4 Enjoyment. When grief play is deliberately intending to disrupt, the motivation involved is often enjoyment at causing misery. One griefer [GP-018] proclaimed in a discussion forum that he was a player-killer. He would kill any other play in any online game, remarking that he loved putting people in misery. Another griefer [UO-007] claimed that since kill-stealing was allowed in *Ultima Online*, there was nothing his victims could do when he kill-stole. He enjoyed such play styles, and described an incident where a mob he kill-stole from another player dropped a treasured item. He then showed off this item to the other player, claiming he did this just to exaggerate the effect of his act on his victim.

Not all grief play actions are malicious in intent even if they are still motivated by a desire to derive enjoyment at the victim's expense. In the case of *Star Wars Galaxies* where a player placed a physical obstruction in a community's player-city [SWG-006], even when players in that city expressed their annoyance, the player remarked that this action had been intended as a friendly 'rivalry' jab. He added that some players have no sense of humor even though it was 'just' a video game. In another case, a player of *EverQuest 2* [EQ2-016a] played a prank on a stranger, and posted his account of this incident in the discussion forum. While acknowledging that his action had been intentional, he defended himself by insisting no exploits had been used, and that it had been in the spirit of role-playing as the class of his character was the ideological opposite of his victim's class. In both cases, the humor element here is similar to that found in teasing (Shapiro et al. 1991), and the actions were enjoyable to the perpetrators. Moreover, the perpetrators in both cases admitted that their actions had been intentional if in the spirit of role-playing. However, that their actions had been carried out for their own personal amusement and that they were disruptive led to perceptions that they had griefed.

4.5 Role-playing. One key experience of virtual environments cited in literature (for example in Bromberg 1996, p. 148; Suler 2002, p. 456) is the adoption of alternate identities. Chapter 1 explained that some participants role-play in MMORPGs. Some players argue that they should be allowed to role-play their characters in a manner that is consistent with that game setting. For example, while exceptions are possible, thieves and murderers are usually 'evil' characters. As such, a player with a thieving character may be motivated by a conscious intent to role-play to the hilt. As a thief, he intends to scam and cheat other players. In one case, a player of *EverQuest 2* on a role-playing server witnessed another player deliberately attacking mobs that he was about to engage. This was in the vicinity of a city populated by players playing evil characters. When

118

queried, the player replied that this was an evil city and this was how evil people act [EQ2-017a]. From the point of view *EverQuest 2*'s rules, this was not considered kill-stealing. The game mechanics 'lock' a mob to an attacking player once engagement starts, rendering kill-stealing thereafter impossible. Until then, any player in the vicinity is free to engage the mob. This did not stop the victim from believing he had been griefed. Some players truly believe an element of chaos is necessary in a fantastic-type of game [R64], and these players may grief for the express purpose of creating some excitement in the game world. Role-playing here is thus cited as a possible motivation.

Having said this, few players and developers believe that griefers as a rule are really role-playing. Most players do not role-play, and the few who do invariably gravitate towards selected servers that have been designated 'role-playing'. For many players, the term role-playing refers only to their choice of a profession with unique skills allowing them access to specific types of activities in-game. This is opposed to their having to behave or interact with *other* players in a specific way. For example, many players play a troll type of character, but not because they wish to interact with other players like one. Rather, they play trolls because a troll is effective in certain types of combative activity. Hence, in the case of kill-stealing in *EverQuest 2* above, few would have believed that the player was kill-stealing because he was 'evil'. Likewise, developers ([R1], [R5]) interviewed remarked that more often than not, when queried by game masters, griefers use the desire to role-play as an excuse to explain themselves. Some MMORPG researchers (for example Oliver 2002) posit that players are not obligated to be consistent in how they play their character classes. Putting it in another way, the belief purported by some respondents that role-playing seems more an excuse to get away with bad behavior seems congruous with Oliver's (2002) remarks— that human motivations do affect how one plays, regardless of 'role'.

Discussion

This section furthers discussion of four aspects of grief player motivations. Specifically:

1. Anonymity as a motivation.

2. Motivation and implicit and explicit grief play.

3. How motivations are interrelated.

4. How motivations are related to existing models of player motivations, bullying, teasing and bad behavior.

Anonymity as a motivation

Chapter 2 discussed literature on whether anonymity leads to bad behavior, and the data in this study cited anonymity as a possible motivator for grief play. Anonymity can result in both good and bad behavior in virtual communities.

In the context of an MMORPG, there is anonymity in its player base. The large numbers of participants—successful games can have as many as a few million subscribers—facilitate anonymity. MUDs with smaller player bases did not see the levels of grief play present today [R1]. When asked if the large numbers of players were encouraging some players to grief, one developer [R33] quipped: "The larger the bowl, the less obvious a single pea becomes."

There is indeed a more than tacit relationship between the degree of anonymity experienced and the size of the community; large virtual environments are less intimate than smaller ones, and it is indeed harder to notice an individual in a large crowd. Moreover, some MMORPGs also allow the creation of multiple characters per player account on one server[81]. While this mechanism may have been intended to allow participants to experience playing a range of character types, this mechanism also facilitates bad behavior. Griefers know that they have multiple characters they can fall back on in the event that one character becomes 'known' in the player body for bad behavior. It also allows throwaway characters created for the express purpose of grief play. In fact, griefers with high-level characters may be reluctant to grief with these characters. Achieving a high-level of

---

[81] As noted in Chapter 1, the MMORPG player body is often divided into different servers to better distribute the player population. Servers are still fairly large, and each server can hold several thousand players. Players choose the server they wish to belong to at the start of character creation, and normally are not allowed to change servers thereafter (although some game operators do provide this service for a fee).

character advancement in MMORPGs is not easy, and griefers may not want to risk the unsoiled reputation these characters have in the game world. They would rather grief with newly created low-level characters with names that bear no resemblance to their high-level characters[82].

All this does not mean that players in MMORPGs which limit players to a single character per server will not grief. They still do. However, the point here is that allowing multiple characters makes it easier to go unnoticed in a crowd. Hence, while the research cannot disprove the more positive potential effects of anonymity, in this case, it seems likely that high levels of anonymity can expedite bad behavior.

Whilst there are indeed general perceptions of participant etiquette in the form of implicit rules, the study could not conclude whether players follow these rules of etiquette because they are anonymous.

No matter what the finer rules of player conduct and etiquette may be, intentional disruption is irksome to players and many will regard grief play as behavior that is unacceptable and not within norms. Moreover, that only a small number of players grief shows that grief play is anything but normative behavior, and the effects of their behavior can be widespread. Still, the majority of MMORPG players get along fine, with many developing social bonds of friendship and in some instances even marriage. The disinhibition that Reid (1999, p. 112) posits seems to be consistent with MMORPGs—that it leads to *both* hostile and intimate behavior. This brings back the argument to the earlier point—that both good and bad behavior can result from anonymity.

Implicit and explicit grief play

An earlier section of this chapter also distinguished between 'reasons' and 'motivations' to grief, although for readability purposes they were collectively termed 'motivations'. This distinction, again, is as follows:

- A reason is a circumstance where a player engages in grief activity as a consequence.

- A motivation is a compelling circumstance that drives or stimulates a player to grief.

The study has proposed that there are two types of grief play: implicit, and explicit. For just the purpose of this subsection, the term 'motivations' will be again distinguished from 'reasons'.

---

[82] See Chapter 8 – 'Other methods'.

Analysis allowed the 16 factors to be separated into motivations and reasons. Keeping in mind the non-positivistic nature of this study, these 16 factors were correlated to implicit and explicit grief play by considering whether players would *likely* consider an activity as grief play if they observed the type (implicit and explicit) coupled with the perpetrator exhibiting the associated factor. A 'yes' in Table 12 and Table 13 indicates that players are likely to view the act as grief play. An 'ambiguous' indicates that players are likely to disagree it is an act of grief play as much as those who agree. A 'not commonly observed' indicates that the activity is not normally associated with the factor. Each pairing of the factor to the grief play type in the two tables below is also designated with a cell indicator. The two tables below are the result of this analysis.

Table 12: Reasons versus implicit and explicit grief play

Reasons	Implicit grief play (greed play)		Explicit grief play (Harassment, Power imposition, Scamming)	
1.1 Anonymity	Cell 1	Yes	Cell 2	Yes
1.2 Boredom		Yes		Yes
1.4 Protest		Not commonly observed		Ambiguous
1.6 Game premise		Ambiguous		Ambiguous
3.1 Ritualization and group identity		Not commonly observed		Ambiguous
4.1 Bad mood		Yes		Yes

Table 13: Motivations versus implicit and explicit grief play

Motivations	Implicit grief play (greed play)		Explicit grief play (Harassment, Power imposition, Scamming)	
1.3 Greed	Cell 3	Ambiguous	Cell 4	Not commonly observed
1.5 Testing		Not commonly observed		Ambiguous
2.1 Spite		Yes		Yes
2.2 Victim vulnerability		Yes		Yes
2.3 Revenge		Yes		Yes
3.2 Reputation		Yes		Yes
4.2 Wanting to feel powerful		Yes		Yes
4.3 Attention		Yes		Yes
4.4 Enjoyment		Yes		Yes
4.5 Role-playing		Ambiguous		Yes

To illustrate these two tables, consider two examples. Firstly, players are likely to view as grief play a player who harasses (explicit grief play) because of boredom (1.2). Secondly, players are divided over whether a player kill-steals (implicit grief play) because of role-playing (4.5).

An explanation of each cell follows.

Cell 1: denotes activities which are implicit grief play and associated with reasons. Compared to the other cells, activities here are least likely to be perceived as grief play. An example of an activity in this cell could be: "A player kill-steals because he genuinely believes this is an acceptable and expected activity in the game."

Cell 2: denotes activities which may be explicit grief play, but are driven by factors other than a desire to disrupt playability for its sake. When activities from this cell are demonstrated, some players may view that grief play has occurred, but not all will. An example of an activity in this cell could be: "A player kills newbies because he genuinely believes this is an acceptable and expected activity in the game."

Cell 3: denotes activities where a griefer engages in play styles that may not be associated with grief play, but because of the motivation involved, he is still likely to be perceived as griefing. The motivations here are likely intending to disrupt. An example of an activity in this cell could be: "A player kill-steals because he wants to feel powerful."

Cell 4: denotes activities closely associated with grief play in literature—that it is intentional and disruptive of player experiences. Grief play here is explicit. When griefers demonstrate motivations in this cell, players will most likely view that grief play has occurred. Griefers themselves will likely be aware that they are griefing. An example of an activity in this cell could be: "A player kills newbies because he wants to feel powerful."

The relationships between factors and grief play types are not exclusive. In each case, a 'likely' relationship has been suggested. For example, newbie-killing—which falls under explicit grief play—is not normally driven by a desire to role-play. However, this does not mean it cannot happen at all. It is still possible that a player kills newbies as he reasons to himself that they are the 'enemy' and he needs to impede their progress into higher level characters where they will be harder opponents in the future. One griefer [R6] remarked:

There are people who did not kill the lower level ones because they felt it is a form of bullying. However, I feel the other way. If you don't kill him/her, he/she will report your location. Soon, someone will come and kill you. It is sort of social ethical issue. If you were in a war and you meet face to face with a child holding a gun. Would you shoot him? I will. Without hesitation. Because if I don't shoot him, he will shoot me!

Table 12 and Table 13 also show the more common relationships. They do not represent the full array of possibilities between factors and the more numerous subtypes. For instance:

1. A player 'wanting to feel powerful' is likely to engage in newbie-killing, rez-killing, and event disruption (explicit grief play). However, he is somewhat less likely to engage in ninja-looting or item farming (implicit grief play).

2. A player 'testing' the game is likely to engage in use of loopholes and trade scamming. However, he is less likely to engage in threatening, eavesdropping, slurs, or intentional spamming.

3. A player seeking to increase his 'reputation' is likely to engage in event disruption, newbie-killing, rez-killing, and trade scamming. However, he is less likely to engage in ninja-looting[83].

Given that there are 16 factors and 19 grief play subtypes, a large number of relationships can result. This makes any tabular representation of factors to subtype unwieldy. The tables above representing broad relationships between factors and explicit/implicit grief play will have to suffice at this juncture. How representative is each relationship would have to be ascertained in a quantitative study.

Motivations interrelated

The third aspect of grief player motivations[84] of interest is if these motivations are interrelated. Analysis of data suggested that the presence of one motivation can lead to another. Examples of cause-effect relationships include:

1. A player who 'spites' a group of players may grief, and in so doing 'feels powerful' in disrupting their gaming experience.

---

[83] This is unlikely (though not impossible) because a player who is intent on gaining reputation as a griefer would find it difficult to get invited into a pickup group. Game rules in many MMORPGs allow only group members to loot a mob's defeated corpse, making it impossible for players outside the group to ninja-loot.

[84] The section here reverts to terming reasons and motivations as 'motivations'.

2. A player who is 'greedy' may believe that the 'game premise' requires him to be fiercely competitive in order to gain the necessary resources to advance. Thus, he engages in item farming or area monopolization.

Extended relationships comprising multiple motivations are also possible. For example, a player who is 'protesting' against a current game mechanic will gain 'attention' from other players, resulting in an increase in his 'reputation'.

The following model presents the 16 motivations and possible relationships among them, and how they are related to 'enjoyment of the game'.

Figure 3: Grief player motivations interrelationships

This model is also not complete. It does not show every possible relationship among motivations. Keeping this in mind, what the model does show is that all motivations are directly or indirectly related to 'enjoyment of the game'. It suggests that griefers act because they ultimately seek to gain pleasure from playing the game, whether this pleasure comes directly from 'enjoyment' at causing misery or some other motivator. Putting aside the factors that are interconnected with 'enjoyment' at causing misery, the remaining factors (for example greed, game premise, and testing) that result in 'enjoyment of the game' are exemplified by the fact that some griefers know that their play styles are disruptive to others, but they are not intending to harm their victims in the physical sense. Rather, they are only playing the game as they enjoy it. For these griefers, a common defense they would cite is that "It's just a game", and they expect their victims to similarly disassociate in-game activities from the real-world.

Player motivation models, teasing, bulling and bad behavior

The fourth aspect of player motivations of interest is its relationships to existing models of player motivations, and studies of teasing, bullying and online bad behavior. The table below shows a focused representation of five categories of player types and motivations.

Table 14: Focused representation of player motivations and types categorization

Motivation /Type	Category 1	Category 2	Category 3	Category 4	Category 5
Lazzaro	Hard fun	Other players	Easy fun		Easy fun
Rouse	A challenge	To socialize	To explore		
Fullerton et al.	Achiever	Joker	Explorer	Competitor	Storyteller
Hallford & Hallford	Treasure hound, Navel gazer		Tourist	Fragmaster	Story chaser
Bartle	Achiever	Socialize	Explorer	Killer	
Yee	Achievement	Relationship		Grief	Immersion
Rozak	Rank/Competition	Hang out with friends; Be part of a group; Meet new people		Griefer	Role playing

Of the 16 motivations, 14 were found to have relationships to existing models. Each of these is explained below.

Game influenced

1.1 Anonymity. Participants in large multi-player game worlds enjoy relative anonymity, which in turn can encourage bad behavior. Suler (1997), Davis (2002) and literature in CMC have noted similar findings.

1.3 Greed. Greed is related to selected player types and motivations in category 1: the 'treasure hound' (Hallford & Hallford 2001), 'achiever' (Bartle 1996), and 'achievement' (Yee 2002).

1.4 Protest. Suler (1997) observes that some participants in virtual communities justify their misbehavior as retaliation against a community that they perceived has wronged them, believing they have the right to express themselves freely. This is similar to the 'protest' motivation.

1.5 Testing. Talin, an observer in the gaming industry (whose commentary on managing deviant behavior in online worlds is included in Mulligan & Patrovsky 2003, pp. 347-360), writes that some players play to explore and test the boundaries of acceptable behavior (p. 353). Suler (1997) remarks that some participants are attracted by the risk of exploring prohibited areas. There is similarity also to category 3: that some players explore the limits of game mechanics, and in so doing they may disrupt another player's gaming experience.

Player influenced

2.1 Spite. The grief player motivation here is similar to motivations revealed in studies of bullying and teasing, and Suler's (1997) study. Land (2003) notes that bullying victims may be targeted because they possess certain attributes, resulting in jealousy towards these targets.

2.2 Victim vulnerability. Suler (1997) observes that there is a tendency to badly treat newcomers in virtual communities.

2.3 Revenge. Shapiro et al. (1991) cite reciprocation as a motivator for teasing, and Suler (1997) cites retaliation as a motivator.

Griefer influenced

3.1 Ritualization and group identity. Shapiro et al. (1991) note that teasing may occur as a result of a desire to demonstrate social status in a group. This is related to selected types in category 2, specifically Rozak's (2005) 'be part of a group'.

3.2 Reputation. Suler (1997) observes that teenage gangs enjoy notoriety, and consider their being punished by MUD game masters to be 'badges of honor'. This motivator is related to selected types from category 1; Rozak (2005) describes a 'rank/competition' motivation, and Hallford & Hallford (2001) describe the 'navel gazer' as a player who is particularly concerned about how advanced his character is compared to others.

Self

4.1 Bad mood. Bartle (1996) remarks that players, can move among all four player types depending on their moods. For example, an 'achiever' may turn 'killer' if his mood changes. Thus, a player who is normally well behaved may grief when he is in a bad mood. Shapiro et al. (1991) cites a similar motivator for teasing. Bosworth et al. (1999, p. 345) have also associated anger with bullying, with the level of anger directly proportional to the level of bullying.

4.2 Wanting to feel powerful. This motivator is observed in other studies. Land (2003) cites the desire to dominate as a motivator for teasing, and Suler (1997) notes the desire to feel superior and powerful for some participants of virtual communities. Similar player types and motivations are found in category 4: Bartle's (1996) 'killer' player type, Yee's (2002) 'grief' motivator, and Rozak's (2005) 'griefer'.

4.3 Attention. Bartle (2004, p. 167) argues that griefers want to be noticed, and Pawluk (1989, p. 161) observes the presence of an audience in teasing. Davis (2002) also notes that people who misbehave want attention.

4.4 Enjoyment. The definition of grief play in literature suggests that griefers enjoy causing disruption (Mulligan & Patrovsky 2003). Suler (1997) also remarks that "playful mischief" is a motivator in milder forms of bad behavior. A griefer who teases and annoys players could also be a 'joker' in Fullerton et al.'s (2004) player types.

4.5 Role-playing. The role-playing motivator is related to Yee's 'immersion', Fullerton et al.'s (2004) 'storyteller', Rozak's (2005) 'role-playing', and Hallford & Hallford's (2001) 'story chaser' player types in category 5.

The two grief player motivators that are not immediate correlations to existing models are 'game premise' and 'boredom'. The game premise—for example whether the game is PvP-centric or not—alongside the strictness in which game policies are enforced influence the general disposition

128

for players to grief. By itself, it is not a 'motivation' or compelling reason for players to grief. It merely facilities and expedites the opportunities to. Boredom tends to also be the initiator or a trigger point for a player to grief. Like 'game premise', an equivalent motivation in existing models could not be found for 'boredom'.

Conversely, there are other motivators in existing models which the study could not validate. Three of these should be mentioned. Firstly, the immaturity of participants demonstrating bad behavior is cited by Suler (1997). Lin & Sun's (2005) player respondents remarked that griefers are typically "junior high school students", and Davis (2002) echoes this by remarking that age is a factor for bad behavior in online games. However, while some of my respondents who suffered at the hands of griefers claimed that their tormentors were immature, there is no indication in data to show if this absence of maturity was a result of their griefers' ages. In fact, while many acts of grief play seem opportunistic (for example because the player was bored), others were premeditated. There was evidence that the Trinsic incident had been meticulously planned in advance, as was also the incident where players wearing plate mail amour were singled out for attack in *Ultima Online* [R5]. These are signs that griefers may not be impulsive. Also, while there were some players who called griefers 'kids' ([DAoC-005], [CoH-009]), others when interviewed did recognize that not every griefer would be a young person, and that the maturity of a player to behave responsibly towards others in the game does not necessarily come only with age.

Secondly, Suler (1997) cites "simple ignorance" as a reason for bad behavior. A griefer may indeed be ignorant of rules if he is a new player, and thus may grief until he knows better. One should also note that ignorance is different from absence of disruptive intention. Ignorance means that the player does not know that the activity is disruptive. However, a player who is not ignorant may still engage in disruptive behavior that is not disrupting for its sake (for example area monopolization). Having said this, data could not validate with certainty if ignorance is a common reason for griefing. With the large player numbers in an MMORPG, players possess varying levels of familiarity with game rules. Hence, it is quite possible that a few persons may unwittingly commit acts of disruption out of ignorance. Still, respondents remarked that griefers hardly ever seemed ignorant of game rules. A player who abuses another because of an ignorance of game rules would be apologetic, or minimally at least hesitant about continuing with his play style when the afflicted players verbalize their unhappiness. Many griefers, however, often either repeat their acts, or verbally taunt their victims as well. Both are criteria from Chapter 4 that can lead a player to believe he has been griefed. In these cases, ignorance does not seem a reasonable premise for their behavior.

Lastly, Suler (1997) notes "culture clash" and that influence from other cultures may be a reason for some people to behave badly in multi-user environments. Personal information was not obtained from respondents in the study, nor is such data available in discussion postings. Hence, the research could not validate or disprove Suler (1997) proposition[85].

Conclusion

What drives a person to exhibit bad behavior seems to be similar no matter what the medium of communication or virtual setting is. The motivations of griefers are not too different from motivators revealed in teasing and bullying, and bad behavior that occurs online. What is telling as well is that griefers can exhibit motivators that are similar to other non-griefing players who play the game. For instance, a "socializing" player joins a community and participates in activities to feel a sense of identity to the group. In the same way, a player could join a griefing group, and subsequently grief with them to feel a sense of identity.

The discussion of motivations for griefing also poses another question: while a number of motivators for grief play have been identified, is there a representative reason why players grief? The general approach of this study—that it is explorative and qualitative—has not allowed a definitive finding on such a representative reason for grief play, if it exists at all. What the research does suggest is that even with the large number of grief player motivations, many motivations seem to be directly or indirectly related back to enjoyment of the game that has been derived from grief play. It can be concluded that for many griefers, enjoyment of the game derived from the disruption of other players' gaming experience is either a motivation in itself, or the consequence of some other factors influencing a person to grief. It could be argued that ultimately, players, including griefers, play MMORPGs for 'fun'.

Finally, it has not been the intention of this research to make moralistic judgments about players who grief, or to suggest that griefers are only harmful to an MMORPG and do not bring benefits to the game. In fact, there is some evidence to suggest the contrary for the latter. Griefers may bring

---

[85] See Chapter 7 – 'Game management'.

130

some positive effects to the game in specific settings. The research will next investigate the third research objective: how grief play affects the game.

CHAPTER 6: IMPACTS OF GRIEF PLAY

Having investigated the perceptions of both players and developers on what grief play means and also the motivations of grief players, the third objective of this research is to investigate the effects, or 'impacts', of grief play. Grief play affects how players behave in the game world and how game developers design their games. Victims of grief play often report their incidents and how their play experiences have been affected in discussion forums. Game sites also routinely publish interviews with developers of MMORPGs in development, with developers queried on how their game will deal with grief play. This chapter has two operationalized objectives:

1. To investigate the impacts of grief play: how it affects players, developers and operators of MMORPGs.

2. To determine if grief play constitutes problematic behavior.

For the purposes of this chapter, an impact is defined as a consequence or outcome of grief play. Occasionally, the impact may create a further reaction. This makes it possible for one impact to be a cause for another impact.

Impacts of Grief Play

There is little material on how grief play can affect the game operator, game development, and players. Amongst a couple of exceptions is the interview with Steven B. Davis (2005). In the interview, Davis remarks that grief play (and cheating) causes players to quit, and new players do not join the game. It also increases the costs of customer service support, and technical support to solve or debug game mechanism exploits uncovered by griefers. The costs of employing customer service staff to deal with grief play can range from USD100,000 to USD300,000 per position per year (Davis 2005). Another example is Bartle's (1996) work on player types. In it, he discusses the effects player-killers have on other player types. He posits that increasing the number of player-killers will result in decreases to achievers and socializers, but will have no effect on explorers (they do not care if they get killed).

As with other aspects in this study, the methodological approach was to let the impacts of grief play surface from data. 20 distinctive impacts were identified. Analysis of these impacts next revealed that grief play can affect players and the developers/operator of the MMORPG. Subsequent work led to a finer categorization. In the player segment, grief play can affect:

- Player sentiments or changes in player attitudes.

- Player behavior or changes in play styles exhibited by players.

- Player communities or changes in how players bond or interact with each together.

In the developer and operator segment, grief play can affect:

- Game design or how grief play affects game mechanisms, and the types of play activities permitted by rules.

- Game service or how grief play affects the customer service representatives who respond to players' petitions for attention.

The table below shows the 20 impacts, categorized into player, and developer/operator segments.

Table 15: Impacts of grief play

Segment	Impact
Players	Player sentiments
	1.1 Annoyance
	1.2 Emotional distress
	1.3 Dissatisfaction
	1.4 Enjoyment
	Player behavior
	2.1 Caution
	2.2 Isolationism
	2.3 Twitching
	2.4 Reputation
	2.5 Herd mentality
	2.6 Inaction
	2.7 Snowballing
	Player communities
	3.1 Bonding
	3.2 Distrust
	3.3 Events
	3.4 In-game activism
Developers and operators	Game design
	4.1 Rules
	4.2 Reduced player interaction
	4.3 Distrust (of players)
	4.4 Stress testing
	Game service
	5.1 Game masters

It should be noted that while Table 15 above is representative of data collected in this study, griefers will find new ways to disrupt play experiences in new MMORPGs. Moreover, the degree to which grief play can impact a player or game depends on specific circumstances that can vary from one incident to the next. Lastly, relationships exist among some of these impacts. For example, one impact can 'lead' to another impact. These relationships will be discussed in a later section.

Player sentiments

1.1 Annoyance. Annoyance is a common reaction exhibited by players who are griefed. When players are annoyed, they express these sentiments in discussion forums and to each other in-game. Occasionally, players complain to the managers of the player community, for example guild or clan leaders, which the griefer may be affiliated to. These complaints are often lodged with the expectation that these managers will reign in their badly behaving members ([R51], [R53]).

The sentiment of annoyance can also get aggravated by the commonly expressed remark from griefers or other players that "It's just a game." Myers (2005) remarks that grief play may not be deliberately intended to be hostile against the victim. Rather, it can be a symbolic act, and the offence caused not intended as a personal affront. However, this does not help victims of grief play feel better. Ironically, their feelings of annoyance may instead be intensified, as victims may perceive that griefers are trivializing the impacts of their actions.

When annoyance is built up long term, it can lead to frustration with the game at large. It can change player perceptions of when an incident becomes grief play. If grief play in a game becomes common place, players may become quick to conclude that griefing has occurred when any incident does not go their way [R76], or when their enjoyment of the game has been impeded. These responses may be merely reactionary. However, petitions are still lodged as a consequence, and they increase the volume of petitions game masters have to respond to.

1.2 Emotional distress. Some players who are emotionally attached[86] to their characters become distressed when griefed. When they are griefed, they feel that the act is a personal attack. When players become sufficiently distressed (or frustrated) by grief play, the pull of playing that comes from other aspects of the game needs to be stronger for them to continue playing. Some of these aspects could be the quality of game content, or more social aspects like friends made or the community that the player is affiliated to. In fact, Koivisto (2003) argues that the game community

---

[86] See section – 'Influencing grief play impacts on player sentiments' in this chapter.

itself may be the most important reason for players to continue playing a game. If the attraction of these other aspects is not enough and yet players continue to be distressed, they may quit ([R40], [R65]). In one case, a player cancelled his account after weighing the cost of the monthly service and the enjoyment he was deriving versus the misery caused by griefers [R29].

Some players believe that grief play can also separate players who are less resistant to distress and therefore play in safer game areas or quit altogether from other players who can put up with the environment and stay on [R25]. Some players call this "natural selection", where only the most emotionally resilient players continue playing long-term. One player remarked that the virtual (game) world necessitates the "survival of the fittest" [R64]. Players who retaliate against griefers often become highly skilled, and are proud of their abilities to retaliate against griefers, as was observed in some interview responses. This is not to say that the players who relocate to a different game area (or MMORPG altogether) are less resistant against the rigors of online gaming. Some players intentionally avoid grief play for other reasons, and this is discussed below. Still, the more experienced players become skilled, and from the stories of how they reacted to griefers, are often capable of taking immediate and direct responses when griefed. In these cases, grief play may still be annoying but less emotionally distressing for them.

1.3 Dissatisfaction. When players are griefed, they often look towards the game operator for resolution. There are numerous cases of players feeling that game masters had not resolved incidents of grief play to their satisfaction[87]. Sometimes, only individual players are affected by grief play. These include incidents of rez-killing, or newbie-killing. In cases where the effect of a grief play incident is widespread, for example the disruption of a player-run event, player dissatisfaction may be increased in proportion to the amount of work and effort invested in the preparation of the event, or the size of the event itself. The Trinsic incident is one such example. When disruption of such scale happens, players can also become dissatisfied with the game operator and may even resent its management [R53] if they believe rule enforcement was lax on griefers. Moreover, the dissatisfaction may become aggravated if players perceive that game rules should had specifically disallowed the play tactic exhibited by the griefer, but yet customer service representation took the side of the griefer [R40]. The expectations that players have of the game

---

[87] See Chapter 7 – 'Game masters' for some incidents related by players.

operation on the enforcement of rules merits a substantial discussion, and this is presented in the next chapter.

1.4 Enjoyment. One player of *EverQuest* in Delwiche's (2003) study remarked that the presence of player-killing on a PvP server provided a degree of 'immersion' not found on non-PvP servers. Some of the players in this study enjoy the presence of grief play; others when queried insist they do not. Whether players enjoy the presence of grief play is influenced by their expectations [R35]. If players are cognizant and receptive of a game environment where danger lurks at every corner, or they retain the ability to respond to that danger (for example by attacking their griefers back in PvP), players are less likely to feel the strong adverse emotions when griefed. They may even derive some enjoyment at retaliating against griefers [R29]. Bartle (1996) notes that the presence of a little player-killing may be good for the game, as it supports "camaraderie, excitement and intensity of experience." The excitement that comes from the presence of danger was echoed by players: one player [R39] remarked that it was exciting to deal with 'bad' players. Unpredictable variables may make the game more exciting too, as another remarked [R25]:

> … So I have to keep an eye out for those when hunt there[88]… and the occasional lone PK raider/thief that could come our way… the possibilities are endless, you always have to keep an eye out for newcomers and the randomness and the challenge that potential human enemies present will never be possible with even the best AI[89] monster ever made.

Occasionally, players start out disliking grief play, but upon getting used to PvP become more tolerant of it. One player [R20] was initially not skilled in PvP, and was frequently player-killed and griefed in *Ultima Online*. He disliked the game as a result. However, upon exposure to *Shadowbane*, he got accustomed to PvP and now enjoys the intense interaction that PvP brings about. He has also become more tolerant of grief play, and enjoys NCsoft's *Guild Wars*, a PvP-centric MMORPG. The tolerance a player can develop for grief play after taking part in PvP can be compared to teasing. Bollmer et al. (2003) posit that individuals who are used to teasing, for example after having been frequently teased as a child, tend to see teasing as nothing more than normal social interaction. They propose that the converse is equally true—individuals who have been less frequently teased are more annoyed by teasing (p. 582-583). In other cases, some players

---

[88] This is in reference to opposing communities who claim game areas as they own and stop other players from 'hunting' in these areas.

[89] Or artificial intelligence.

simply get used to grief play and accept it as an unavoidable part of the game ([R46], [R51], [R61], [R73]), although their dislike for the activity was still evident from their responses.

The absence of grief play can also result in some players enjoying the game *less*. Several players of *Ultima Online* reminisced about the loss of interaction with griefers from the point when the game world was split into the Trammel and Felucca aspects. Grief play may be enjoyable to those targeted only if they have some means of direct response—for example, via PvP, or grief retaliation (see below).

Player behavior

2.1 Caution. Anonymity itself already contributes towards a state of diminished trust when online (Johnson 1997, p. 64). Grief play can cause players to be even more cautious in game activities that involve people they do not know or have yet to gain trust for. These activities include player trading of items or in-game currency, forming pickup groups, or inviting new persons into an existing player community. In games which allow players to own persistent housing or accommodation, for example *Ultima Online* and *The Sims Online*, players often only allow persons they have developed trust for to share premises [R39]. Players are less trusting of the sincerity of unknown persons, for example passer-bys, who may honestly just want to help when opportunities arise [R42]. A player of *City of Heroes* complained how they were supposed to be heroes, but given the potential for misunderstanding, they now had to think twice about helping out other players [CoH-008]. In general, when grief play is widespread, players seem to become more suspicious of any good intentions they come across [R69].

2.2 Isolationism. When there is widespread distrust among players, some players can become insular ([R66], [R71]). Players will avoid adventuring in or traveling through areas where griefers are known to appear. Players are also less willing to speak to others for fear that they are griefers. Some even turn into 'hermit'-like players who limit their in-game interaction to friends they know.

2.3 Twitching. Some players become so wary of other players in close proximity when they are engaged in an encounter that they may exhibit what one player called "twitching" behavior [R50]. Twitching is a more intense form of player 'caution'. The nervousness felt can be so acute that a player who is fighting a particularly challenging mob may instinctively move his character to a safer area whenever a stranger runs past him. An ex-player of *Ultima Online* even believed his behavior in the game was schizophrenic. He recalled that the feeling of fear was so pervasive for

137

him he continually looked over his shoulder to see if he was about to be attacked [DAoC-005]. A milder version of twitching can also be observed when players instinctively take an offensive stance when others wander nearby. The passer-bys are often warned that this is "their kill" and are told to move along [R62].

2.4 Reputation. A consequence of players losing trust is the corresponding increase in the importance of player reputation. Player reputations are a way of managing virtual communities (Jensen et al. 2002, p. 448). One such system was implemented in *Ultima Online* (Pizer 2003, p. 434). The system initially involved the use of 'notoriety' tags that were added to each player. As a player killed more players, his tag gradually turned from blue to red. Player-killers soon found ways to get round this system, such that the tag no longer became representative of how likely a player would continue killing others; for example a 'blue' player could really be a player-killer. The difficulty of ascertaining player intentions using reputation systems implemented this way can lead players to become altogether skeptical of the usefulness of any reputation system that is built into a game. Players instead rely on informal reputation systems, for example word of mouth when players chat and warn each other [R66]. Occasionally, players even create informal networks that report on untrustworthy players [R49]. Players also make discussion postings of grief play incidents, often citing names of perpetrators. These incident reports are used by players to gain awareness of the more notorious griefers. In essence, players find it prudent to keep tabs on who the griefers and player-killers are around them [R20][90].

2.5 Herd mentality. Another possible impact of grief play is how it changes implicit rules. One player [R54] related a case in *EverQuest* where a new PvP server had just been made public for play. Players were initially polite and gracious enough to let their defeated opponents recover themselves without further attack. The early player norms included demonstration of fair-play, for example avoiding the use of overpowering force to attack small groups of opponents. However, these norms gradually broke down when PvP encounters became more intense and competitive. Players did not allow their defeated opponents to recover their equipment. They started attacking in overwhelming force, and even used NPCs to train and kill their opponents [R54]. The new priority of players in PvP zones became to win at all costs. Moreover, when players began griefing in these ways, their victims would retaliate using the same tactics. Some cited this as herd mentality since

---

[90] See Chapter 8 – 'Reputation' for further discussion on reputation systems.

"they did it to us first." ([R54], [R60]) Widespread grief play causes the "wall-sitters" to grief as well [R71], and courtesy is regarded as "a waste of time" [R58].

Still, not every instance of herd mentality occurs as a reaction to having been griefed. Some players who have not griefed before may start doing so upon observing how others have griefed. One griefer of *Ultima Online* [R6] remarked:

> I see my friends and guild mates do it. (So) why am I not joining in the fun? So I joined my friends going around earning cheap points killing hapless low-levels and terrorizing them.

2.6 Inaction. Some players do not respond to grief play at all. Sometimes, this is because players become so used to grief play that they believe nothing will come out from directly confronting the griefer, petitioning the incident to game masters, or reporting to their peers in discussion forums. Sometimes, the player may simply not be skilled enough to retaliate against his griefer. Alternatively, the victim may feel that an aggravating response will worsen matters with the griefer (for example he griefs even more intensely), or that a demonstration of frustration will only embolden the griefer. A player may walk away from an incident of grief play without response on his part as he chooses not to let grief play become an integral part of how he plays the game. Alternatively, he just may not want to become emotionally affected by grief play [R55].

2.7 Snowballing. Players of MMORPGs with PvP, for example *Shadowbane* and *World of Warcraft*, do not need a specific reason or excuse to attack another. They are by game rules and Law of code allowed to do so. When players are griefed in PvP-centric games, the feelings of annoyance may be sufficient enough to spur the victim to respond in a confrontational manner. For example, one player [R64] of *Ultima Online* related how he had his friends nearby when he played in game areas frequented by griefers. When he was griefed, his friends arrived on the scene quickly, ambushed the griefer so that "justice was carried out." Retaliation can become grief play when the player retaliating engages in similar griefing activities. For example, a player who has his mob kill-stolen may attack the perpetrator, and upon victory, emote abusive insults or taunts on the player's corpse. The study proposes that these activities be called 'grief retaliation', and that grief snowballs when it happens.

There are also other ways players can 'grief retaliate' without immediately attacking their attackers. For instance, the same player who has his mobs kill-stolen may train surrounding mobs on his griefer, or return at a later time with a more advanced character to rez-kill [CoH-013]. The remarks made by players who grief their griefers back hint at how satisfying they find these acts of retribution. One player [R76] remarked: "When I first started playing five years ago, I would go about business like most other players. Over the years, I grew tired of griefers and began having more fun griefing them back." Another [R28] remarked: "When someone tries to grief me, I will grief them. If someone starts trying to steal my kills, I will ICQ some friends and party with them." Yet another player [R60] would mimic exactly the same play style back at the perpetrator, calling it "reverse griefing".

Smith (1999, p. 147) posits that user retaliation against disruptive behavior can escalate disputes. Some players I spoke to certainly realized this potential for escalation. While some players readily retaliated against their griefers, others also recognized that apart from the satisfaction gained, direct retaliation of the griefing kind may indeed escalate matters. Sometimes, grief snowballing results in spill-over effects where bystanders get affected too. A train of mobs created by an angry player responding to grief play could attack other bystanders who are in close proximity [R51]. A player who has been griefed could even grief uninvolved players because he lacks the skill to retaliate against his very own more skilled tormentors [R80]. Grief retaliation can also confuse the situation when game masters respond to the petition for assistance (which may be lodged by the same bystanders caught up in the incident). In these cases, the game master may just mete out punishment to both persons—griefer and the victim who retaliated [R55].

PvP and grief retaliation as a means of responding to grief play are important issues in this study, and will be discussed further in Chapter 8.

Player communities

3.1 Bonding. One issue of grief play that sees polarized points of view among players is whether grief play builds camaraderie among player communities or it instead fosters distrust. Kim (1998) in her commentary of *Ultima Online* for *Wired News* notes the case for bonding:

> The paradox of violence in online worlds is that while it generates moral outrage, it also encourages players to band together into tightly knit groups of trusted comrades.

Just as players who disrupt will band together to cause mayhem, those who want to play in more harmonious fashion will bond together in a similar manner ([R64], [R69], [UO-009]). With reference to Kim's comment above, when players are sufficiently annoyed or distressed by grief play, they may, not unreasonably, band together for mutual support. Bartle (1996) notes that a little player-killing can support camaraderie among players. One player [R25] remarked that he felt "a much stronger sense of community in a world where danger lurks at every corner." Experienced players may even form player communities to help newbie groups, for example by passing on game-centric knowledge so that these new players are less vulnerable to grief play. One such example of a community in *Ultima Online* was a guild called "Skara Brae Rangers"[91], whose namesake came from a city where grief play was widespread. This guild was established specifically to counter the PKing of newbie players. Over time, the guild developed its own unique tactics to counter these player-killers. Even after the game world was split into Trammel and Felucca aspects, similar guilds continued to set up in Felucca to counter and fight player-killers [R68].

Examples have also been observed elsewhere that grief play can result in strangers helping each other out. One player of *City of Heroes* related a story of how he had high-level mobs trained on him. Nearby players subsequently rushed to help stop the griefing [CoH-015]. Sometimes, players in opposing factions may even temporarily stop attacking each other to hunt down a griefer in the play area, as one player's community did in *EverQuest*'s PvP server [R54]. In *Ultima Online*, one griefing guild would camp an area known as the "Yew duel roof". They would kill people in the middle of their duels, and then leave the area quickly. This resulted in other guilds that normally disliked each other banding together, and systematically attacking and killing members of this griefing guild whenever they showed up. Eventually, the griefing guild disbanded [R68].

3.2 Distrust. While grief play can result in players bonding together, it can also lead to distrust among players. Players who are distrustful of others become more cautious as well. Some players remarked that they tend to be more helpful of strangers and other players early on, but are less so when grief play becomes common [R78]. Players can also become more calculative. As a result of kill-stealing in *Ultima Online*, the game became more item-centric for some players ([R61], [R63]). Some players also hesitate joining pick-up groups comprising strangers. Instead, they prefer to join groups comprising persons they know or are affiliated to their own player community. For the latter, there is avenue for recourse from player community management if one of their own members griefs within the group.

---

[91] The identity of this player community has been cited with permission from the player who established it. However, the guild was short-lived. Internal disputes within the guild resulted in the community fragmenting and losing its effectiveness in its efforts to combat player-killers.

Grief play can also act as a catalyst in the fragmentation of a player community. In one case, a guild in *Ultima Online* saw five instances of groups splintering off to form separate communities [R78]. All five instances were apparently the results of grief play incidents from players within this community. The five groups deliberately misinterpreted rules of play within the community and engaged in player-killing and rumor mongering. One could speculate that players in a community may internally dispute for many other reasons. However, that grief play can elicit strong emotions from players hints that the players in this instance may have had already sufficiently polarized sentiments of grief play. This in turn served as a trigger point for them to split from the community and form separate groups. In this way, grief play may have precipitated the fragmentation.

Ultimately, the presence of danger and facing challenges brought upon by grief play may indeed bond some players closer together. However, the same kind of bonding can also be built through more communal types of activities, for example player-driven events or other types of collaborative activities. This sentiment was expressed by a player [R43] who provided the following analogy. The argument that grief play may bond players closer for him was similar to how hazing in college fraternities can bind the fraternity males closer together. However, in his case, he was in a non-hazing fraternity, and was proud to be in it, as his fraternity did not condone hazing behavior on its members. Collaborative activities do foster rapport and build mutual trust among players [R62], and some players would rather bond through these activities than through having to face griefers.

3.3 Events. Events in-game are often organized by players, and are a common way for player communities to advance the narrative element of the game world. They also enhance the communal aspects of the game. These events can be well attended, but they also frequently become targets of attacks by griefers intent on creating the largest amount of disruption. The amount of work involved in planning and running an event can be considerable. For example, the player event in the Trinsic incident had been in planning for months by its organizers. The events where non-invitees can easily get into tend to be vulnerable, as these are public events where any player can join. Data revealed several players who once organized events less keen to do so in games where grief play is observed ([R41], [R59], [R71]). Some have stopped organizing public events altogether for fear of outsiders disrupting their events. When events do get organized, contingency plans often get developed as well. This is so that the event can quickly move to another location if griefers show up ([R66], [R69]). Other players stopped attending events for fear of getting griefed ([R65], [R59]).

3.4 In-game activism. In-game activism from players against the game operator is another possible impact of grief play. Activism can take place when players are dissatisfied with the game. For example, players may believe there are rules that condone or even encourage grief play, or they perceive that management is not taking adequate action on loopholes that are exploited by griefers [R48]. An ill-chosen or implemented game mechanism that is exploited by griefers may see many rounds of irate postings in the discussion forum, complaints to customer service, and player-initiated protests. For example, a group of players protesting against a rule or the inactivity of the game operator towards grief play may 'sit-in' and physically obstruct access to an area[92]. Ironically, this kind of activism can result in disciplinary action against these 'anti-grief play' players.

Game design

4.1 Rules. Bad behavior can be influenced by the permissibility of the environment. As noted before, permissibility is determined by two things: the kind of rules in the game, and to what degree those rules are enforced. An example can illustrate this. *EverQuest* was released in 1999, a time when grief play in *Ultima Online* was rampant. *EverQuest* was more restrictive in the kind of activities permitted to players, for example in player-versus-player conflict. Game masters were also vigilant in rule enforcement. As it turned out, *EverQuest* became a more successful game in terms of player subscriptions and retention when compared to *Ultima Online*[93].

A possible impact of grief play on game design is the inclusion of more restrictions on player activities. In *EverQuest 2*, mobs that have been engaged by a player group cannot be further engaged by another player outside this group. Sony Online Entertainment has stated that an encounter 'lock' allows a mob to be specifically designed to suit a group's capabilities without having additional variability added, for example in the form of interference or assistance from external players. However, many players believed that this mechanism was designed in part to eliminate kill-stealing and training that were common in the earlier game, *EverQuest*, and they expressed these sentiments on discussion forums. Whether the mechanism was really intended to

---

[92] On one occasion, players in *Ultima Online* protesting against the number of game bugs that had gone unfixed banded together in the hundreds, and had their characters strip naked. They proceeded to storm a prominent and public establishment in the game world (Kim 1998), creating a noisy and boisterous scene in protest.

[93] Kosak (2002) in his commentary of the 2002 Game Developers Conference for *GameSpy.com* equates an MMORPG with heavy restrictions to Disneyland. He likens a Disneyland MMORPG as a 'controlled environment' with every trace of undesirable elements removed.

address kill-stealing and training or not, it stands to reason that if players are making use of a game mechanism to grief, a more restrictive game mechanism can still render the subtype impossible.

4.2 Reduced player interaction. A more specific instance of restrictive rules is reduced player interaction [R37]. For instance, in *World of Warcraft* and *Dark Age of Camelot*, players cannot communicate with players on the opposing faction they are fighting against. This makes it normally impossible for opposing players to communicate within game. For example players in one faction cannot utter battle chants against the opposing faction, even if it is intended in the best spirit of role-playing. It also means players cannot grief by harassing, taunting or hurling continuous abuse on opposing players.

The employment of restrictive mechanisms governing player interaction is not without debate. Specifically, these mechanisms can alter game play, and there is debate on whether communication among players should be restricted at the expense of game playability, or should players be given greater control in deciding who they interact with. One mechanism at the centre of such debate is 'instancing'. Instancing is a game mechanism that allows small groups of players to have their own unique copy of a small game area, for example a zone, that becomes private to them. It allows players to selectively choose who they want to play with, and in so doing reduce the possibility of getting griefed by strangers. Instancing has increasingly become more common in MMORPGs. One design benefit of instancing is that it allows encounters to be tailored to suit specific groups, as one developer explained [R82]. However, a game that is heavily instanced also feels less "multi-player-like" [R88]. It could be argued that both friends and strangers should become an integral part of a multi-player community [R81]. The use of instancing as an impact of grief play in this sense limits the community from becoming very communal ([R34], [R85]).

There are also other consequences of insulating players from each other. Many players make new friends by meeting strangers and helping each other out on incidental circumstances. Many friendships in-game are formed this way. Instancing makes it harder to meet new people and by extension make new friends. This in turn makes it easier for players to leave the game [R35] since the social pull of playing with friends in the game is reduced for them.

A final consequence of instancing is that having a unique copy of a game area for groups to play in removes competition among multiple groups for that encounter. For example, *EverQuest* 6 years after release is now a game populated with high-level players who are each loyal to their respective

144

player communities. At one juncture, the competition for 'end-game'[94] encounters was so intense that kill-stealing among player communities for these mobs was observed. While such mob competition is on the one hand despised by many high-level players, it also keeps these very same players motivated [R35]. A community comprising these high-level players which succeeds in getting to and defeating the mob ahead of other communities obtains not just the powerful items that the encounter will reward them with, it also obtains the bragging rights that Rouse (2005, p. 2) cites. These rights in turn add prestige, and can be used as a recruitment poser to attract other players to join their community. Instancing removes that competition, and for some players an important element of the high-level game for them—intense player interaction and inter-community activity.

4.3 Distrust (of players). Some developers believed that players cannot be trusted; one developer [R34] even remarked that players will abuse freedom if it is given to them. *Ultima Online* is an example of a game that had been designed with the intention of allowing players to self-police, as designer Raph Koster remarked (Koster n.d.). However, it turned out that more players wanted to play bandits and bullies than players who attempted to play police[95]. As a result, the bandits and bullies could overwhelm those who tried to police them, as noted by Kolbert (2001) in *The New Yorker*. In other cases, game design concepts that may be integral to the setting of an MMORPG do not get implemented because of fears it would get abused by griefers. One example of this is the 'virtue' system in *Ultima Online* that Kim (1998) notes for *Wired News*. The predecessor of *Ultima Online* was a series of single-player CRPGs called *Ultima*. A story telling element of the series was how players would undertake and complete quests of virtues like honesty, valor, humility, and compassion. This system of virtues, while prominent in the single-player version of the game, was not included in the MMORPG version for years. One difficulty game developers faced in this case was that this system would not always reflect the real personality of players. A player of *Ultima Online* who completed a series of virtue quests and attains an 'honest' tag may still lead astray a newbie unaware that this tag is only an in-game construct [R34]. In sum, well-intended concepts do occasionally get shelved because of fears that they will be used to grief.

---

[94] These are usually encounters with very hard mobs that can only be defeated by large raid groups of high-level characters.

[95] See Chapter 8 – 'Policing or banditry'.

4.4 Stress testing. Many games during development undergo 'beta testing'. Typically, the game operator recruits expert players to identify problems with the game software so that they can be corrected before release (Davis et al. 2005). Similarly, some griefers are on the lookout for game mechanisms that are poorly implemented, and will exploit possible loopholes in these mechanisms to give themselves added advantage. One consequence of such code scrutiny by griefers is the increased awareness of poorly implemented game mechanisms in the general player base. Players want to be aware of exploits, for example in trade scams, so that they cannot be taken advantage of by griefers. As such, news of how griefers exploit mechanisms can circulate quickly. As one player explained, he needs to "be one step ahead of the scammers" [R61]. The awareness of exploits can lead to other effects. Players irate at the existence of loopholes will log petitions identifying these loopholes. Moreover, other players may even attempt to exploit these loopholes themselves as well. Game operators expend effort to improve code and game mechanisms in order to make them resilient to exploitation.

Still, the propensity of griefers to exploit game mechanisms can be harnessed to the betterment of game design. Specifically, the rigor that players attempt to find loopholes in code can be employed as a means of testing a game under development (Myers 2005). Denegri-Knott (2003) remarks that in the context of consumer-producer relationships on the web, consumers who behave badly may in fact be creative in how they come up with new ways of manipulating a system. One developer remarked that the intensity of which a griefer will scrutinize every nuance of a game mechanic should be respected, as they see the game in a "more complete way than most players" [R33]. In this sense, grief play does have an advantageous impact—it can eventually lead to a game becoming more robust.

Game service

5.1 Game masters. As described in earlier chapters, players are able to request assistance or attention from game masters during a game session or customer service representatives when outside it[96]. There can be numerous petitions at any one time with the size of the player-base and the number of players logged on simultaneously. Given the high cost of employing customer service staff, mechanisms have been developed to better manage the large number of petitions.

---

[96] Mulligan & Patrovsky (2003, p. 237) note that prior experience with MMORPGs demonstrated that at least one game master is required for every 5,000 anticipated subscribers at the launch of the game. The operator for a large MMORPG may require a large department of game masters (p. 236).

These range from engaging player volunteers to handle the less critical requests for help[97] to the outsourcing of customer service support. Interestingly, the outsourcing of customer service support has actually led to some players alleging lower quality of services. For example, Sony Online Entertainment, which operates several popular MMORPGs including *EverQuest, EverQuest 2* and *Star Wars Galaxies,* has outsourced part of its customer service operation to India[98]. While the spreading out of customer service representatives around the world enables the service to run more robustly—for example, players in the United States who play in off-peak hours can continue to receive customer service from representatives stationed in India—this has not stopped players from feeling disgruntled. In particular, some players have remarked in discussion forums that the CSRs cannot speak proper English [EQ2-028].

Players who are griefed will often lodge petitions for game master attention. When grief play is common, a large number of petitions get lodged. Davis (2005) remarks that 25% of petitions are caused by griefers. CSRs in *Asheron's Call* spend 40% of their time dealing with griefer issues (Pizer 2003, p. 431). The problem can be compounded when grief play affects a large number of people. For example, event disruption, player blocking or training are likely to affect a larger number of players simultaneously, compared to newbie-killing or trade scamming which affect individuals or smaller groups of players. When incidents of this scale take place, multiple petitions for game master attention may be lodged. These petitions can be lodged independently of each other. For example, a training incident which results in a group of players getting killed can result in every player of that group petitioning. Players sometimes do this with the hope that with every person calling for attention, game masters will either respond more promptly, or become more likely to resolve the incident in their favor. Whether this happens or not, when players lodge multiple petitions for game master attention on the same incident, it extends the queue of petitions that game masters must respond to. This further delays petitions from other players who may have asked for assistance on matters unrelated to grief play.

Some players are also dissatisfied with customer service on grief play resolution, and express a lack of confidence in the management of the game. The reasons cited for such dissatisfaction include

---

[97] See Chapter 8 – 'Player volunteers'.

[98] As announced by Sony Online Entertainment on 6 April 2004 (see http://eqforums.station.sony.com/eq/board/message?board.id=TSArchive&message.id=5).

inconsistent application of game rules (for example a game rule disallows a play style that has been assessed as a legitimate play style), game master resolution based on an incomplete understanding of circumstances, and slow response (for example game masters take too long to arrive at the scene). In one case, a group of ten players in *City of Heroes* lodged forty petitions requesting game master attention when an extended series of training incidents occurred. Game masters did not respond even after seven hours, as posters into the discussion thread alleged [CoH-017]. For some, it is a waste of time to petition for game master attention when the incident concerns grief play [TSO-031]. Mulligan & Patrovsky (2003, p. 122) note that customer service in MMORPGs suffer from bad reputation; data certainly suggests how this can happen as an impact of grief play.

There are also other consequences that grief play can have on game masters. Like players, game masters have only so much time or patience. Players who harass and cheat can drive game masters "buggy" (Mulligan & Patrovsky 2003, p. 241). One developer even cited game master "burnout" as a consequence if game masters have to deal with an endless supply of griefers [R87]. Moreover, when game masters attempt to enforce game rules and discipline, for example against the usage of loopholes exploited by griefers, players may conclude that the game service is fascist-like. Goodwill can potentially be eroded [R87].

Clearly, the customer service representation function of an MMORPG is run at expense to the game operator, both in terms of monetary and social costs when players do not agree with the resolutions. In the case of *Ultima Online*, Kolbert (2001) at *The New Yorker* writes that this expense had not been anticipated for its game operator as the game was intended as self-policing. If nothing else, game operators are concerned with methods of reducing the load grief play exerts on its game service.

Discussion

Even though the number of players who grief in an MMORPG may be small, there are several circumstances that can exemplify the effect of actions from a few. Firstly, if the ratio of perpetrators to victims is large, i.e. a small group of players griefing many players simultaneously as they did in the Trinsic incident, the effect of a grief play incident can be large. Secondly, if there is widespread publicity of the grief play incident, for example in discussion forums, players may believe that griefers are overrunning the game. This in turn can lead players into believing that a grief play incident had a much larger effect than in reality, and can in turn influence their perception of whether or not the game operator is in control of the situation.

One intended outcome of this study is to better understand if grief play constitutes problematic behavior. As described in Chapter 3, while anecdotal evidence observed prior to the study suggested that grief play is a damaging type of behavior, the study avoided adopting this perception at the onset. In the analysis of grief play impacts, of interest was if a particular impact was perceived by respondents to be 'harmful', destructive and negative, versus 'beneficial', constructive and positive. These perceptions were coupled with an understanding of how the impact affects the players, developers and operators of the game. The table below reports the placement of each impact:

Table 16: Impacts placement

Placement	Impact
Negative	1.1 Annoyance 1.2 Emotional distress 1.3 Dissatisfaction 2.1 Caution 2.2 Isolationism 2.3 Twitching 2.5 Herd mentality 2.7 Snowballing 3.2 Distrust 3.3. Events 3.4 In-game activism 4.1 Rules 4.2 Reduced player interaction 4.3 Distrust (of players) 5.1 Game masters
Neutral	2.4 Reputation 2.6 Inaction
Positive	1.4 Enjoyment 3.1 Bonding 4.4 Stress testing

18 of 20 impacts of grief play have been categorized into negative and positive outcomes. In the case of 2 impacts—reputation and inaction—the impact is neither wholly negative nor positive. Firstly for reputation, a reputation system can be abused (negative) if a griefer extorts from a victim and threatens to smear his reputation if he does not acquiesce to his demands. Alternatively, a reputation system can also allow griefers to be identified (positive). Secondly for inaction, a player

may not react to grief play because he feels helpless (negative), or he simply does not want to let players who are intent on disruption interfere with his personal enjoyment of the game (positive). For these two impacts, their effect is regarded as neutral.

Chapter 3 recognized a limitation of the study: that the players who participated in the interviews and also those who posted into the discussion forums are not necessarily representative of the player base. In order for a representative determination to be made on whether participants view grief play as harmful behavior compared to those who feel it is constructive and a necessary aspect of an MMORPG, quantitative methods of research would be required. Recognizing this limitation, one has to look for other ways of making this determination. One way of deriving a position on whether grief play should be seen as problematic behavior is by considering if there are numerically more negative impacts than positive ones. With the analysis of data and findings emerging at this juncture, it is now possible to propose a general observation of grief play: that grief play can be said to be 'problematic' as it causes more negative impacts than positive ones.

This position is also supported by considering why people play games, and the chain of events that emanate from grief play that inhibit their needs and wants from being met. Essentially, games are intended to be fun for players. If they continually experience annoyance, on a basic level, the game becomes less fun and enjoyable. While some players will relish the opportunities offered in the game to address those feelings of annoyance (for example they retaliate against griefers), others either cannot or prefer not to. On the basis that there are emotional costs experienced by these afflicted players which in turn reduces the amount of 'fun' derived, it can be argued that grief play constitutes problematic behavior.

In the course of data analysis, some of the impacts affecting players also seemed to be interrelated. For example:

- When players are 'annoyed', they may become 'dissatisfied' with the game operator.
- When players are 'annoyed', they may grief others as 'herd mentality'.
- When players 'distrust' each other and their trust for others becomes eroded, they may become 'isolationist'. They may also become increasingly 'cautious', which may lead to 'twitching' behavior.
- When there is 'herd mentality' among players to grief, it can lead to grief 'snowballing'.

These relationships are of cause and effect. The following figure illustrates a collection of such relationships, with arrows denoting cause to effect between impacts. For example, in the figure below, 'distrust' can be a cause for 'caution'.

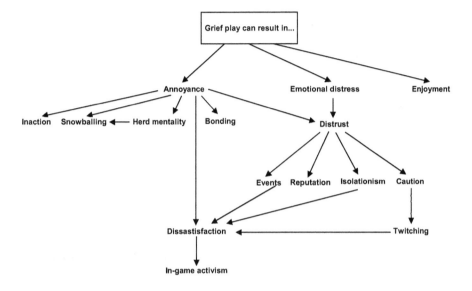

Figure 4: Impacts interrelated

The figure also illustrates another observation of impacts: that some impacts are immediate outcomes of grief play, while others may only occur after an extended period of griefing and other intermediary impacts have taken place first. For instance, when a player is griefed for the first time, 'annoyance' may be experienced immediately. When the same player has been griefed repeatedly, this can result in the player becoming 'distrustful'. The lack of trust with other players can further lead to 'caution', or 'isolationism'.

Also, of note in the figure is that all three of the first tier grief play impacts—'annoyance', 'emotional distress', and 'enjoyment'—are player sentiments. This suggests that player sentiments may be the basis where long term effects of grief play extend from. Put in another way, if player sentiments can be understood and managed, then the better the (subsequent) impacts on player behavior, communities and design/operation can be controlled. Sentiments can be managed through the adjustment of expectations so that players are less likely to become 'dissatisfied'. A player who knows what to expect in a game is less likely to be surprised, annoyed, frustrated or distressed by grief play. Understanding how player sentiments can be influenced is the subject of discussion in the next section, and player expectations the topic of discussion in the next chapter.

Influencing grief play impacts on player sentiments

How players react to grief play also varies from person to person. The intensity and the subtype of grief play itself can influence the sentiments experienced. However, data analysis revealed four other factors that can influence player sentiments. They are:

1. The ability to respond directly or retaliate.
2. The level of association to the character.
3. Player gender.
4. The expectations of the game operation.

Firstly, players get angry when they cannot retaliate (Lin & Sun 2005). From data, players who can retaliate against griefers expressed satisfaction at exerting some measure of justice on their tormentors. While they still felt some annoyance, feelings of helplessness were less commonly experienced compared to players who did not or could not retaliate. Grief play can become more tolerable when players can retaliate [GP-016]. Moreover, players who can retaliate are also more likely to derive enjoyment in the increased risks posed by grief play.

The ability to retaliate is influenced by the game knowledge and skill that the player possesses. For example, an awareness of a particular exploit will mean that the player is aware of how a scammer may attempt to trick him. An experienced player with a more advanced character (in terms of prowess and equipment owned) can better retaliate against griefers who 'cross' his path. Similarly, if he is well connected to other players, for example he has friends in his player community, he can gather a band to help retaliate.

Secondly, the level of association the player has to his character also influences his sentiments when griefed. A player can play a single character throughout the years he spends in the game. Over time, some players develop emotional bonds with their characters and the equipment they possess. The latter is particularly true if the items had been rewarded for completing a task that required extensive effort and problem solving. If their attachment to characters and equipment are strong, players will feel a real sense of loss when their characters are defeated and equipment lost as a consequence of defeat. The subtype of grief play imposed on them coupled with actual

152

circumstances, for example if players perceived that griefers employed unfair tactics, can further their distress. This has the potential of exacerbating the effect of a grief play incident.

Conversely, players who maintain detachment from their characters and equipment are less likely to feel distress or annoyance when griefed. However, unlike players who are able to retaliate, players who feel detached are also unlikely to feel satisfaction or enjoyment upon retaliation. In fact, because they do not care what happens to their characters, they are more likely to demonstrate inaction than retaliation. The same detachment can also be experienced by griefers. Some griefers do not care what happens to their characters. Some players grief with the full preparation that their characters would be killed. Hence, while a player who retaliates and kills his griefer may result in him gaining satisfaction and enjoyment, the griefer in turn may not feel annoyed or distressed at the death of his character. The griefer's detachment is perhaps best illustrated by remarks often heard in discussion forums that are similar to this: "It's just a game. Get over it." ([TSO-015]], [UO-008], [WoW-008]) A griefer who tells his victims not to take their characters' deaths seriously is likely to treat his own character's demise as trivial too.

On the same line of argument, one could also posit that some players are not griefing to cause annoyance or distress to victims. This can happen in two ways. Firstly, grief play is a metagame for them. They play to test game mechanisms to their limit. That they are distressing players is a consequence of their play styles, but not their objective. Secondly, these players are merely engaging in competitive play, and engage in implicit grief play because there is some in-game incentive to. An example of such an incentive could be a valuable item reward from defeating a mob, with greed play attendant.

Thirdly, the gender of the victim[99] can also affect player sentiments when griefed. Au (2002) at the *Salon.com* magazine presents anecdotal evidence that grief play affects female players disproportionately more than male players. The interviews in this study involved several respondents who revealed themselves to be women[100]. The method of study does not allow for general conclusions to be drawn on how women gamers are responding to grief play, nor does the study intend to psychoanalyze women in gaming. However, the perspectives offered by the women

---

[99] *The New York Times* estimates that at least 20 to 30 percent of players in three popular MMORPGs (*Ultima Online*, *Asheron's Call*, and *EverQuest*) are female (Laber 2001).

[100] A few respondents agreed to be spoken to on the phone. Their genders were verified this way.

respondents are still illuminating, and suggest that women gamers are responding to grief play in ways that are different from the other respondents who are either male or whose genders are not known for certain[101].

Literature shows that there are different attitudes exhibited by women in online gaming compared to men. Men tend to minimize personal interaction with other players, whereas female gamers communicate and socialize more frequently (Cloutier 2004, p. 16; Gorriz & Medina 2000, p. 47). Women are drawn towards games with a narrative (Gorriz & Medina 2000, p. 44), and the presence of social relationships and characters as constructive elements of play can also draw women to play these games (Laurel 2004, p. 74). Moreover, a female player when faced with an obstacle in the game will tend to analyze and discuss it first, then attempt the best solution they can think of. Male gamers prefer to break down obstacles as rapidly as possible and move onto the next test (Farmer 2001, p. 64).

In this study, one female player [R18], who plays several MMORPGs with a regular player community comprising of people she knows in the real-world, noted that her reactions to getting griefed were more emotional than those of her male player friends. When queried further on why she reacted this way, she remarked:

> Generally, when women play an MMORPG, they try to create in the game an ideal sort of life. When their game characters are happy, they're happy. When their game characters are sad, they're sad, and so on.

It would stand to reason that when an activity such as grief play disrupts the idealized lives they lead as characters, they would potentially feel very disturbed and personally offended. This bond they feel towards their characters is similar to the emotional attachment described earlier on. Another woman player noted that she herself, alongside other female MMORPG players known to her in the real-world, see "the game a bit more seriously than as 'just a game'" [R20]. Yet another admitted that female gamers take the game more personally than men [R23].

While there is no data in this study to prove (or disprove) that male gamers feel less emotional attachment to their characters than women, what is revealing are the perceptions of these female players and how they differ from their male counterparts'. One remarked that male players are

---

[101] When queried, the women respondents cautioned that their sentiments were not necessarily representative.

more likely to respond to grief play in the same way they respond to real-world challenges—they do not stop to internalize or analyze the incident [R18], an observation that seems similar to that made by Farmer (2001, p. 64) earlier. When male gamers have been griefed, it will not take long for them to form an action plan, for example a course of retaliatory response. When they have retaliated and gained satisfaction or resolved the incident in some other way, for example inaction, they are likely to put the incident behind them, and move on ([R18], [R23]).

Lastly, the sentiments felt by players when griefed are closely tied with their expectations of grief play management and the game. This is a large topic that merits its own discussion in the next chapter.

Of the four influencing factors, some are not within the game operator's sphere of control. For instance, a game operator can find it difficult to control whether male or female players buy their game. What the game operator can do, however, is to influence subscriber demography through advertising the game to attract a specific player segment. The association felt by a player towards his character is also somewhat difficult to control, as this association stems from the length of play time and personal goals for playing set by the gamer. What is within the game operator's control is the management of expectations. Also, the game operator can empower players with abilities to respond directly or retaliate against griefers, since these involve rule sets and game mechanisms governing the types of player to player interaction permissible. These will be discussed in Chapter 8.

Conclusion

This chapter has investigated how grief play can affect players, developers and operators of MMORPGs. It identified 20 possible impacts, and suggested that relationships among them can exist. The impacts themselves have ranged from ones that are beneficial—for example that griefers do stress-test the game—to harmful, for example the distrust players have of each other.

The methods employed in this study do not allow for a representation on the degrees to which grief play can affect players, game design and operators. For instance, even though annoyance has been cited as an impact of grief play, a quantitative study is necessary to ascertain the extent to which players are indeed annoyed by grief play. Still, two characteristics of grief play suggest that the play style should be constituted as 'problematic' behavior. Firstly, there are more harmful impacts than beneficial ones. Secondly, data shows that many players experience the sentiments of annoyance and distress when griefed. The game is intended to be enjoyable for players. That they instead feel the sentiments of annoyance and distress point to that grief play is a 'problem' at least for those who are affected by it.

The impacts of grief play on player sentiments also seem to be key in understanding and better managing grief play. If player sentiments can be understood and influenced to desired outcomes, the adverse consequences of grief play on player behavior, game design and operation can be better managed. The next chapter investigates the fourth research objective: what players expect from grief play management.

CHAPTER 7: PLAYER EXPECTATIONS

The last chapter argued that the impacts of grief play on player sentiments can be influenced by several factors. One is the player's ability to respond directly or retaliate against griefers. Another is the player's expectations of the game operation.

Game operators do attempt to set and maintain what they see as appropriate expectations for their game. After all, games that can properly communicate and deliver on expectations retain their subscribers. They also benefit from good publicity through word of mouth that can spread from current to potential subscribers (James et al. 2004, p. 67). However, anecdotal evidence from discussion forums and observation within game environments prior to formal data collection revealed player dissatisfaction with game operation in several MMORPGs. For example, players expressed unhappiness in public forums about how game masters had resolved a grief incident, or how the game operator had not responded towards a mechanism that had been exploited for abuse. Other players responding to these threads of discussion argued that the unhappy players complaining about the incident should have expected these acts as part of normal game play. In other cases, game masters answering a petition would advise players on how they should respond to grief play incidents. However, some players still remain dissatisfied as they expected game masters to resolve incidents in some other way. All these incidents are oriented around player expectations of the game.

The fourth objective of this research is to study player expectations on how grief play should be controlled and managed by game operators. This chapter has two operationalized objectives:

1. To investigate player expectations of grief play management.

2. To investigate the issues surrounding the setting of expectations by the game operator.

Before player expectations can be discussed, it is necessary first to put in context the recourse that players have when they are dissatisfied with the game operator. The next section looks into the boundaries of power that exist between the game operator and players.

Players and game operation

Organization-sponsored and commercial virtual communities require the operator to foster relationships between customers and employees (Porter 2004). Even then, MMORPG management does not owe players something that was not promised at the onset. For example, if players are told

157

that a particular game server will be unregulated, i.e. game masters will not be available to resolve or mediate player disputes, the game operator does not then owe its players anything in this regard. Like other types of virtual communities, ultimate power lies with the administration (Smith 1999, p. 144). In the case of an MMORPG, this would be the game operator. Producers of services do what they can to limit a consumer's chances to act against them (Denegri-Knott 2003), and these measures can come as statements of policy. The ROCs of many MMORPGs will remind players each time they log into the game that the game operator can restrict or disallow a player from accessing the service for any behavior the game operator judges as inappropriate. For example, one statement of *EverQuest 2*'s EULA[102] reads:

> We may terminate this Agreement (including your Software license and your Account) and/or suspend your Account immediately and without notice: ... (iv) upon gameplay, chat or any player activity whatsoever which we, in our sole discretion, determine is inappropriate and/or in violation of the spirit of the Game.

The statement above favors the game operator. In fact, taken prima facie, it alludes that players have, in principle, no representative rights in the game. Taylor (2002, p. 239) notes that *EverQuest*'s repeated use of the tagline "You're in our world now" to describe the sense of immersion into the game world has been perceived instead by some players as a problematic management stance. As one game developer remarked [R87], the power of the administration to run the game as they see fit is close to a fascist state, an observation that is also echoed by Smith (1999, p. 144). The relationship between game operator and players can become hostile in this fashion (Scholder & Zimmerman 2003, p. 219). According to Timothy Burke, an MMOG researcher, this antagonistic relationship is partially because players are functioning in a virtual world whose internal workings are not transparent to them[103] (Burke 2004). Both Wisebrod (1995) and Grimmelmann (2005) acknowledge that there is an imbalance of power between players and management. Some players will continue to regard as grief play any player behavior that interferes with their enjoyment of the game [R1], regardless of the game or implicit rules that may be existent in the play area. If players are still not satisfied with the service—even if they have been advised of adopting the right expectations in these game areas—their options for recourse are limited to their

---

[102] See http://eq2players.station.sony.com/en/support_article.vm?label=EQIIEULA.

[103] Burke (2004) adds that the lack of transparency is defended by game developers for various reasons, including the sensitivity of game mechanisms for business reasons and that players can misconstrue design concepts that are still hypothetical as promises of actual implementation.

leaving the game. In other words, the players can only vote with the dollars they pay in their subscription. This is regardless of whether that dissatisfaction comes from an incident of grief play that was not resolved to their expectations, or from some other reason, for example boredom of game content.

Having said this, Grimmelmann (2005) argues that players are not exactly powerless if they can leave the game. The ROCs allow game operators to alter any aspect of the game or player access to the service as they wish. However, in reality, any change of a game mechanism that proves unpopular among players may cost the game operator in subscriptions—sufficient players may just leave after all, which can hurt revenue considerably. The larger responsibility charged of the game operator is that any issue in the game operation that impacts revenue must be aggressively managed—this is both its legal and moral responsibility to stakeholders, as one developer remarked [R38]. This gives pause to the game operator from making changes that will alienate or upset the majority of its player base without putting it through careful consideration first. In the context of consumer-provider relationships that exist online, Denegri-Knott (2003) describes as paradoxical the (apparent) victimization and simultaneous empowerment of consumers.

Having said this, it is not easy for players to quit even when they are emotionally distressed, annoyed or dissatisfied with the game. The longer a player plays a game, the more accomplishments, status and equipment are accrued by the player. Game operators do not offer compensation when players quit the game. A player who wants to quit has to consider the loss of all he has attained and the investment of time to progress his character this far. It is comparatively easy for newbie players to cancel their new subscriptions if they are griefed barely minutes after character creation, since similar investments of time have not yet been made. Game operators thus strive to create conducive environments for newbies to play in and become familiar with the game [R5]. This has the effect of increasing the association felt by player to character.

It is in this framework of a power-play between players and the game operator from which player expectations towards the grief play management exist. As vociferous as players can be when they have been griefed and the game operator has not resolved the incident to their expectations, what change they can effect is limited until they actually cancel their subscription and leave the game. As one developer [R35] quipped, "...if the actions of one player causes two players to quit in disgust, it would be grief play." For game operators, grief play is of particular concern if they lose customers. So, while players can still take their grievances to public forums or complain to each other, apart from sufficient numbers of players quitting the game, the power of players to effect change can be limited.

Player expectations

Anecdotal evidence prior to the commencement of interviews revealed a range of player perceptions of the expected responsibilities of game operators insofar as grief play management is concerned. Thus, respondents were asked several questions about their expectations of the game operator. Initially the questions were general, but as data collection progressed, the questions became more specific as tentative themes surfaced.

Data revealed 9 player expectations of grief play management in all, and subsequent analysis led to the categorization of these expectations into three aspects of the game operation. They are: firstly, player expectations of game management; secondly, player expectations of game features, mechanisms, or rule sets; and thirdly, player expectations of customer service representatives and their attempts to resolve incidents of grief play. These expectations are categorized into three aspects of game operation: game management, game design, and game masters.

Table 17: Player expectations

Aspect of game operation	Expectation
1. Game management	1.1 To manage grief play 1.2 To set accurate expectations and enforce rules 1.3 To understand grief play from their point of view
2. Game design	2.1 To be empowered to respond directly against griefers 2.2 Be able to consent and un-consent to PvP 2.3 Equal access to areas 2.4 PvP encounters to be fair
3. Game masters	3.1 To properly understand the circumstances of a grief play incident 3.2 To track player behavior

A first look at this table may suggest that there is overlap among the three game aspects. Specifically, the expectations of game design and game masters could reasonably be categorized under game management. However indications from data hint that the finer categorization makes sense. For example, in some cases, players remarked that they expected the game master responding to a grief play petition to resolve the incident in a specific way. In other cases, remarks were made that game design should include specific mechanisms allowing players to better respond

160

to griefers. Lastly, remarks have been made about game operators and if they are listening to player feedback. Hence, it makes sense to differentiate between player expectations of different game operation aspects.

An explanation of each expectation follows.

Game management

1.1 To manage grief play. Even though players expect to be empowered to respond to grief play on their own, they ultimately still expect the game operator to take ownership of the 'problem' and play the lead role in its management. When players were asked whose responsibility is it ultimately to manage grief play, the following sentiment was common:

> The (MMORPG) company is I feel responsible for doing what they can to make the paying customers happy or appeased to want to continue to pay their salaries. It is not our job to play policeman in a game we pay them to play. [R65]

Other players also stated that they have a right to proper service when they encounter trouble-makers. The remark made by the above respondent [R65] that it is not the player's responsibility to regulate the play environment stands in contrast to Roberts' (1998) comment that virtual communities are self-regulating and should be able to self-police (p. 361). In PvE-centric games at least, the sentiment that the game operator should play the lead role in resolving player disputes seemed common. That the typical MMORPG is a paid subscription service was a common reason for this sentiment: as one player remarked, "I pay the money every month to play the MMORPG and if I request help because of griefing, I think I have the right to get some kind of decent service." [R20] Developers interviewed in the study agreed as much ([R2], [R35]), with one even quipping: "That is like asking, who should take ownership of the problem of muggings in a city park, the visitors, or the city?" [R2] Moreover, discounting the player expectation of the operator to provide good service, there are often many different groups of players and their diverse interests to appease in disputes [R62]. Notwithstanding difficulties of determining intention, some players believe a neutral third party is needed to mediate their disputes, as mediation by players can be vulnerable to bias [R69]. There needs to be consistency in how rules are applied in the mediation of disputes, and some players believe that staff employed by the game operator is more likely to be fairer enforcers of rules[104].

Having said this, many players note that while the game operator should ultimately take the principal responsibility of managing grief play, they do want to help and expedite that management process. For example, players can report on griefers [R23] and alert management to the use of exploits. They would also like the game operator to facilitate their assistance by providing tools to help collect or collate data on griefer activities [R75].

Lastly, while players expect game operators to address grief play, they recognize the difficulty task faced by game operators. Game masters cannot be expected to wander the game world looking for griefers [R28]. The number of griefers is small compared to the overall size of the player base in a typical MMORPG, which make them hard to spot. Since there are limited numbers of game masters, their time would be more optimally used by relying on informative player petitions that are lodged when grief play does occur, with additional descriptions on where it occurs. In this way, game masters do not have to monitor every part of the game world.

1.2 To set accurate expectations and enforce rules. Players expect the game operator to state their stance on grief play (for example in the ROC), and in particular, what is grief play, its examples, and how it will be dealt with by the game operator. One developer [R5] stressed the importance of making clear what is considered grief play in the game, stating that players should not be naturally expected to understand what acceptable or unacceptable behavior is. When game rules describing behavior and how game mechanisms should be used have been stated, players expect game operators to rigorously enforce these rules as well ([R11], [R18], [R40]).

Interestingly, not only do players want game rules on behavior to be properly stated, they also expect the game operator to define the implicit and social rules expected of the player base ([R29], [R51]). In virtual communities, there are often lists of frequently asked questions, or FAQs, compiled that explain the forum guidelines on courtesy and good behavior. One could argue that participants in virtual communities—MMORPGs included—should not need to be told to apply in the game environment common sensibilities of courtesy and fairness that exist in the real-world. However, some players believe that such statements on implicit rules are necessary because there is

---

[104] See the 'Game masters' section in this chapter.

162

a range of diverse cultures and backgrounds across users ([R67], [R74]). The variety of cultures in the melting pot of virtual communities is an observation also noted by Smith (1999, p. 145). Moreover, Suler (1997) cites "simple ignorance" as a reason for the continued existence of bad behavior in virtual communities, although data could not show for certain if players in MMORPGs grief from ignorance. Given the large numbers of players, there is just that possibility that a few players grief because they are not aware of common sensibilities and courtesy that is expected from the player base.

Given these dimensions of the player base in a typical MMORPG, it does seem reasonable that the establishment of a set of social rules and etiquette expected in the game by the game operator can only help. This is even at the risk of belaboring the point and having to state what may already be obvious to other players. Defining implicit rules could be even more important in an MMORPG when compared to non-gaming virtual communities. This is because MMORPG activities can be more intense (for example in PvP). Lee (2002) in his essay on deviant behavior in MMORPGs notes that interaction among participants occurs in real-time. The effects of an action in an MMORPG is more immediate and visible than a discussion posting, and the game premise already creates a perception that violent activity is a normal part of game play. Properly defining a culture unique to the game can avoid the instances of grief play that might arise from ignorance of implicit rules, and also remind players that notwithstanding the environment being a fantasy role-playing game, there is still a thing known as player etiquette. Defining implicit rules will however not be easy—a casual survey of discussion postings will reveal that many players do not believe that game operators are cognizant of prevailing moods or perceptions of the player base. Some games, for example *Star Wars Galaxies*, have been successful in appointing player representatives to gather feedback on class-specific mechanisms from discussion forums. Such player representation could be useful in assisting the game operator in establishing a set of implicit rules.

Having said this, any game operator statement of implicit rules by its very nature will not be binding on players. An implicit rule that demands player compliance stops becoming an implicit rule. It becomes a game rule instead and therefore is binding. Other non-formalized implicit rules are also superseded in game operator consideration of any incident purported as grief play. As it is, implicit rules may have to be presented as statements encouraging players to be sensitive to prevailing expectations of player conduct. For example, there is an implicit rule in *EverQuest* that

163

new groups entering a dungeon zone should ask for a 'camp check'. Such an implicit rule could be stated in the ROC, with players encouraged to adhere to it.

Finally, game masters can be inconsistent in how they rule on grief play incidents, as one developer remarked [R35]. The reasons for this include the difficulties of determining intention, and the subjective perceptions that will exist among the victims, perpetrators and witnesses of any grief play incident. This is not counting also the possibility of game master fatigue and issue of individual skill in resolving disputes.

One way of sidestepping these issues is to simplify the incident arbitration process. Every petition of grief play is invariably centered on the perceived permissibility of the activity imposed. So, one solution is not to subject a rule of play to human interpretation. A rule of play that is enforced in Law of code is not subject to ambiguity. Not all rules of play however can be implemented as Law of code[105]. Still, the rules of play that can be implemented as Law of code are easier to arbitrate with, since they eliminate the subjectivity of intention or other mitigating circumstances. For example, in order to stop a griefer from kill-stealing, encounters can be 'locked' to the first player who engages the mob (or vice versa—the first player that the mob engages). *EverQuest 2* is an example of a game that implements encounter rules this way. Having a clear rule that is written into code eliminates any argument. Whoever lands the first blow on the mob—as registered by game software—has the right to finish that encounter. In the eyes of the game master, there should not be any ambiguity or dispute among players on who got to the mob first. While this does not stop players from petitioning game masters regardless, that there is a rule of play stated as Law of code does make it easier for game masters to resolve disputes of this nature if they occur.

1.3 To understand grief play from their point of view. Players expect the game operator to understand grief play from their point of view. This expectation was cited many times in data: "… a game company and admins (administrators) should be constantly trying to understand what players are currently regarding as unacceptable griefing" [R49], "Griefing should be set against general player expectations of behavior in the game" [R57], and "The company needs to talk to their customers about what their customers deem grief play." [R61] In fact, given how difficult and draining is the development of an MMORPG, game developers may not have the time to play the

---

[105] See Chapter 1 – 'Rules in an MMORPG'.

game with the same intensity as more active players can muster. This can further the lack of congruity between developer and player perceptions of the same game [R81][106].

The issue of differing perceptions between players and game developers can result in emergent game play [R81]. In Lucasfilm's *Habitat*, an incident arose where one player equipped with a weapon started randomly shooting people. When participants were polled, half of them believed that murder in *Habitat* should be treated as a crime. However, the other half believed it added an element of fun to the game. Morningstar & Randall (1991) in their commentary of *Habitat* describe this lesson learnt in the game design of large multi-user virtual worlds:

> The more people we involved in something, the less in control we were. We could influence things, we could set up interesting situations, we could provide opportunities for things to happen, but we could not predict nor dictate the outcome. (p. 288)

In this case of *Habitat*, developers had not expected the consequences of a game mechanism. Emergent game play refers to such play styles that are not initially predicted or intended by the game developer. Examples of emergent game play include the different types of interaction among players that were not expected beforehand by developers. These could include the rights to a mob or camp, or player etiquette. This is not to say that game developers do not expend effort in attempting to predict how players will react to a game mechanic. However, with the very large number of players in each game, how players eventually end up behaving may not be what was originally envisioned.

Game design

2.1 To be empowered to respond directly against griefers. Many players want to respond directly against griefers, and when players are not equipped to deal with a grief play situation, they will turn to the game operator for resolution [R5]. Sentiments expressing the desire for player empowerment like "The devs (developers) should be endeavoring to incorporate self-protection solutions for players as new content is introduced" [R49] were observed in data. Prominent in the list of player-driven responses cited by players is the PvP form of response against griefers. Evidence of this player expectation can also be observed by player remarks that games without a PvP component are

---

[106] Lin & Sun (2003) offer a contrasting argument. In their study of MUDs, they note that often, MUD designers wonder about the perceptions of players, without realising that their viewpoints may already be representative of those very perceptions (p. 81). Often game designers themselves have often played other games. In this sense, they argue that the gap between designer and player perceptions may be actually less distinct than one might think.

"care-bear" games ([WoW-001d], [R68]). The remark can be derisive, with the connotation that players who play in non-PvP-centric game areas need to 'whine' and get game masters to resolve their problems.

Also, a PvP mechanism is not the only way for players to respond to griefers on their own. Many MMORPGs allow a player to add another player to his 'ignore' list. This mechanism is similar to that found in chat rooms and used by participants to exclude misbehaving persons from further communication and interaction in the chat room (Evans 2001, p. 201). Likewise, adding an MMORPG player to an ignore list squelches all further utterances from that person. Such a mechanism is effective in resolving the verbal types of grief play (for example slurs, intentional spamming, threatening), but they are not effective for many other types, for example rez killing, ninja-looting, or player blocking.

Another player-driven response is the avoidance of a griefer altogether. There are several possible game mechanisms to facilitate avoidance. Players can be empowered to eject or ban offending players from their establishments. Players expect to be able to remove players from spaces designated as private to themselves (for example player owned houses in *The Sims Online* or *Ultima Online*) if these players are detracting from their enjoyment of the game. Other players avoid griefers by interacting or playing only with people they want to [TSO-020]. Instancing also allows players some control over who they want to play with, and in so doing avoid the players they believe are potential trouble-makers.

Lastly, another form of player response that was discussed in data is a player-driven tribunal system. In this hypothetical system, griefers are brought before a group of appointed players who will judge the offence and mete out appropriate punishment. This player response was extensively remarked upon, and merits its own discussion in Chapter 8.

2.2 Be able to consent and un-consent to PvP. Central to this study is PvP, since several forms of grief play involve PvP. Players expect to consent to participate in PvP, and also be able to withdraw their consent from it ([R19], [CoH-010]). In the context of PvP-centric forms of grief play, for example newbie-killing or rez-killing, the ability to consent and un-consent to PvP can affect both game operator and player perceptions of whether grief play has taken place. Take *Ultima Online* as an example and its two aspects; Trammel (non-PvP), and Felucca (PvP). Players who play in or travel to Felucca are in essence consenting to PvP, and if they are killed there—through newbie-

166

killing or rez-killing for example—the game operator may not see it as grief play [R3]. Some players' expectations even extend beyond this: they remark that there is no such thing as 'grief play' in Felucca [UO-001]. In this sense, the game operator and some players believe those who play in Felucca consent to PvP, and since players now have the ability to both defend themselves or retaliate, they cannot claim to be griefed when viciously attacked. By game design, the converse is also true—players who stay in Trammel are signaling they do not consent to PvP.

Now, contrast this to *Ultima Online* when it was released in 1997. The game had not been divided into Trammel and Felucca aspects then. The whole game world was open-PvP, i.e. PvP that does not need to be consented to once players enter into the game[107]. As far as game operation was concerned, any person choosing to play *Ultima Online* at that time was consenting to PvP upon entering the game world, even as a new character. However, players still complain if they feel their characters have been 'violated' (Bartle 2004, p. 408). This is regardless of whether they have given consent to PvP upon entering the game world or not. Similarly, several *Ultima Online* players who were interviewed recalled how badly they reacted when they were first killed in griefing-like ways. This suggests that even though the game was open-PvP, players did not feel that their playing *Ultima Online* implied their consent to PvP [R3]—no matter what expectations the game operator had set from the beginning. Others possibly did not know what open-PvP was really like. One player [R85] when recollecting his perceptions of early *Ultima Online* remarked:

> Even if that player knew beforehand that the game was open-PvP and even if he might not have seen it as a problem, now he learned what it actually meant. And many players learned not to like this aspect of the game very much.

Clearly, game operator and player perceptions were different in the regard of consent.

The expectations that *Ultima Online* players had before can be compared to more recent PvP MMORPGs like *Shadowbane*. *Shadowbane* is open-PvP and players today play the game with the expectation that they can be viciously attacked and killed [SB-001]. The same kind of killing tactics employed in *Ultima Online* back then may not be considered grief play in *Shadowbane* today by the game operator or its players. The change of player perceptions could be in part a result of the timing in which these games were released: *Ultima Online* in 1997 and *Shadowbane* in 2003.

---

[107] While there were areas in the game world where players were reasonably protected from attack by other players, the size of these safe havens was a small fraction of the total playable area in the game.

Ultima Online was the first successful MMORPG that attracted a large number of subscribers (Bartle 2004, p. 21). The successful initial following came about in part from the game adopting an already popular setting from its single-player equivalent, *Ultima*. *Ultima Online* saw the infusion of a large number of players who while familiar with single-player computer role-playing games were less familiar with the multi-player equivalents, and thus possibly unaware of what it meant to play in an MMORPG with open-PvP [R85]. Hence, there may have been a general lack of familiarity with the kind of violent interaction permissible in such game environments. There were also few other MMORPGs that players could subscribe and play in at that point in time, and a player did not have many other MMORPGs to turn to even if he was dissatisfied with *Ultima Online*.

The situation is different now. Today, there is enough variety to satisfy the range of gamer persuasions. There are MMORPGs which are non-PvP (for example *EverQuest 2*), open-PvP (for example *Shadowbane*), or allowing PvP only if explicit consent is given (for example *Star Wars Galaxies* and *Dark Age of Camelot*). For instance, in *Star Wars Galaxies*, a player must declare his affiliation to either of the game's factions in order to engage in PvP. Such an act has to be deliberate. In *Dark Age of Camelot*, PvP is allowed only in specific parts of the game world—a player who travels to those areas is seen as consenting to PvP. The difference between consent systems present in open-PvP and explicit consent-only PvP-centric games can be small, but it influences player expectations. Players in open-PvP know that the majority of game content will be accessible only as PvP players (PvPers), while explicit consent-only PvP-centric games tend to be either still dominantly PvE, or that the perceived amount of PvE content is as large as that offered through PvP. Lastly, consent-based systems can weed out unwitting or unwilling opponents, since players must consciously opt in to take part [CoH-011]. Such differentiation may be preferable for players who regard themselves as bona fide PvPers, as they prefer to combat others who engage in the same activity willingly.

2.3 Equal access to areas. Related to the consent of PvP within an MMORPG is the access of game areas. As discussed above, some players do not consent to PvP or want to play in a PvP area. However, if they perceive that the PvP area has services, goods and activities that are not available in the non-PvP area, they may complain of unequal access of areas. Interestingly, in the eyes of the

168

game operator, they may have a valid argument [R5][108]: if players are paying similar subscription fees, it is reasonable for them to expect access to similar areas of play.

Greed play is sometimes associated with these expectations of equal access to areas. For example, a dungeon which spawns a highly contested mob will tend to be heavily camped. Occasionally in these areas, competition may be so intense that players may grief, kill-steal, or player block to monopolize the dungeon for their exclusive use. Now, if the area where this dungeon resides in allows PvP, players may challenge the incumbent groups already there by attacking them and pressing them to leave or to share the area. In some cases of area monopolization, powerful PvP player communities are able to kill all competing groups with ease, and hoard the best areas for themselves [CoH-011]. On the other hand, if players do not want to, or cannot engage in PvP because the area disallows it by Law of code, players may still demand equal access to this dungeon if they cannot get the incumbent groups to share. They will petition to game masters to force the groups already there to share the area. Alternatively, they may take their expectations to the discussion forums and demand the dungeon be instanced so that they can enjoy uninhibited and grief play-free access.

Such expectations of game areas in the context of PvP tend to happen in explicit consent-only PvP-centric games with large or dominant PvE areas. If the game is open-PvP, i.e. the majority of game content is geared towards PvPers, it is unlikely there will be many arguments that PvPers are getting privileged access compared to non-PvPers since there would be very few of the latter. Even then, there could still be players petitioning over area monopolization. While Law of code allows and implicit rules will likely expect PvP player communities to wrestle for control of the game area, expectations on such contesting for the same area are still predicated on perceptions of fairness[109].

2.4 PvP encounters to be fair. One circumstance in a PvP act that can lead players to believe they have been griefed is if the fight had been unfair[110]. A PvP rule set may not distinguish among player levels and thus allow player engagements across both ends of a prowess range. A player who

---

[108] Developer [R5] added that these areas do not have to be perfectly identical. It is adequate if they are equivalent. For example, goods for purchase in both areas are approximately of the same effect, there is game master support in both areas, and the play areas are of comparative size and complexity.

[109] See Chapter 8 – 'Player justice'.

[110] See Chapter 4 – 'Player and game operator perceptions of grief play'.

is better equipped or more advanced in character ability has the advantage over a weaker player in PvP. Even then, players still expect an even chance of countering or defending against griefers in PvP-centric encounters ([R35], [CoH-011]). Players expect PvP rules to be designed so that players cannot attack someone else of vastly inferior prowess. For example, players expect that a high-level player should not be able to attack a much lower level player, since the lower level player will not stand a fair chance of winning the encounter. Lower level players are often new subscribers, and exposing them to a harsh system where they are not accorded some protection even when they are new may simply result in their becoming distressed enough to quit. From the game operator's point of view, the expectation that newbies should be afforded some initial protection is sensible. While 'total' PvP should allow any player to kill any other player—and they do not need a reason to begin with—it is just not good business sense for new players to be victimized [R5]. Moreover, players want classes to be balanced against each other such that no one character class possesses an overwhelming advantage against others in PvP encounters. Players expect the outcome of PvP encounters to be determined by superior tactics [R85] rather than through PvPers inadvertently benefiting from poorly implemented game mechanics or character class imbalances.

Game masters

3.1 To properly understand the circumstances of a grief play incident. Players do note if game masters are empathetic when they respond to petitions for attention (James et al. 2004, p. 68). However, the dissatisfaction noted in players is still alarming. Many players reported incidents where they were dissatisfied with game master resolutions either because of the (lack of) timeliness in the response, the inconsistency of resolutions, or the perceived lack of understanding of circumstances. The timeliness of a response is dependent on many factors, including the number of petitions already lodged, game masters online at the moment, and time taken to resolve each petition. The consistency of resolutions depends on factors that include the clarity of game rules, the skill of the game master, and if the incident was properly understood. Several players related incidents where they felt game masters had failed to properly understand the circumstances of grief play incidents. Some of these incidents are as follows.

Firstly, in *Ultima Online*, one player who was harassed in his own (game) house by a griefer was told by the game master to leave his home, even though he was the owner of that very establishment [R59]. This led to the player complaining that the game master had 'standardized' messages which were used before the incident is understood. In a similar incident, a player in

EverQuest 2 was scammed off an item by another player [EQ2-022]. Despite the inclusion of a Reimbursement Policy[111] explaining how scamming should be reported, the game master responding allegedly told the player that all trades between players were final and nothing could be done by customer service. The player complained that the game master had not considered the evidence submitted as required by the Reimbursement Policy, and had only provided him with standardized responses. The guidelines to reporting scams created the expectation that there would be reimbursement upon investigation of the evidence accompanying the petition, even though the policy itself did state that all player trades are final.

Secondly, the player who turned himself invisible in the 'invis' incident to escape from a mob was deemed to have griefed when the mob attacked other nearby players. The player concluded that the game master had applied a rule that treats any player who turns himself invisible while bringing a mob to other players albeit accidentally as training, without first understanding how the accident had occurred [R63]. In another incident, a player who was walking circles around another player was threatened with banning for physical harassment by a game master. This is even though no words had exchanged between the two players, nor did the petitioning player sound out his discomfort [UO-008]. The player reporting the incident in the discussion forum expressed frustration on the inconsistency of game master resolutions. He accused game masters of responding harshly to an incident even when it was not clear if grief play had occurred. To further prove his point, he claimed that game masters did not respond when his real-life partner, also another player of the same game, was verbally harassed by others with messages of a sexual nature. Lastly, a player had a petition lodged against him by another player, who alleged he had used a non-approved third party program [R61]. He was subsequently banned from the game. The complaint in this case was the perceived absence of proof, and the readiness of the game master to take a stranger's petition without first investigating if a third party program had indeed been used.

_____

[111] The Reimbursement Policy of *EverQuest 2* (see
http://eq2players.station.sony.com/en/support_article.vm?label=EQIIReimbursementPolicy) states: "If you would like to provide evidence of a trade scam based on an agreement with another player, please use the /report command to record the appropriate text and send that text directly to the GMs."

The intention of this study is not to investigate each reported incident of grief play and determine if game masters had erred or were correct in their assessment[112]. The five cases presented above cannot be taken as representative evidence to conclude that game masters do not attempt to understand the circumstances of a reported incident. While Sage (2003, p. 93) posits that the persons who can best understand the intention behind an activity are those involved in it, this should not be taken as a lack of trying on the part of CSRs. The stories related here are also possibly biased. This only underlies the importance of the game master having access to as much information as possible when determining who said what and when in order to understand the circumstances of an incident [R88]. He can then make the best attempt to determine probable intention and circumstances behind an activity.

Moreover, the dissatisfaction with game masters may not always be the result of what players perceive as incorrect resolutions. Rather, players could be dissatisfied because they perceive an imbalance of power between customer service and themselves. Players by game design play to be heroes who are successful, powerful, and glamorous. One developer remarked that players can get disappointed not only because in a grief play incident this fantasy of being heroic has been diminished, but also because the dispute has been resolved by a game master, who as form of "deus ex machina" is more powerful than a player can hope to be [R87].

3.2 To track player behavior. Players expect game masters to be able to track players, particularly those who have a history of causing disruption. As it is, petitions are often lodged on-site immediately when an incident of grief play has occurred. Player dissatisfaction can occur if they perceive game masters have not adequately punished a player who is believed to have griefed previously. Sentiments such as "he is a known griefer but he still got off scot-free" were commonly observed both in respondent remarks and discussion forums. In one case in *EverQuest 2*, a griefer who gained the trust of his peers in a player community turned on them one day by systematically removing half of the community's members. This destroyed a substantial amount of prestige points and progress accrued by members of this community [EQ2-019]. The player even posted up pictures of his actions, and displayed no remorse. A fortnight later, the trade scam petition was lodged against this same player [EQ2-022] (see above discussion on "*3.1 To properly understand*

---

[112] In the case where there is such a study objective, the researcher would need players to identify themselves to the game operator for petitions to be retrieved, chat logs to be made available, and other players and arbitrating game masters to be interviewed to "hear the other side."

the circumstances of a grief play incident"). However, game masters did not reimburse the victim despite the existence of a prior petition complaining of this griefer's activities. Players who posted into the discussion thread remarked that this griefer already had a bad reputation prior to the trade scam, and questioned why customer service had not taken into account previous petitions in their assessment.

In essence, players do expect game masters to retrieve player histories and they become dissatisfied if they perceive this is not done. If the reported player has had petitions reporting disruption previously lodged, players expect game masters to review those prior petitions and judge the new incident of grief play in that context.

MMORPGs are usually capable of tracking the number of petitions lodged and warnings given out to individual players. Such numerical tracking of selected aspects in a user's behavior is similar to that found in an administrator-operated reputation system (Jensen et al. 2002, p. 448). Even then, game masters have limited time to resolve each petition. Game masters are already burdened with petitions from players asking for help on game mechanisms, item reimbursements, cheating and harassment (Mulligan & Patrovsky 2003, p. 241). Game masters would prefer the dispute in a grief play petition gets resolved quickly and for both parties to go on their separate ways, as one developer remarked [R88]. It is not cost effective for the game operator to have their game masters spend hours monitoring or spying on a player alleged to be a griefer, or searching through chat logs in order to find evidence to justify the punishment of just one player.

Having said this, many MMORPGs do use some form of tracking. In order for it to be effective when game masters deal with grief play, the tracking has to be comprehensive but yet capable of summarizing that information into a succinct form to expedite speedy assessments. Not only should chat logs be maintained, events between two players that range from simplistic ones—for example a player initiating an attack on another player; to more complex ones—for example a mob that is chasing a player changes his target to another player—should be maintained. Such information will help the game operator piece together evidence in order to properly evaluate complaints made against players.

Discussion

Based on data, player expectations of grief play management can be distilled into the following:

1. Players expect game rules to be made clear.

2. Players expect effective enforcement of those rules.

3. Players expect to be able to respond or retaliate against griefers.

The first two of these player expectations cited above are tightly coupled with one another. Every game has rules and there is usually some enforcement. However, if players *perceive* rules to be unclear or not enforced, even if they already are, players will be dissatisfied. However, many game operators will maintain that their rules are clear, and that there is adequate enforcement. The source for this difference in perception can be distilled to two considerations: is the game operator stating and communicating the right expectations, and are players adjusting to the expectations stated by the game operator?

Firstly, whether the expectations of both players and the game operator can be congruous is dependent on whether expectations from the game operator can be set and communicated properly. Setting expectations for an MMORPG can be difficult. Ideally, the expectations of behavior and settings for the game must be stated in clear language with no ambiguity, and at the same time take into account emergent play styles that will surface later. The expectations must be communicated in a way that will make hundreds of thousands of players across cultures cognizant of what they will be exposed to upon subscription. Moreover, MMORPGs are dynamic entities (Cornett 2004, p. 704). Game mechanisms and content do not remain static, but instead undergo continual revision from improvements made to code and inclusion of new content to attract new subscribers. The game is in a persistent state of change. With Law of code changing, game rules must change in tandem, and those changes need to be communicated to players.

Ultima Online and *EverQuest* can be contrasted to each other as an illustration of game operator attempts to set and communicate expectations. *Ultima Online* was initially sold as a game where players could choose non-combatant and peaceful professions to play. For example, players could be blacksmiths, tailors and even fishermen. However, players who bought the game quickly discovered choosing such non-combatant professions did not lead to their avoiding combat, unless they never left the safe boundaries of cities where NPC guards would protect them from player-killers. Worse still, the non-combatant classes they played were particularly vulnerable. At one juncture, limited skill point pools available to each character meant that a player who spent his skill points in tailoring would be less effective in combat. This ultimately led to players feeling that the game operator had failed to deliver on the promise of a fun non-combat experience [R35][113], even though it had been promised as such.

EverQuest on the other hand was designed primarily as a PvE MMORPG, and it was stated as such. Initially, there was also a small PvP component in the game, and players were required to explicitly give consent to engage in this limited PvP element. Hence, from the start, the game did not have to deal with PvP-centric types of grief play on a large scale. Moreover, the game operator was also more aggressive and successful in disciplining players who disrupted others' gaming experiences. Rules were more restrictive and enforcement more strict, both which influenced expectations. So, while *EverQuest*'s tagline "You're in our world now" may had been snorted at in derision by pundits, player behavior was better managed, expectations were better set and players were more aligned to what the game operator had in mind. *EverQuest* ultimately enjoyed greater commercial success than *Ultima Online* did.

As for the second question, even when expectations are correctly set by the game operator, players can continue to be dissatisfied when it comes to grief play. There can be two explanations for this:

1. Players are ignorant of the game operator's stated expectations.

2. Players are aware of the game operator's stated expectations but do not adjust to those expectations.

Player expectations of the game and its operation will evolve over time [R18]. Not only can this come about from game design changes and addition of new content in an MMORPG, it can result from increased familiarity to the game and other similar games that get released over time. As players become more experienced with MMORPGs in general, what is 'surprising' and 'unexpected' behavior to players may become commonplace, and evolve into implicit rules. In this sense, a player new to one MMORPG but has played others extensively may be unfamiliar with game rules and Law of code as of yet, but he may already possess his own expectations of what the game 'should' be like. This will be especially true if the game belongs to a similarly broad type compared with others he has played (for example if the game is PvE or PvP-centric), or if it is designed by a studio or maintained by a operator whose games he has already been exposed to.

---

[113] It is still quite possible to avoid combat. One just has to be skilled at avoiding trouble spots where griefers are known to hang out and avoid them, but this can in turn bring about expectations of equal access (see the "Game design" section in this chapter).

Notwithstanding these difficulties, how can players become more aware of the expectations set by the game operator? There are cues in MMORPGs where potential customers can both gather or infer expectations from. Players can infer expectations from the game box. Core game mechanisms, for instance if the game allows PvP, are commonly noted on the game box. Games in development are also publicized by interviews with game developers or by previews of the game in gaming magazines or web sites. Occasionally, games still in development are also released in limited fashion for the public to try out (simultaneously helping developers test game mechanisms). Moreover, some game operators make available demonstration versions of their MMORPGs for players to try over a limited period of time for free[114]. Lastly, expectations can also be gathered through game rules that may be included in accompanying documentation with the game purchase, or through the ROC that may be displayed each time a player logs in. However, not all players visit discussion forums or web sites managed by the game operator that may present game rules [R88]. Hence, players should not be expected to go to the web to look for game rules. Ideally, these rules should be accessible from within the game client at all times.

When players are aware, do they still adjust to the expectations set by the game operator? *Ultima Online* was open-PvP at the onset and the game operator at that juncture seemed to adopt a tolerant stance towards aggressive types of game play. Consider Richard Garriott's remark[115] for *Wired News* (Kim 1998) that *Ultima Online* was designed to let evil players have legitimate roles in the game world. The game world became populated with what Kim (1998) calls "evil players who talk like Snoop Doggy Dogg, dress like gangstas, and act like rampaging punks." These players played in ways that were disruptive to the rest of the player base. Even players who were conscious that the game was open-PvP complained about getting griefed, harassed and killed repeatedly. Open-PvP or not, players did not respond well. Compounding the problem was the apparently slow response to the existence of bugs, which encouraged the proliferation of third party programs[116] that exploited loopholes in code. Griefers used these programs liberally to disrupt, which further increased the disillusionment players had with the expectations set by the game operator on PvP.

---

[114] Many MMORPG titles come packaged with a 'free' month of access into the game upon initial purchase, after which players can decide whether to continue their subscription.

[115] See Chapter 1 – 'Role-playing and grief play'.

[116] One such program in *Ultima Online* was "UOExtreme". Developers at one juncture were fixing bugs in the game to stop this program from code exploitation (see http://uohoc.stratics.com/logs/1998-07-30-pub.shtml).

Apart from continuing to state and inform expectations, there seems to be little else a game operator can do for players who are aware but do not adjust their expectations accordingly to what is stated.

It is important to note again that players expect to, in some way, take matters of justice into their hands. When players feel they have been griefed, harassed, or violated in some way, a feeling of helplessness and inability to directly respond or retaliate against their griefers contributes towards their emotional distress, frustration, or dissatisfaction with the game. For many, their natural inclination is to retaliate in some way. When players can retaliate and render comeuppance to griefers, the negative sentiments felt are typically mitigated to some degree. Player-driven mechanisms of managing grief play will be discussed in the next chapter.

Finally, players today can choose from a range which MMORPGs to play. The variety of choices has also led to changes in player expectations. On the one hand, player expectations are influenced by the first MMORPGs they play in [R3]. As they become more experienced and exposed to other games, some become more tolerant of bad behavior or better able to respond. On the other hand, as more games become available, players who are unhappy in one game are less bound to remain in that game. This is notwithstanding the time investments involved in developing one's character, and the level of association to the character that grows over time. One commonly observes in discussion forums disgruntled players of an MMORPG saying they will quit as soon as what they believe is a better game gets released. The study could not say for certain if players today when griefed are more likely to stay as they are better able to handle grief play (being more experienced in MMORPGs in general) or leave because they have a choice to play other games. However, whether their final resolution is to stay and deal with it or leave, these players will still complain when they are griefed.

Conclusion

This chapter has sought to explore player expectations of grief play management, and to investigate the issues surrounding the setting of expectations by the game operator.

Ideally, if players have appropriate expectations of a game, they would be more tolerant when they are exposed to occurrences where someone plays in a way they find disruptive to their gaming experience. If players are fully aware that their setting foot into the game world meant they could be harassed, abused, or killed in exaggerated fashion, they would be less likely to view such play styles as non-normative and demanding of game operator attention.

177

As it is, data has shown that player expectations are not always congruous with expectations from the game operator that may have been presented in game advertising, publicity, or stated game rules in the ROC. There are two possible reasons for this: players are ignorant of those expectations set by the game operator, or cannot or do not adjust to them. Other factors, for example the response accorded by game masters to petitions or the ability of players to respond directly or retaliate against griefers, can also influence player expectations.

Ultimately, what seems agreeable by both players and the game operator is this: it is important for the game operator to set the correct expectations, and to properly enforce its stated game rules. Players also want to be empowered to respond to grief play on their own. These methods, alongside game operator-driven mechanisms, are discussed in the next chapter as the fifth and last research objective: to investigate grief play management.

CHAPTER 8: GRIEF PLAY MANAGEMENT

Having explored player expectations of grief play management, the discussion now moves to how grief play is actually managed—which is the fifth and final objective of this research.

To begin the discussion, it is important first to understand the necessity of managing bad behavior in these communities. One developer of MMORPGs, Damion Schubert[117], compares the importance of managing bad behavior to the Broken Windows 'theory'. This theory is cited by Wilson & Kelling (1982) in their commentary on police and neighborhood safety for *The Atlantic Monthly*. They argue that if one window in a building of the neighborhood is left broken and not repaired, it will not take long for all the remaining windows to be broken too. The theory posits that in a populated neighborhood, when incidents of vandalism and harassment are not resolved quickly, the perpetrators and other possible offenders of similar crime will be encouraged to intensify these acts. This leads to further deterioration of the neighborhood. Similarly, if bad behavior is not managed in an MMORPG, it can create impressions in the player base that such behavior is a normal and permitted aspect of the environment. *EverQuest*'s more rigorous enforcement of rules by its CSRs can be compared to the lack of similar enforcement in *Ultima Online*. Players may have perceived greater 'lawlessness' in *Ultima Online*, and emboldened to further grief as a result.

The operational definition of 'manage' used in this research is 'to exert control over'. From the onset, there are two primary stakeholders in an MMORPG that would be interested in seeing grief play managed: players whose experiences are affected by the behavior, and the game operator who can either be directly impacted (for example creation of restrictive rules), or indirectly impacted by the behavior (for example players become dissatisfied with grief play management). Published interviews in popular media with game developers of new MMORPGs frequently report on how grief play is managed in their games. The chapter on player expectations also noted that players expect to be able to respond or retaliate against griefers. Hence, there are also two broad categories of grief play management methods, and each is driven by the stakeholder interested to see grief play managed: players, and the game operator. This chapter looks at these methods, and has two operationalized objectives:

---

[117] See Damion Schubert's commentary at http://booboo.phpwebhosting.com/~ubiq/index.php?p=290 for this.

1. To investigate player and game operator-driven methods of managing grief play.

2. To investigate grief play management in relation to management approaches of virtual communities.

Five methods of managing grief play will be discussed in this chapter. Each poses different challenges. Some of the five methods have already been instituted or designed into games, while others have only seen limited implementation or have been suggested and discussed by participants of MMORPGs. Data collection was interested in exploring both player and developer perceptions of the usefulness of each method. In most cases, respondents were asked to comment on a method. In a few cases, a method was suggested by a respondent—these will be noted as such in the course of discussion.

The five methods are:

Table 18: Managing grief play

Driver	Method
Player-driven	Player justice
	Player volunteers
	Social networks - Reputation - Player interdependency
	Player judiciary
Game operator-driven	Punitive systems - Out-of-game punishment - In-game punishment

Lastly, the 'driven' descriptor in each method refers to the amount of control exerted by the stakeholder. Most of the five methods to be discussed here still operate within the confines of the game environment. Hence, while a method may be 'player-driven', it does not mean that the game operator has no involvement in it. Some player-driven methods—for example player justice, player judiciary and player volunteers—make use of rule sets, game mechanisms, constructs, or instituted procedures in the game. In this sense, even if the method is marked as player-driven, the game operator can still be an influencing factor by expediting its use—for example providing a

180

mechanism that lets players act on griefers—or inhibiting its use—for example making it impossible for a player to act on a griefer. The exception is social networks, which can make use of any communication media, for example privately run discussion forums. Hence, social networks in some forms may not be within the sphere of influence of the game operator.

Player justice

Whether incidents of grief play are well responded to by game masters or not, players expect to be empowered with mechanisms in-game to deal with grief play on their own. In fact, some developers remark that player-driven methods of response are the best ways to manage grief play [R5], an observation not dissimilar to that made by Phillips (1996, p. 59) in that Usenet members preferred peer rather than administrator-driven approaches to managing problematic behavior. MacKinnon (1997, p. 208) in the context of virtual environments describes a process called "just adjudication", which emphasizes the importance of "local context" when assessing punishment for the virtual offender. Such local context will involve persons of the community persecuting the offender (p. 209).

In the context of MMORPGs, many games allow 'player justice' methods, or allowing players to seek immediate satisfaction against each other when grievances occur among them. In one sense, a player justice system is comparable to that of a 'frontier' town where the law does not reach. Inhabitants of such a town would be expected to resolve on their own any matter of dispute. If an inhabitant perceives he has been slighted or offended, he will employ 'just cause', and inflict punishment on the person who has offended him. The following figure illustrates a possible reaction from a player when he has been griefed, and the interplay among the impacts on player sentiments, player expectations, and player justice.

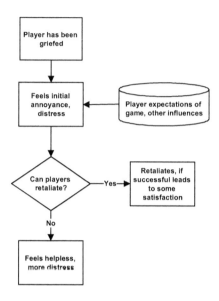

Figure 5: Impacts, player expectations, and player justice interrelated

In MMORPGs, player justice methods are implemented as "retribution systems", as one developer called it [R5]. These systems keep track of what it considers 'hostile' acts inflicted on a player, and 'punishment' opportunities which become available as a method of response. A simplistic mechanism could be as follows: the game keeps track of actions that player A inflicts against player B. When the actions of player A against player B meet a predefined condition, the game allows player B to employ a set of retaliatory actions against player A in 'retribution'. An example of such a predefined condition and its accompanying retaliatory action could be:

Game code does not permit player A to attack player B in the city, and vice versa.

However, if player A steals from player B in the city, player B gains the ability to attack player A.

Typically, such systems would include other considerations as well. For example, player A may have the element of surprise and hence advantage. Hence, in order to even the odds, the system could allow players in nearby proximity to also attack player A for a limited period of time.

Having said this, the retaliatory actions available to the victim need not be violent. Hypothetically, non-violent retaliatory actions could include character penalties instituted on player A. For

182

example, player A could be inflicted with a slower movement rate (how fast he can traverse through the game world), or decreased character prowess. Having said this, when players were interviewed and queried on their perceptions of player justice, many were inclined to think of violent methods of retaliation and particularly through PvP. Given this notion, the chapter will focus on PvP as the 'main' mechanism to render player justice. Player justice is in fact most commonly associated with PvP. Such rule sets do not normally consider the presence of intention in an aggressive act nor do they distinguish whether an attack is the outcome of a player wanting justice. Rather, players can undertake violent action against any other without particular regard to reason, just so long as conditions have been met—for example all parties have agreed to PvP under the consent system used or criteria has been met in a retribution system—and the area of play allows PvP under Law of code.

PvP mechanisms of allowing players to seek satisfaction and claim justice when griefed have also been the subject of debate in discussion forums. One commonly cited argument is that PvP deters grief play since a player who can retaliate aggressively or defend himself is a less attractive target than one who cannot. Some griefers take pause if they know they can be killed in return by their intended victims either immediately or later once the victims have recovered. In this sense, grief play is at least managed on the individual level without further involvement from the game operator. Some developers, for example *Ultima Online* designer Raph Koster (Koster n.d.), have also remarked that PvP will actually deter if not prevent grief play as it will give players the tools they need to self-police. Kim (1998) at *Wired News* likens these methods of retaliation to "vigilante justice", since players are not relying on the game administration to resolve matters of dispute, but instead take them into their own hands.

Having said this, there are some considerations in any implementation of PvP methods of response that limit its effect, or even potentially increase rather than decrease the level of griefing. The next section looks at three of these.

Might is right

Firstly, these methods of response place the ability to render justice squarely on the PvP skill of players. The gap between skills can widen across the player range, and correspondingly the ability to administer justice stretches across both ends of the range. The system would work very well if PvPers on the highest end of the ability scale behave. However, there is no guarantee they will. At the player level, individual PvP skill can become the only way of countering griefers. In one case in

Meridian 59, two skilled PvPers took over a section of the game world called "The Main Gate to Tos[118]", and killed at least dozens and perhaps even hundreds of players over several hours, as one player related [R68]. Players attempting to fight back were unsuccessful. The two PvPers only stopped when game masters intervened, summoning a difficult mob to fight against the two.

The unequal ability in PvP can be the result of differing player dispositions. Some players do not enjoy PvP, nor do they play a highly advanced character equipped to retaliate against a griefer. Some players play non-combative professions, and are helpless in combat [R59]. One could argue that these players can join player communities for self-defense and protection, or avoid PvP game areas. However, some players prefer not to be affiliated to any player community[119] [EQ2-023]. MMORPGs are designed to let players play in styles they want (excepting grief play). Players may believe that the game operator is setting requisites to access game content if they are forced to join player communities just to play non-combatant roles or in PvP areas.

The same power disparity can exist at the player community level as well. If the strongest community comprising the highest level players possessing the most powerful equipment griefs one of the weakest communities, there is little the latter can do in response. In one case in *EverQuest*, one guild had the majority of high-level players on the PvP server. This guild controlled access to the preferred game area (a dungeon) for players to game in [R43]. The guild did whatever they wanted to other players, for example training mobs on members of other guilds. Many players wanted to 'police' this guild, but no guild had the equivalent power to do so. Eventually, the next two powerful guilds on the server banded together in an attempt to drive out this powerful guild and free up access to the dungeon for all players. They succeeded, only to result in one of the two guilds breaking their mutual agreement to share. They instead took over access of the dungeon themselves, and monopolized its access for their own members. This is even though they had originally agreed to stop the earlier guild from doing just that.

Sometimes, the strongest PvP communities intent on griefing do not even need to monopolize area access. With their might, they can threaten weaker communities to get their way. One player [R43] posed one scenario where the leader of a powerful community says to the leader of a lesser

---

[118] Tos is a city in the game that many players visit.

[119] Anecdotal data revealed that many players of MMORPGs prefer not to be affiliated in player communities, but instead play alone or with just a friend or two.

community that a player in their ranks has trained (griefed) them, and must be removed immediately. If not, they must be prepared to be singled out for repeated attack until this player is removed from their community. The weaker community cannot issue the same kind of demand if a member of the stronger community griefs them, because their threat will hold no sting. These scenarios do sound like blackmail. But outside a possible game rule where players should 'play nice', no other game rules have been broken.

In summary, one problem of self-policing through PvP is that there is no way to police the strongest. Coupled with the potential for power to corrupt, player communities with the most power and skill can become the ones which need the most policing, and simultaneously are also the most difficult to police.

Policing or banditry

Jensen et al.'s (2002, p. 447) observe that policing systems in online spaces are reactive by nature. The reactive nature of policing systems is an inhibitor for players in PvP-centric games to play police. The second consideration in the use of PvP was demonstrated in pre-aspect *Ultima Online*: that it was a lot more fun playing a bandit who griefs than a security guard who polices. *Ultima Online* allowed the establishment of player cities, which comprised players banding together and building in-game homes in proximity for social purposes. These player cities became the targets of organized griefer attacks, and the players in these cities found it difficult to mount an effective policing force to protect themselves.

While open-PvP allows players to protect their player cities through the creation of militia or policing forces, it is more fun to disrupt than to stand around like a security guard waiting for something to happen, which is less fun, as one developer remarked [R35]. As Rogers (2003, p. 465) remarks, one problem with combating player-killers is the lack of incentive for those that attempt to control them. Griefers can log on, attack other players in the often unguarded city, create mischief, and log off before a substantial group of player-'police' can organize themselves to counter them. Hence, it is not surprising that some players feel that their limited game time is better used griefing. As it is in MMORPGs, there is more incentive to be an entity that acts rather than an entity that responds to that act.

Game operator perceptions in PvP

The third consideration is this: the game operator may be less willing to view an incident as grief play if a PvP response is available. Some developers believe there is more grief play in a PvP-centric game like *Shadowbane* than in non-PvP-centric games like *EverQuest* [R34]. Game masters may be less alert and responsive if the game environment is permissive. For some, an action is only grief play if players cannot defend themselves or retaliate against the griefer ([R23], [R78], [R86]). Put in the converse, there is a perception that grief play does not exist in PvP-centric games, since aggressive methods of recourse are available to the player. For example, in the Kazzak encounter of *World of Warcraft*, players complained about the suicidal tactic[120] employed. The tactic was observed by some players to be a clear demonstration of grief play. There was no reason for a low-level character to be there apart from a desire to disrupt the event, even if for role-playing reasons. The game operator recognized this tactic as a legitimate play style since a PvP response was available[121]. Such a stance was announced to players in April 2005:

> When a group of players has engaged Lord Kazzak, any players of the opposing faction interfering in the encounter are free to do so as a PvP resolution is available to the victims.[122]

However, a PvP response was impotent in this case, because a low-level character of opposing alignment who rushed in will be killed immediately by Kazzak himself. This rendered difficult any kind of PvP response on the part of those disrupted, since the suicidal player was killed too quickly for them to react. In this case, while PvP was available for players to resolve acts of grief play on their own, there were mitigating circumstances that rendered the use of such PvP responses ineffectual.

Summarizing player justice

From the discussion of the three considerations above, there seems to be four criteria for PvP to be an effective way of managing grief play.

---

[120] See Chapter 4 – 'Harassment' and Chapter 5 – 'Player influenced'.

[121] The terms of use in *World of Warcraft* do state that such tactics are legitimate: "Blizzard Entertainment considers all valid play styles in *World of Warcraft* to be part of the game, and not harassment, so player-killing the enemies of your race and/or alliance, including gravestone and/or corpse camping, is considered a part of the game." (Blizzard Entertainment Inc. 2005)

[122] See http://forums.worldofwarcraft.com/thread.aspx?fn=blizzard-archive&t=27&tmp=1#post27, although this policy has since changed.

Firstly, PvP encounters should be fair. This requires meticulous balancing of player classes so that one class does not possess game unbalancing advantages over the others. It may also require the creation of rules that disallow considerably more powerful players from attacking weaker or vulnerable players. For example, it has been suggested that players who have just been killed and are in a weakened state should not be exposed to further attack (and possible death) again for a limited period of time. Alternatively, players can be allowed to attack any other. But if they are more powerful, they will not be able to derive any benefit from killing those who are much less so.

Secondly, players should have equal access to the administration of justice without forcing them to dramatically change their play styles. For instance, some players prefer to play non-combatant classes. It does not seem fair to force them to engage in PvP in order to (reasonably) access game areas. The concept of a bounty hunter in a city-state can address this, and is discussed in a later section.

Thirdly, PvP encounters among players should eliminate as much as possible the possibility of accompanying abuse. PvP should be impersonal, and be centered on factional or group-wise types of conflict as opposed to individual PvP encounters.

Fourthly, PvP should still be supported by vigilant game mastering.

The fourth criteria requires further elaboration. The Kazzak encounter of *World of Warcraft* showed that the game operator may regard certain tactics to be legitimate play activities when a PvP response is available. However, the discussion there revealed that there may be mitigating circumstances. There needs to be an avenue for third party arbitration even in a system where members are expected to resolve disputes among themselves. The importance of human arbitration to determine if an act is grief play has been explained in Chapter 4, and some element of this need remains in player justice systems. Player justice systems that use software tracking to determine whether an action belonging to a defined set of actions is undertaken eliminates human consideration of intent in that action. In principle, the intention to disrupt or merely engage in play allowed by game rules can be inferred by sophisticated tracking mechanisms. For example, the tracking mechanism could check if a high-level player—player A—has been attacking a low-level player—player B—repeatedly. When this happens, it may treat player A as a person who is potentially griefing, and thus award player B with a larger array of retaliatory actions beyond those offered under normal PvP. However, such inference from tracking mechanisms would still not be foolproof. Hypothetically speaking, what if player B has been verbally tormenting player A with abuse, which resulted in A initiating an attack on B, and continuing to do so relentlessly? The tracking system may not have considered information on such surrounding circumstances, only that player A has attacked B from a considerably advantaged position.

Bartle's (2004, p. 409) remarks that the degree of PvP allowed can be dependent on tolerance for its abuse and the level of support customer service staff can handle hint that PvP should not mean an abdication of responsibilities on the part of game operators in resolving player disputes. It is difficult to create game code that can accurately determine intent and circumstances in an action. Assuming that the presence of intent to disrupt is still key in the determination of whether an act is grief play or not, the best way then to determine intent and context is through human judgment. In this sense, each petition still needs to be resolved, and it may not be sensible to simply abandon players to manage among themselves solely through the use of force.

Player volunteers

The discussion in Chapter 7 noted that customer service can be expensive to run. One method that can help alleviate the work load faced by game masters is to find players who can discharge selected roles of game masters. Many games have programs that allow players to volunteer their time to help game masters resolve petitions, organize in-game events (Mulligan & Patrovsky 2003, p. 256), or provide counseling and assistance for players. These player volunteers are known by different names depending on the MMORPG. For example, they are known as guides in *EverQuest*, as counselors in *Ultima Online*, and the program itself as Interstellar Services Department in *EVE Online*. Game operators can delegate specific types of petitions to player volunteers. Some of these can be petitions asking for clarification or knowledge of an in-game mechanism that often come from new players. They can also handle implicit grief play (for example area monopolization) by counseling players. The game masters will still handle petitions of more severe nature: for example explicit grief play or other disruptive incidents involving large numbers of players.

Insofar as grief play management is concerned, there are indirect and direct benefits of engaging player volunteers. One indirect benefit is that by passing less critical petitions to player volunteers, player volunteers can at least lighten the petition load faced by game masters. This in turn gives game masters more time to handle the other petitions, and possibly increase the quality of their responses. A direct benefit is that properly chosen and trained player volunteers can help manage

188

grief play by having them inculcate among new players the social context of the game and expectations of behavior. This can possibly reduce or at least delay the potential for some players to grief. While this may not prevent players with extensive experience in other MMORPGs and who already exhibit their own distinct play styles from griefing, it may still help reduce the propensity of other players to grief out of opportunity.

Player volunteer programs are however not without controversy or issues to counter. In 2000, several player volunteers in *Ultima Online* sued the game creator, Origin Systems, Inc. (OSI), and game operator, Electronic Arts, for the exploitation of volunteers in the customer service program (Mulligan & Patrovsky 2003, p. 249; reported also in the *GameSpy.com* magazine by Haumersen 2000)[123]. Moreover, like player judiciaries (see below), there is the potential abuse of power since there are players with special privileges and powers that the rest of the population do not have [R5]. It is important that players are screened when they apply to become player volunteers. Mulligan & Patrovsky (2003, pp. 252-255) propose a set of suggestions to consider in the screening of volunteers. Among other guidelines, they encourage game operators not to select players who demonstrate the most vociferousness in their desire to become player volunteers. They argue that these players are likely to abuse their powers. Also, player volunteers should not be utilized without having a paid employee overseeing their participation and ensuring that volunteer privileges and powers are used responsibly (James et al. 2004, p. 74). The need to supervise player volunteers negates in some part the benefits of such a mechanism, which is to free-up customer service.

Player volunteers are an interesting hybrid between player-driven and game operator-driven methods of managing grief. Notwithstanding fears of volunteers abusing their powers or threatening legal action against game operators for labor exploitation, the use of players as volunteers bears considerable potential.

Social networks

Environments which do not reward participants with social capital for good behavior may not see them behaving well. Similarly, environments where there is little social cost in behaving badly can see increased occurrences of participants behaving badly. Jakobsson & Taylor's (2003) study of

---

[123] This lawsuit rippled through the MMORPG industry, and many developers interviewed in the first year of data collection declined to comment on player volunteer programs. In April 2004, one web site (see http://www.gamerifts.com/news/archives/arc4-2004.shtml) suggested that the lawsuit was finally settled out-of-court.

social networks in *EverQuest* note that social capital is important for high-level players to progress towards more advanced areas of the game. In particular, individual players can "do good deeds in the name of their guild as a way of boosting its reputation." (Jakobsson & Taylor 2003, p. 86)

In the context of grief play management, one player-driven method that can manage grief play is social networks. There are social networks present in all MMORPGs. The growth of these networks is often encouraged by the game operator. For example, the game operator-managed discussion forums are popular sites for players on the same server to interact outside the game. There are also smaller social networks within player communities themselves. For example, many player communities have their own private discussion forums. If social networks can be used to emphasize the importance of maintaining good reputation with other players and also player interdependency, it can help manage grief play.

There are two uses of social networks described here: as reputation networks, and as a means of increasing player interdependency.

Reputation

A reputation system can be informal in the form of player feedback that exists on social networks, or formal if they are built into the game as a game mechanism.

With regards to informal reputation systems, it is advantageous for a player to maintain a good reputation among other players. The presence of feedback creates an expectation of that person's disposition (Pizer 2003, p. 434; Resnick et al. 2000, p. 46). It can influence whether others will interact with the person or not (Jensen et al. 2002, p. 447). Trust is a key component for developing social capital, and is built among participants having favorable interactions with each other (Preece 2004, p. 38). Informal reputation systems can provide incentives for good behavior. For example, a player who is placed in high regard by his peers can receive personal invitations into play sessions. They can also provide disincentives for bad behavior. A player who is widely known to grief may not be invited to join small groups in a play session, or into player communities. However, the efficacy of informal reputation systems as a deterrent for grief play can be influenced by two things: the size of the social network, and also if players themselves make good use of information on the network.

190

Firstly, the player base for an MMORPG is large enough for a griefer to disappear into the crowd[124]. This in effect makes it harder for players to pay attention to or watch out for a specific player who griefs. The size of the player base also allows a range of player dispositions. The worse offenders may be shunned by some players, but they are likely to find others of their ilk to play with and thus not feel the sting of isolationism. Moreover, keeping in mind that the large player base of an MMORPG is distributed among servers, a griefer who is inflicted with poor feedback for his actions may be unknown on a different server of the same game. Feedback itself on a participant's reputation is not portable across online environments either, as Resnick et al. (2000, p. 48) notes. Even if a griefer becomes widely known for bad behavior on his server, he can leave the game, adopt a different character name in another game, and effectively erase his past (Friedman & Resnick 2001). In this sense, reputation as used to manage bad behavior may work better in smaller online role-playing games like *A Tale in the Desert*.

Secondly, not every player avails himself of information channels—for example the discussion forums maintained by the game operator [R88]—to keep himself informed of griefers, or to understand expectations of player etiquette for that matter and recognize that a behavior he has witnessed is non-normative.

The two problems of informal reputation system in other words are visibility and also access to information. Formal reputation systems that are built into the game can to some degree address both problems. For example, a griefer may be tagged with an irremovable descriptor in-game that warns other players about him. Such a tag could be put onto the player if he has received past a certain number of game master warnings for bad behavior, or it can associate a general play style to the player by utilizing numerical tracking for his in-game activities, for example number of players he has killed. With reputation tags, players do not need to use information channels outside the game environment to check a player out, since the reputation label is already there in-game. The problem of anonymity among players is somewhat addressed as well since the tags are visible, although the effect is still diluted in a large player base.

---

[124] A player (or player community) of bad repute does not necessarily need to face ostracism. He can, occasionally, move to another server in the same game and leave his bad reputation behind. There is discussion on this at Terra Nova where a game master was alleged to have expedited the movement of a poorly behaving guild to another server: http://terranova.blogs.com/terra_nova/2005/05/reputation_capi.html.

Having said this, game-instituted and formal reputation systems have their own challenges. For one, they may embolden players to grief. This is possible if the griefer is motivated by the desire to gain attention, or if the reputation system awards a notorious player with 'cool'-sounding titles even if they are intended to warn players instead. This is not to say that an informal reputation system (on the social network) in comparison is not vulnerable to players who desire notoriety. Rather, a formal reputation system can actually *provide* incentive for players to behave badly. One example of this is the reputation system used in *Ultima Online*. At one juncture, the system tagged players with titles, for example "Dread Lord". These titles were awarded based on numerical tracking of play events. While it gave some players a hint of the titled player's disposition, some players with the title griefed to associate action to a very 'evil' sounding title. Gaining the title itself also became the incentive for others then to engage in mass player-killing, particularly newbies since they were easy to defeat [R63]. Another issue was that these tags could be misleading. A player with the title "Glorious Lord" in *Ultima Online* was not necessarily a well-behaving player.

One way of improving a formalized reputation system could be to do away altogether with numerical systems that monitor the frequency of play events, since they can very well end up providing incentives for specific in-game actions that are commonly associated with grief play. Formalized reputation systems could be based only on the number of game master warnings received for bad behavior. While some griefers may end up griefing even more to compete among themselves on who gets the most warnings, there is at least a larger deterrent effect if they cross the limit of warnings, since the punishment turns to account banning or suspension. Formalized reputation systems can also be improved by using written feedback rather than numerical tracking that awards players with labels. One game developer [R87] suggested a reputation system that lets players write snippets of personal feedback of other players, and for these snippets to be privately displayed whenever they encounter these players. This idea could be extended by having these snippets sent to and collated by game servers. Such feedback can then be retrieved from within the game client by any player. Such written feedback systems make sense, and similar models have been implemented to good effect in other virtual communities. For example, eBay allows buyers to post feedback of the persons they buy items from (Preece 2004, p. 60). A further refinement could be for players to be able to view feedback on the persons writing these snippets themselves, so that they can judge for themselves whether the feedback seems genuine, or it is an attempt to smear their reputation. In essence, this creates a network of feedback snippets that players can make use of. Written feedback systems have one other advantage: they have the potential to become a carrot rather than stick type of reward system in managing behavior. A player who receives glowing praise from his peers would be better recognized, and possessing a good reputation could very well be an incentive for others to also behave well.

Player interdependency

Social networks can also be emphasized through increasing player interdependency. Newbies are often targeted by griefers because they are weaker in character prowess, less familiar with in-game mechanisms, and have few friends. They are less able to resist griefer attacks, and are easy targets for them to bully. As it is, though some players as good Samaritans still help newbies, there is typically no incentive to help. There is little social capital to gain in-game for helping others (although the written feedback based reputation system above could address this). If the presence and retention of newbies could be made more important to player communities, there would be a more robust response from others to their being griefed. One way of doing this is to make newbies important to experienced players. Koivisto (2003) cites a mechanism in *A Tale in the Desert* where one goal for players to attain is to be a mentor to newbies. This idea can be taken even further. Game mechanisms that automatically invite all newbies into existing player communities [R87] or social communities out-of-game could be implemented. Incentives could also be created in-game for player communities to welcome newbies. For instance, the presence of newer players opens up game content or player community-oriented events that are not available to player communities without newbies.

Player judiciary

The last player-driven method of managing grief play is through a player run judiciary body. The ability for players to make and enforce laws has been suggested in discussion postings by players, and a player judiciary is one such form of player-driven governance. There has been limited implementation of player governance in older MUDs like *LambdaMOO* and recent small-sized games like *A Tale in the Desert*. In *LambdaMOO*, players could initiate petitions for change, and upon gathering sufficient support send it to administrators for consideration (Mnookin 1996). In *A Tale in the Desert*, players are allowed to propose their own laws[125]. If these laws gain enough support among their peers, the law can be implemented into the game by developers if it is

---

[125] See http://www.atitd.com/man-lawmaking.html.

technically possible to do so (Burke 2004). Beyond this, player judiciary systems have not seen widespread implementation in MMORPGs. Hence, the discussion here is hypothetical. However, its premise as a way of empowering players to manage grief play was interesting enough to warrant investigation in interviews.

A player judiciary arbitrates player to player disputes, including incidents where a player griefs another player. It is empowered by game design to mete out limited forms of punishment to offending players. Player judiciaries can be contrasted to player justice. While both methods are responsive, player justice is retaliatory whereas a player judiciary is not. Another key difference is possible player participation in the formation of policies. In the context of virtual communities, Andrews (2004, p. 67) refers to member participation in the development of policies and practices as volunteerism with incentives, and that it can encourage greater online interaction.

A possible model involves firstly setting up a body of rules governing behavior. Existing game rules can be used as a base, with the most commonly accepted implicit rules formalized and added on top of it. This in essence creates a 'governance'. In principle, while the game operator could establish governance without player participation, this will not be ideal if the intention is to get player buy-in. Next, players are selected, and solicited by the game operator to setup a tribunal. Tribunal players can then be trained in their roles by the game operator. When sufficient complaints are lodged against a player, for example for griefing in relation to the rules established in the governance, the tribunal can require the player to appear for trial. Evidence is heard, and the player is required to account for his actions. If the player is found 'guilty' of bad behavior, punishment can be meted out. These punishments are meted out with the intention of providing disincentives for other players to engage in similar behavior. However, player judiciaries are not intended to replace game master arbitration in game rule-breaking. They are best utilized as an avenue for players who are disputing over implicit rules or milder forms of grief play to take their grievances to, and seek resolution or redress.

For a player judiciary to be effective, it requires empowerment by game design to mete out punishment [R2]. Game systems would also be needed to pass along evidence required by the tribunal to judge fairly. Such information would include chat logs, event listings that track a player's actions, and even a player's past history to see if the 'accused' is a repeat offender. Assuming that verdicts can be reached timely, examples of punishment that could be meted out by the tribunal include:

1. Removal of privileges: for example the player is squelched and can no longer chat with others in game.

2. Limitation of character prowess: for example the player's combative abilities are reduced for a limited period of time. Alternatively, the player is required to pay an in-game fine.

3. Jail time: for example, the character is required to spend a period of time locked up in an in-game cell.

On the punishment of 'jail time', an incarcerated player may attempt to undermine the effect of the punishment by logging on and leaving his character unattended on the computer. For example, he could leave his character logged on overnight. He then waits for the jail term to expire at little play time cost to himself. Jail time types of punishment can be refined by instituting checks to make sure that the player has not left his jailed character unattended. For example, a game master can check in on the jailed character periodically. Alternatively, an automated mechanism that sends messages to the jailed character and expects specific responses within a defined time frame can ascertain if players are properly serving the terms of their sentence. A system that generates random characters on-screen and requires the jailed character to type these characters as a response can also work.

These punishments are necessarily mild, given that the rules broken are likely implicit than game. These punishments are also similar to game operator-driven in-game punishments described later in this chapter. Unlike out-of-game punishment like account banning, the punishment meted out in player judiciaries is less severe. Still, any kind of system that allows a player to mete out character specific types of punishment would require 'buy in' on the game operator's part that it is necessary and appropriate.

In addition, there would have to be player participation in the selection of the tribunal if players are to recognize their representatives. The initial pool of candidates could be selected through player voting, and the game operator further chooses the final player representatives through consideration of its own criteria. The tribunal players would need to continually maintain an acceptable level of respect with the player body through their keeping high standards of social behavior. A homage type of system may need to be built alongside the tribunal, and used by tribunal players to gain ground support from players. There would also need to be some way for the game operator to periodically 'judge the judge'. This is to ensure that the tribunal does not abuse its given powers. The inclusion of implicit rules in the governance on what is acceptable player etiquette and behavior takes on heightened importance, since the tribunal can enact upon its statutes. Given how

195

player expectations can change as the game progresses from birth to maturity, such governance would necessarily be continually evolving.

Time would also be needed for a tribunal to prepare itself. Given the nature of such an event, all participating players have to be present for the hearing at the stipulated time. One can envision a scenario where the accused refuses to appear, but this problem could be solved by either game mechanism and established process. For instance, having been already informed of the time and venue of the event, game design could allow the tribunal to forcibly teleport the accused to the trial if he tried to stay away. If the accused player is not logged on in the game altogether, the established process could allow the tribunal to mete out punishment to the accused *in absentia*.

There are advantages to a player judiciary system. Firstly, players have the expectation that game masters understand grief play from their point of view. It makes sense then if players are allowed to have greater input in determining whether an incident qualifies as grief play or not. The judgment of intention and context is passed to players in a player judiciary system. A group of tribunal players can collectively possess wide enough insight and awareness on the perceptions regarding player etiquettes and both game and implicit rules to render fair judgment. If player perceptions of grief play are oriented around implicit rules, it makes sense to allow players to seek peer-mediated arbitration based on implicit rules. Secondly, a player judiciary can provide a basis for players to create their own narratives and story telling. It invites greater participation among players to partake in community activities, and potentially build up a greater sense of ownership of the game world. This can in turn restrain some of the more opportunistic players from engaging in grief play. Thirdly, allowing players input into the governance of their virtual world would influence the player perceptions of empowerment to effect change, and possibly alleviate some of the hostility that stems from the perceived imbalance of power between players and game operators.

Having said this, developers cited three challenges that would be present in any implementation of a player judiciary system, with players echoing similar concerns.

Firstly, the anonymity accorded to players in an MMORPG can hurt the system. For example, it would be difficult to be absolutely certain if the players on the tribunal possess the dispositions or personalities to render fair and objective judgment. In the real-world, professional qualifications can be ascertained. Without infringing on player privacy considerations, how can qualifications be ascertained in an MMORPG? The selection of potential candidates into the nominee pool may well turn into a popularity contest if voting is used, a danger Smith (1999, p. 140) also cites in the election of MUD user representatives to a citizen's council. The 'hardcore' and visible players may get selected [R18], and their selection may not be representative of their ability to be objective in listening to evidence and passing judgment. Some players revealed fears that a sufficiently large body of players sympathetic or loyal to a player who has the disposition to grief may result in the nomination of that player into the tribunal. Moreover, it would be difficult to detect activities outside the game that can possibly circumvent the judiciary process. For example, players in the tribunal may be bribed by the accused *outside* the game to pass favorable judgment [R25]. One could argue that these difficulties are also experienced in the real-world, but that these activities are online will at least add another layer of complexity. The crux of the debate seems to be that the system is open to abuse ([R18], [R35]). This emphasizes the importance of vigilance by the game operator if any such system is implemented. There would need to be rigorous and regular checks instituted in the selection of the tribunal and that these players continue to uphold high standards of social behavior.

Secondly, there is also the risk of tribunals arriving at judgments that are not agreeable with the game operator. The potential for this happening is increased if the judgment hurts subscription revenue. The aggrieved victim could cancel his subscription if he feels the tribunal has not adequately punished the griefer. Alternatively, the accused may feel he has not had a fair hearing, and likewise leave the game. If sufficient players quit the game because of judgments rendered, it could jeopardize the support the tribunal needs from the game operator. To be fair, both of these circumstances are similar to disgruntled players, whether griefer or victim, who are dissatisfied with game master resolutions. The risk of players becoming unhappy could be somewhat reduced by the kind of punishment that is meted out by the tribunal. These punishments are limited. Tribunals cannot suspend or ban player accounts, because it is unlikely any game operator would be willing to turn over issues of revenue generation to players [R3]. Finally, there is no guarantee that the game operator is obliged to follow through whatever rules or judgments decided upon by a tribunal. Virtual worlds are not usually democratic (Grimmelmann 2004, p. 176). Game operators can hold elections or voting for players to offer their input on one matter or another. But unless the game operator and players have agreed to a binding contract demanding compliance to decisions as in the case of a player judiciary, the game operators are not bound to abide by any promises made to support the decisions reached by the tribunal.

197

Thirdly, there is also a potential problem on the lag time between the grief incident taking place and the carrying out of punishment decided upon. Players are already remarking that game masters take too long to respond to a grief play incident. A process where players need to be summoned, evidence to be collected, the accused to be heard, and with decisions finally reached could take so long it just cannot keep up with the scale of grief play. There is argument on this basis that swift punishment for griefers works better—it allows players to mete out immediate justice on their own, i.e. through PvP.

There are also other considerations. Some MMORPGs allow players to create more than one character on the same server. If one character is punished through a time limited sentence, the player can let this character sit out the punishment and play another character. This problem is similar to that of the virtual jail. In one sense, short of player account banning or suspension, the punishment that is meted out punishes the character but not necessarily the player. The alternative is to replicate punishment on every character owned by that player, but other persons who may be playing different characters on that account will be punished alongside the guilty.

There is also the issue of mindsets. Some players remarked that they do not want players making or enforcing policies that affect their game play. One griefer [R12] remarked that since players are paying common subscription fees, some believe that "you (other players) have no right to tell me what I can or cannot do in the game." Some players are more receptive to punishment decided upon and administered by the game operator, but are hostile to any system that allows the same punishment to be decided and inflicted by fellow players. This is possibly because their ability to defend themselves in a tribunal hearing is based on their arguments, and these arguments are exposed to the subjective perception on the part of their peers. Some players prefer to resolve their differences using PvP (player justice). This is because the outcome of a PvP resolution would be one based entirely on their skill in it, which they are probably confident of. These players would rather not trust a system which depends on perceptions of other players—something they have less control over. However, such sentiments seem to be centered on unfamiliarity with untried processes, and such resistance may be countered by gradual changes in player culture that will result if player judiciaries are implemented.

Ultimately, the main challenges in player judiciary systems are in the selection of appropriate players to assess their peers, the ability of players to arrive at fair assessment and the full support any such tribunal will require of the game operator. If these three challenges can be dealt with, there is promise in this system.

Having presented current and possible player-driven methods of managing grief play, the discussion now moves to game operator-driven methods.

Punitive systems

Game operators institute punitive systems to manage grief play. These are administratively-driven mechanisms (Bruckman et al. 1994, p. 183), and are disincentive types of systems which can curtail grief play when coupled with rule enforcement. There are two types of punishment: out-of-game, and in-game[126]. Both out-of-game and in-game punishments are also preventive[127] since there is a deterrent effect—it discourages other players from griefing. Punishment typically follows after a badly behaving player has received game master warnings. Instrumental also to punitive systems is the use of chat logs and other tracking mechanisms when game operators investigate incidents of bad behavior. Evidence is important: when players are caught for bad behavior, they may protest and claim innocence. Occasionally, the punished player gains popular support among players that can in turn lead to a public outcry. When this happens, the game operator may need to produce recorded evidence to explain why the player was punished [R88].

Out-of-game punishment

Out-of-game-punishments have been implemented in the management of many games. These punishments include player account banning and suspension. Player account banning and suspension are differentiated by the length of the punishment: banning is 'final' and permanent, while suspension is temporary. Final systems of punishment are not unique to MMORPGs. Bungle's misbehavior in "*A Rape in Cyberspace*" (Dibbell 1993) resulted in the erasure of that person's character. Such removal of participants is regarded as the most extreme form of

---

[126] In the context of *LambdaMOO*, MacKinnon (1997, p. 231) proposes a hierarchy of culturally relevant punishments that make for an interesting comparison here. For example, "deprivation of existence" in his hierarchy is similar to account banning, "deprivation of participation" to account suspension and the virtual jail, "deprivation of status" to public 'shaming' displays and reduction of movement rate, and "deprivation of property" to in-game fines.

[127] Suler (1997) argues that strategies for managing online bad behavior can be preventive in that they stop the act from occurring, or remedial in that they attempt to correct the problem after the act has occurred. However, administrative punishments in MMORPGs are not corrective. In fact, they are not intended to rectify the effects caused by grief play to begin with. Rather, they are intended as preventive mechanisms to stop a player from griefing again, and to deter others as well.

punishment (Mnookin 1996). Suspensions on the other hand are always temporary—players just cannot access their characters for a limited period of time.

When players are banned or suspended, characters that belong to that account are no longer accessible. Both punishments are preventive since they stop a player from further griefing, and permanently in the case of account banning. Having said this, while banning will close the player's account, the player can still create a new account by purchasing another copy of the game and starting over. Creating a new account, however, results in monetary costs and character loss incurred, and thus can still deter a player from griefing.

The suspension or banning of accounts can also occur for actions in-game other than grief play. These include actions that are disallowed by game rules: for example, the use of third party programs, the exploitation of a weakly implemented game mechanism, or eBaying.

The suspension and banning of player accounts can be effective in the management of grief play. If there is a real chance of a player getting caught and summarily punished for behavior explicitly disallowed by game rules, the behavior gets reduced, as several developers remarked ([R1], [R3], [R38]). There is no punishment currently more severe than that involving account access. Since the number of persistent griefers is small (Pizer 2003, p. 431), player account banning does not create its maximum effect through the elimination of these players. There are a larger number of potential or opportunistic griefers who may or may not grief depending on their perceptions of the game environment's permissiveness, which are in turn influenced by the rules governing behavior and their enforcement. Catching and banning persistent griefers can of course eliminate the hardcore griefers, but the larger effect of such punishment is in its effect on the potential and opportunistic griefers.

The effect on potential and opportunistic griefers, however, introduces the issue of whether punishment should be publicized or not. There is disagreement among respondents if public announcements of out-of-game punishment should be made. One perception is that the effect attainable through suspension or banning depends on the presence of publicity of the event. Some developers remarked that when the player community socializes and knows that players have been punished for specific behaviors disallowed in the game with attendant explanations on why it was necessary, there is an immediate and significant reduction in that behavior ([R1], [R3]). If punishment is publicized, it alters other players' perceptions of the permissiveness of the game environment against grief play. This in turn can discourage players from potential griefing. Moreover, stealthily or quietly suspending or banning players can create other difficulties. For example, the punished players can go outside the game and publicize the event on their own [R2], explaining their side of the story first. Frequently, they will do so in a manner that is biased to their advantage. If players are punished for various infractions with no attendant publicity associated with the event each time, they can claim that they had quit the game.

Two cases illustrate the risk of not publicizing punishment. The first case was cited by a game developer [R3] regarding a game that did not have a policy of providing details on why an account had been banned. When one player admitted he had been banned for one type of bad behavior, there was protest from the other players why this one person had been singled out when no one else had "ever been banned", untrue as it was. The game operator changed their policy of player banning to one of full disclosure, announcing who had been banned, and why they had been banned. In the second case, disciplinary action was taken against a player community that was caught exploiting a bug in order to defeat a game encounter in *EverQuest* [R88]. 28 members of the community were suspended or banned. The game operator did not comment on the disciplinary action after it was taken. Members of the community posted their side of the story in several popular discussion forums, which led to an uproar among the player base. Eventually, Sony Online Entertainment had to post portions of the chat logs involving members of the guild to prove that these members were consciously aware that they were engaging in game exploitation. In essence, if punishment is not announced, players may perceive inaction on the part of the game operator against rule breakers. The rule breakers themselves may also put their spin on the incident. Furthermore, if explanative reasons are not provided, players may speculate.

Having said this, there are also arguments *against* publicizing out-of-game punishment. The most persistent griefers may actually thrive on the publicity of getting punished by the game operator. Getting caught and banned is a "badge of honor" for some griefers. These players undertake the worst kind of actions possible in-game with preparation that they would be banned when caught. When the punishment is announced, they will ride on that publicity [R34]; after all, attention is a motivation of some griefers. If the objective is to get the griefer to leave the game as quietly and harmlessly as possible, it seems logical to be covert when punishment is meted out [R87].

Furthermore, there are also concerns of player sensitivities when the circumstances of the punishment are made public. For example, the victims who have been griefed may not want others to know for fear of repercussions or ostracism. Information divulged on the account holder of the banned player, for example account names, may also be considered private to him [R5]. Moreover, there are concerns that full disclosure on why punishment was meted out may result in consequences that go beyond what banning is intended to achieve. *Lineage* has a large proportion of its several million subscriber base playing in South Korea. In one case, it was reported in *TIME* magazine that some players playing *Lineage* at a Seoul Internet café got upset over the actions of another player in-game. They identified the player and sought revenge through real-life violence (Levander 2001)[128]. It is hard to imagine that game operators would want to be in any way responsible for or even implicated in such incidents if players could somehow be identified through publicizing the punishment.

Ultimately, the issue lies in the amount of accompanying detail in any announcement, and I argue that it is better to announce with some details rather than not announce at all. The announcement of punishment does not require full disclosure of details associated with that account or the incident. Moreover, the benefits of gaining player confidence that rule breakers will be dealt with outweigh the risks that a small group of persistent griefers are further motivated by attention-seeking. It seems sensible for the game operator to at least announce when punishment has been meted out and the number of players punished, with succinct explanations on the infringements and the type of punishment meted out. As a rule, personally identifiable information just should not be included in any such announcement.

Finally, whether punishment is publicized or not, game operators are mindful that a heavy-handed approach to player banning can result in adverse effects. For example, if players are banned for the smallest infractions, players may take their unhappiness to the discussion forums and insist they were punished "for no reason". Such unhappiness can stem from the belief that player banning should be reserved for the worst kinds of bad behavior. For example, a player who sexually harasses may deserve a banning. But banning a player who uses an exploit that is already widespread or a player who is not "playing nice" could result in bad publicity [R34]. In the former,

---

[128] Lee (2002) has another explanation for such acts of violence. In his essay on deviant behavior in MMORPGs, he notes that every player in the game perceives himself to be on equal footing. There is some logic to this, since all characters do start off equally in an MMORPG, although depending on their play styles and time invested into play, the pace of character development differs thereafter. Still, when their characters are harmed or offended, players are emboldened and believe they should not have been treated like this. He posits that they turn to violent behavior offline against their offenders as a result.

there may be perceptions that specific players have been singled out, and that the game operator should expend their time to make game code more robust instead. In the case of the latter, the player could have been merely having "a bad day". If this player is also well liked by the community, this will result in the player base losing sympathy or respect for the game operator even if the intent is to run a clean game. It is thus sensible to issue warnings or implement suspensions for the minor infractions, with banning reserved only for the more severe infractions or when persistent rule breaking is involved.

In-game punishment

In-game punishment inhibits or disables a griefer's ability to act without disallowing access into the game itself. In order to discuss in-game punishment, one needs to understand how grief play subtypes are facilitated through game mechanisms. Grief play is mainly facilitated through three forms of communication or action in a game:

Table 19: Expediting grief play

Communication or action	Grief play subtype
Action imposed on a game construct (mob, mechanism):	2.1 Use of loopholes 2.4 Training 4.1 Ninja-looting 4.2 Kill-stealing 4.3 Area monopolizing 4.4 Item farming
Action imposed on a player	1.3 Spatial intrusion 1.4 Event disruption 1.5 Stalking 1.6 Eavesdropping 2.2 Rez-killing 2.3 Newbie-killing 2.5 Player blocking 3.1 Trade scamming
Verbal communication	1.1 Slurs 1.2 Intentional spamming 1.7 Threatening 3.2 Promise breaking 3.3 Identity deception

The subtypes of grief play expedited by verbal communication are not difficult to curtail. Many games allow a player to add a griefer to an ignore list, and in so doing further utterances or notification of events from that griefer will not be seen or heard by the player. While this does not help a player from getting griefed for the first time by someone he has not already been alerted to, it can help for repeated behavior. Still, even though players can ignore utterances from others, customer service has noted that many players continue to complain about verbal harassment [R88]. Apparently, the presence of mechanisms that allow players to manage some subtypes of grief play does not mean players will use them.

The subtypes of grief play expedited through actions imposed on a player or game construct are harder to curtail. This is because these subtypes involve the employment of game mechanisms that are technically allowed by Law of code, but in ways that are not intended by game design. They become only disallowed by game rules when they surface as emergent game play[129]. Davis' (2005) definition of grief play is pertinent here again: he remarks that grief play is an act which is technically legal under Law of code. In these cases, one option is to change code to render impossible a grief play subtype. The other option is to manage this behavior through in-game punishment. Some examples of in-game punishments that can be employed to deal with griefers include:

1. Squelching the griefer's public chat channels.

2. Disallowing name changes.

3. Disabling the griefer's ability to act on the abused game construct (for example player trading).

4. Disabling the griefer's access to the game area.

5. Turning the griefer invisible to players so that no one can see or hear him.

As illustrations, the following tables list each of these in-game punishment examples and how it can affect the griefer's ability to act. Each table relates the punishment to the grief play subtype. A punishment that will disable the grief play subtype is denoted by "D". A punishment that will inhibit the subtype is denoted by "I". Explanatory notes are enumerated, and explained after the tables.

---

[129] The continual improvement of code to make a game construct less exploitable does help, but it does not have the deterrent effect of the punitive systems discussed here.

Table 20: Actions imposed on a game construct

Action imposed on a game construct	Use of loopholes	Training	Ninja-looting	Kill-stealing	Area monopolizing	Item farming
1. Squelching the griefer's public chat channels.						
2. Disallowing name changes.						
3. Disabling the griefer's ability to act on the abused game construct.			D (1)	I		
4. Disabling the griefer's access to the game area. (2)	I	I	I	I	I	I
5. Turning the griefer invisible to players.			I (3)			

Table 21: Actions imposed on a player

Actions imposed on a player	Spatial intrusion	Event disruption	Stalking	Eaves-dropping	Rez-killing	Newbie-killing	Player blocking	Trade scamming
1. Squelching the griefer's public chat channels.	I	I						D
2. Disallowing name changes. (4)		I						I
3. Disabling the griefer's ability to act on the abused game construct.					D (5)	D (5)		
4. Disabling the griefer's access to the game area. (2)	I	I	I	I	I	I	I	I
5. Turning the griefer invisible to players.	I	I	I				I	D

Table 22: Verbal communication

Verbal communication	Slurs	Intentional spamming	Threatening	Promise breaking	Identity deception
1. Squelching the griefer's public chat channels.	D	D	D	D	D
2. Disallowing name changes. (4)				I	I
3. Disabling the griefer's ability to act on the abused game construct. (6)	D	D	D	D	D
4. Disabling the griefer's access to the game area. (2)	I	I	I	I	I
5. Turning the griefer invisible to players.	D	D	D	D	D

Explanatory notes follow:

(1) The griefer can lose the ability to loot mob corpses. This makes it impossible to ninja-loot. This may also remove the incentive for a griefer to kill-steal, but not make it impossible to.

(2) Disallowing the griefer's access to the game area will make impossible his ability to grief in that specific area, although the griefer may still act in other game areas.

(3) Since the griefer cannot be seen or heard, it will be difficult for him to join groups. If game mechanics allow only grouped players to loot corpses of defeated mobs, it can also stop ninja-looting altogether.

(4) A griefer may become notorious through his actions. If his reputation for bad behavior is publicized, coupled with the inability to change his name, his ability to cause some subtypes of grief play is inhibited.

(5) The griefer can lose the ability to initiate an attack on another player.

(6) The griefer can lose the ability to chat and emote.

Based on the three tables above, two more observations on in-game punishment and its relation to grief play subtypes can be made. Firstly, the use of loopholes should be dealt with by account suspension or banning. These actions are always disallowed by game operator, regardless if they are used to expedite grief play. Secondly, disabling the griefer's access to the game area—for example a starter city where new players tend to gather—will make impossible for the griefer to act in that game area. This is similar to the suspension of a player account, although implemented in a more limited fashion. It cannot stop a griefer from going elsewhere to act, although further areas can still be made inaccessible to the griefer.

Apart from the five examples of in-game punishments listed above, other punishments can also be used. Firstly, punishments can diminish the griefer's resources. For example, a griefer can be put into a virtual jail (which costs game time), or be forced to pay a fine (which costs game money). Neither punishment can stop a griefer from acting, but there is still a deterrent effect. Secondly, punishments that diminish the griefer's prowess can also be used. For example, a griefer can have his movement rate slowed, or suffer a reduction in character abilities similar to character 'debt' imposed upon death in games like *EverQuest 2*. These punishments are preventive. For instance, having a griefer's movement rate slowed can reduce his ability to train mobs on other players since it will mean his certain death if he tried. Also, reducing a griefer's character abilities will impact his ability to kill-steal and to engage in PvP types of grief play (for example newbie-killing and rez-killing). These punishments can also be worked into the game narrative. For instance, messages that inform the griefer that "you have been disfavored by the Gods" can appear when the griefer uses one of his diminished abilities.

Compared to out-of-game punishment, an observation of current popular MMORPGs reveals that in-game punishment is not as often employed as a method for managing griefers. There are several reasons for this. Firstly, punishing offenders in-game can draw immediate attention from surrounding players to that offender's behavior. In-game punishment in this sense may be an incentive for griefers who enjoy the attention of getting ostracized or punished in-game where a lot of other players can see them [R88]. Moreover, public shaming targets the character, but given anonymity, it does not necessarily punish the player behind that character to equal effect. If the player does not feel a strong association to his character, the player may not feel punished at all, a sentiment that Williams (2000, p. 101) observes when commenting on the effect of ostracism in MUDs. The second reason could be expediency on the part of the game operator. It can be administratively easier to suspend or ban player accounts than have to choose from an array of in-game punishments based on the grief play subtype committed. Thirdly, in-game punishment requires game master monitoring to ensure that the player does not further grief while serving his sentence. Out-of-game punishment does not require such monitoring. Lastly, in-game punishment is surgical: it may stop a player from griefing in one way but not others. Suspending or banning a player account stops a player from griefing in any way possible.

Other considerations

In the course of the investigation of game operator-driven punitive systems, two further considerations surfaced.

The first consideration is the efficacy of player account banning. As noted earlier, a player who has been punished for bad behavior at worst will suffer the punishment on the account he is playing for that game. A player who gets banned can erase his past by buying another copy of the game and creating a new account to play on. This can happen if the account is closed and the characters associated with it deleted, but the payment detail used for account subscription, for example the credit card number, is left unattended to. If his payment detail has been marked, he can always use another payment detail to start the new account. In the worst case, he can start over in another game—game operators do not share account or person details of badly behaving players. In this sense, expulsion of a griefer from one game in this sense can be ineffectual (Grimmelmann 2004, p.

169) since the griefer can roam free elsewhere. If there is some way where badly behaving players caught and banned could be publicized across games, the effect of player account banning to manage grief play would be more effective.

Simultaneously marking the payment detail alongside the banning of the account can also pose other issues. If two players are paying for both accounts using the same credit card detail (for example they are partners in the real-world), the banning of one player will result in the other player unable to access his own account. Either way, for persistent griefers who are not discouraged by the costs involved in starting over when caught repeatedly, there has been discussion on MUD-Dev on how these griefers can still be identified so that they are not allowed to create new accounts[130] altogether.

A second consideration comes from a discussion point in interview data. The discussion concerned the extent to which game operators can implement punitive systems where their subscribers have to accept real-world consequences for their in-game actions. Mnookin (1996) in the context of *LambdaMOO* argues that participants of the environment should be able to invoke real-world legal systems if actions in the online space damage the person and not merely the persona. In a sense, there is already a very limited invocation of real-world systems in MMORPGs. Specifically, players can be disciplined by out-of-game punishment, i.e. they lose access to the service, for bad behavior. These are, however, currently limited to suspension and banning of player accounts. Interestingly, there have already been some instances of players *arrested* in the real-world for online behavior in games, but these seem to take place when real-world laws are also violated. In one case, BBC News reported of a player who used bots to steal items in *Lineage 2*. He was subsequently arrested by police[131]. The initial report itself did not reveal for certain if the player had been arrested because he was using bots or for stealing. A later discussion at Terra Nova[132] suggested that the player had gained unauthorized access into a game server, and that this was the premise for the arrest. It is interesting to ponder if players can one day be arrested for their in-game activities, for example scamming, as it will surely change the propensity of participants to behave

---

[130] Some of the discussed mechanisms involve the blocking of Internet Protocol addresses, and verification of identities for alternative payment schemes for subscription in the event that credit card numbers have been blacklisted. This study does not intend to present a detailed discussion of these mechanisms, beyond noting that there are difficulties in comprehensively stopping griefers from returning to the game by purchasing new game accounts.

[131] See http://news.bbc.co.uk/1/hi/technology/4165880.stm.

[132] See http://terranova.blogs.com/terra_nova/2005/08/online_muggings.html.

badly in virtual settings. As it is right now though, game operators seem reluctant to get involved with law enforcement agencies to prosecute behavior that occurs in a 'game' environment. It is also hard to imagine that players will be comfortable in the knowledge that they could be arrested for grief play.

One possible real-world punishment that is wholly in the control of the game operator would be monetary fines for bad behavior. Hypothetically, these would not even need to be called fines. They could be called 'additional fees' charged to a griefer's subscription bill, and to be paid in view of the additional customer service support required to resolve the petitions lodged from complaints of grief play. However, respondents were not in favor of imposing monetary fines when the question was posed. One concern cited by developers is the potential fallout in public relations. One developer remarked that there is already a perception among players that game operators are "rolling in money" making these games [R88]. The public relations fallout from game masters inconsistent in rule enforcement (remarked earlier on by another developer [R35]) can be exacerbated when real-world monies are involved. Another developer [R3] suggested a different concern: imposing monetary fines may not deter but instead provide incentive for players to grief. Some potential griefers are already deterred by social types of punishments, for example shame or ostracism, or administrative punishment like account banning and suspension. Monetary fines may be less costly to the offender than these other types of punishment. To date, no MMORPG has instituted a system where players pay real-world monetary fines.

In any case, any argument for the institution of real-world punishments beyond account access for in-game activities would have to be reserved for grievous types of bad behavior. These would include the most explicit subtypes of grief play, for example racial or sexual harassment and scamming, and non-griefing but bad behavior that is strictly disallowed by game rules, for example account or server hacking. Instituting real-world punishment seems less reasonable for the subtypes of grief play that see argument over whether the concerned activities are legitimate play styles or not. Examples of these include rez-killing, newbie-killing, area monopolization and training.

Other methods

Having discussed player-driven and game operator-driven methods, this section looks at two other grief play management methods that can be designed into the game. The two methods here are preventive methods that address a key factor in grief play: the anonymity of players in the game.

209

Characters per server

Some MMORPGs allow players to create more than one character on the same server, a design feature that many players enjoy. Multiple persons—for example a pair of players who are partners in real-life—can play on the same server. Each will own their distinctive characters, but pool and share their resources when need be. It also allows individual players to try out multiple classes without having to change servers to start anew, since this would be time consuming as new characters start off with very little resources.

Players of MMORPGs with large subscriber bases already enjoy a layer of anonymity. Allowing more than one character per server in turn allows players to maintain unique personalities for each character played without other players ever realizing that the same person is playing those characters. This is advantageous to griefers, as it allows them to harass with an additional layer of anonymity. Throwaway characters created specifically to grief can be created at little cost to the griefer. This practice of griefers owning multiple characters to fall back on was an observation made by several player respondents. However, when griefers are banned or suspended, the additional anonymity becomes moot since the griefer will not have access to any character on that account.

One way of allowing players to legitimately enjoy the advantages of having multiple characters on the same server, but not let it become an expedient for griefers at the same time, is to create mechanisms where a player cannot act badly on one character and not feel its effects on his other characters. Two mechanisms that were suggested are as follow.

1. Using 'family' names. Here, all characters created on an account are required to use the same last name. A player who griefs will be known to others by his last name. His bad reputation will persist through his other characters even if he deletes the character he used to grief.

2. Using 'shared karma'. Here, all characters on the account will suffer the same in-game punishment meted out. For instance, access to a game area is disabled for all the characters on the account. However, this can incur the same problems of shared accounts cited in the discussion for out-of-game punishment.

The intention in both mechanisms is similar, although they go about implementing it differently. The use of family names as a persistent identifier for each player no matter what character names are used can limit the degree of anonymity enjoyed by griefers. A player who owns high-level characters may be reluctant to grief using newly created throw-away characters since there is now association between the two. In comparison, the use of shared karma is a harsher deterrent. Not only can surrounding players learn which characters are owned by a griefer if they pay close attention to who is being punished—which in turn enhances the effect of any social network mechanism to manage griefing—the punishment also affects all characters owned by that griefer.

In-game news bulletins

While discussion forums maintained by the game operator do inform players of game-centric matters, including occasional announcements of punishment that has been meted out to griefers, not every player frequents discussion forums [R88]. Another method is, simply, to improve awareness of grief play incidents in the game. In-game news bulletins [R38] that are viewable whenever a player logs into the game can inform players on new grief play subtypes. It can also warn players of notorious griefers that may have been recently disciplined so that players become aware.

Discussion

Even with the grief play management methods that are in use now and taking into account the merits of those that have been discussed hypothetically, it seems that no MMORPG will be able to fully eradicate grief play. The games where grief play cannot possibly exist in any circumstance would be single-player. As long as the environment allows players to interact with one another under a layer of anonymity and where some level of competition and aggression is part of the game, grief play can exist, and possibly even thrive depending on the permissibility of the environment. All game operators can do is to provide ways where grief play can be controlled and its effects limited.

With this in mind, there are two aspects of such grief play management:

- Managing player expectations.
- Managing grief play behavior itself.

Player expectations have been elaborated upon in Chapter 7, but a summary is appropriate here. Player expectations on grief play management can influence or mitigate the effects of grief play. Players in particular expect the game operator to set expectations and better manage grief play through enforcement of rules, be cognizant of their viewpoints of grief play, and empower them to respond in direct fashion against griefers. While game operators do imply or make explicit what they intend their game to be like, their expectations are not always congruous with that of players. One example of this is the permissibility of a PvP game environment. In these games, the game operator may expect players to resolve incidents of grief play, or any dispute among themselves for that matter, on their own. However, players continue to feel that the game operator needs to step in. Sometimes, the mechanisms that allow players to seek recourse on their own are not equally accessible to all players. The lack of congruity may be because stated expectations from the game operator have not been communicated effectively and hence players are ignorant, or players are aware but do not adjust to those expectations. The latter can be particularly true if the player has had exposure to other MMORPGs which he believes are of similar premise.

When players are dissatisfied with the game or the operator, their options to seek change are in reality also limited. Many games include terms of use that are favorable to the game operator and not the player. Game operators are not obligated under their terms of use to change the game in order to comply with player expectations of the service. Hence, until sufficient dissatisfied players quit the game—which turns the issue into one of revenue from subscriptions—it is not easy for players to effect change in a game, no matter what their expectations of the game are.

As for the management of bad behavior, if we view MMORPGS as organization-sponsored and commercial virtual communities (Porter 2004), it could be useful to investigate managerial approaches in virtual environments in order to see if comparisons can be drawn. However, it is important to keep in mind that there are dimensions in MMORPGs that set it slightly apart from other types of virtual communities, for example that of a discussion forum. The dimensions are the context of a multi-player role-playing game, the rules of conduct that govern what is permissible, and that an MMORPG is typically commercialized.

Firstly, the context of many MMORPGs almost demands that players expect some degree of violence as they play against each other, and competitive play as they jostle for the same content. There is a sufficiently high degree of interactivity among players that it is impossible for players to avoid imposing on one another. That the game is "role"-playing creates perceptions that some of these impositions are even expected. The range of permissible activities and hence ways for participants to impose on each other in a discussion forum community would be limited in comparison.

Secondly, like other virtual communities, there are rules governing play activities in an MMORPG. There are both specific game rules disallowing particular activities, and there are general game rules disallowing certain conduct. However, given the large range of activities and the permutations of activities possible, as described earlier, it is difficult to assess if an incident is normative game play unless the circumstances surrounding the activity is also understood. In other words, while rules can still be enforced, in all but the most straight forward incidents of grief play (for example sexually oriented harassment), players are likely to contend with the game operator's assessment or resolution of the incident. In comparison, bad behavior in other online environments like flaming or hacking do not normally need to take into account similar considerations of whether the act is normative, or there was 'just cause' in the act. Many flaming acts take place in the public forum for all to see, and inflammatory postings remain visible until they are removed. Participants in the discussion forum have access to the same evidence. They can recreate the act by reading the posts involved in a flaming incident, and make their assessments based on similar information. In comparison, an act of grief play is witnessed only by players in the vicinity, after which its recounting to others can be subjected to the vagaries of individual remembrance and personal bias. While game tracking does record every event, activity and utterance made by a player, the game master arbitrating the incident does not normally have the time to use such information to recreate the act in order to fully understand circumstances and make assessments to see if rules were broken. Moreover, such tracking information is not typically available to players as well. This means players who comment or debate on the incident can never be absolutely certain what really happened unless they fully saw it for themselves.

Thirdly, most public virtual communities are not commercialized entities. This does not stop its members from having expectations of service standards, but that the service is free means they may have a lesser basis to insist on good service when they do not get it. In comparison, MMORPGs are typically commercialized services, and this creates in players the expectation that game operators are obligated to provide good service. It is a truism to say that every player will have their unique, and probably selfish, perceptions of acceptable service standards. One could argue that game operators have better access to information on whether game mechanisms work[133]. For example,

---

[133] Timothy Burke (2004) in his essay on developer sovereignty in MMOGs provides an interesting counterpoint to this. He argues that such quantitative mechanisms of measuring player activity are "crude", and the result of poor communication between developers and players.

server-side data pertaining to the percentage of players belonging to a character class defeating players of another class is more useful than subjective discussion postings from players complaining of how 'weak' their class is compared to someone who has just crushed them in a PvP encounter. In this sense, the game operator is in a better position to judge the health of game content and its mechanisms. However, such reasoning can be lost for unhappy players when they perceive an encounter as unfair. And unlike non-commercial virtual communities, player perceptions that they are paying monies for the game will intensify the vehemence of their complaints.

Keeping in mind these differences, what can we learn from the management of bad behavior in online environments? Smith (1999, p. 147), Bruckman et al. (1994) and Preece (2004) all note that there are social and technical approaches to management of online environments. With reference to online bad behavior, Bruckman et al. (1994) ask whether bad behavior is a social problem and if it is, whether technologically-based approaches are really effective in managing it. Technological approaches refer to mechanisms built into the environment. These would include user account suspension and banning, and adding selected users to an ignore list. Social approaches include feedback from other users or the administrator as a means of managing badly behaving users. Bruckman et al. (1994, p. 184) argue that community-based methods are useful in preventing and managing social problems, and claim a psychoanalytic approach has been more successful for them in dealing with problem users of virtual communities. A select group of users that maintains high standards of social behavior can be formed, and becomes the deciding authority in the arbitration of minor cases of bad behavior. User involvement in community management is also echoed by other authors, including Ostrom (1990) and Werry (1999). Recognizing that there is a high degree of member-generated content and interaction in commercialized online communities, Werry posits that an "organic management" style can be used by the operator. Such a style would include "'planting' conversations and provocative ideas, and allowing a high degree of self organization." Ostrom argues also that the most successful communities are those where participants are allowed to modify rules governing behavior and also monitor participant compliance to those rules.

With reference to Bruckman et al.'s (1994) question on whether bad behavior is a social problem, grief play could indeed be more a social than technological problem. There are several reasons. Firstly, many of the factors that lead to grief play—for example attention seeking and the spite of other players—are social in nature. Secondly, its impact on players—for example annoyance,

214

emotional distress, and isolationism—are personal responses, and these impacts influence the way players react to others in the community. Thirdly, any sort of game mechanism that allows players to communicate, interact, or act with or on each other can be subject to abuse by griefers. Fourthly, the arbitration of player disputes on grief play is by game masters, and subject to the vagaries of participant perception and what they tell them, and individual skill and knowledge of rules on the part of the game master. These skills and knowledge in turn impact their ability to discern between fiction and fact and render fair judgment. All these support the proposal that grief play is mostly social in nature, even if its management can still include both social and technological approaches.

According to Bruckman et al. (1994, p. 183), approaches to managing deviant behavior lie along two axes: each approach is decentralized or centralized, and technological or social. Bruckman et al.'s model will be used for the purpose of comparing the methods of managing grief play presented earlier. The following graph adopts their diagrammatic comparison, and shows how each of the five methods of managing grief play described in this chapter are differentiated along both axes. CSR responses have also been added to the graph for further comparison, even though it is not a grief play management method per se.

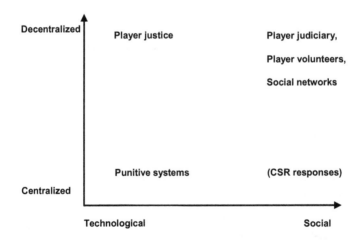

Figure 6: Decentralized/centralized vs. technological/social approaches

Centralized systems: Centralized and technological approaches are administrative—i.e. game operator-driven—and built into the game for use. For instance, the forcible squelching of a griefer's utterances or the suspension of a player account is game operator-driven and expedited by game technology. Other technological approaches include the continual refinements to game code to make them more resilient to the use of third party programs or game exploits to expedite grief play. On the other hand, CSR responses to a griefer who has had complaints lodged against him can be social in nature. CSRs may provide feedback to the griefer on how his behavior has affected others, and warnings can be issued.

Decentralized systems: Player justice methods are not very social in nature—they make use of activity mechanisms built into the game (technological), and are player-driven (decentralized). Some players do prefer to respond to griefers through PvP. Not only is there satisfaction to gain by retaliation, the PvP form of player justice can be a deterrent to potential griefers. Grimmelmann (2004, p. 168) notes that this situation is paradoxical: since the "unpleasant and wrongful" acts are deterred through PvP activities that can be equally unpleasant and probably violent. Data has supported this observation: some acts of grief play are motivated by revenge from having been attacked, and grief can snowball when a victim responds in a violent fashion after having been griefed. Two other player-driven methods—player volunteers and social networks—are social and decentralized approaches, as they employ a high degree of user involvement (decentralized), and apply pressure on griefers to behave in a manner that is acceptable to others (social). A player judiciary system is decentralized in its involvement of users, but is more social than technologically-driven. While the punishment decided and meted out by the player tribunal can be technological in nature, the process of arriving at that punishment is undertaken by players and exposed to subjective perception and individual skill.

There is also a social similarity among all decentralized approaches. Player judiciaries, social networks and player volunteers when delegated counseling responsibilities are really community-centric responses to grief play. There is even a small social element to player justice. Player justice makes use of game mechanisms as a means for recourse. However, consider if the targeted player belongs to a powerful player community. A griefer may hesitate if he knows his victim is affiliated to a powerful association of players committed to help and defend each other against grief play. This could be social pressure at work.

The city-state government

The concept of such mutual protection in player communities described in the last section can be extended in the context of self-organization (Werry 1999). Consider a player-driven online government in the management of griefers by the player community at large. Rogers (2003) proposes a democratic city-state form of government participated in by players, and argues that there could be advantages to gain by its formation. Newbies could gain citizenship in the city-state government upon joining the game, and this would help nurture a sense of belonging and community from the onset. Not only would this make newbies less vulnerable targets for griefers, it could inculcate in the new players the game's social context and implicit rules. This could potentially reduce a player's tendency to grief out of ignorance of implicit rules and player etiquette. Another advantage comes through the creation and empowerment of a bounty hunter class[134] of players to control player-killers (Rogers 2003, p. 470). A bounty hunter is a player who is appointed to and sanctioned by the city-state government to hunt and kill player-killers. Incentives (for example in-game rewards) could be provided for hunting bounties. The profession would remain under strict control of the appointed city mayor through game supported mechanisms (for example bounty hunter tracking to monitor their movements and activity levels) to ensure the system does not get abused. A problem with self-policing described earlier on is the lack of incentive—it is more fun to grief than police. A bounty hunter system could provide that incentive for players to meet the challenge of policing. In one sense, such a city-state is similar to a player judiciary. They both involve the nomination of player representatives to positions of responsibility, and subsequent empowerment with that responsibility to act on players who behave badly.

The city-state also presents an interesting hybrid of a social and decentralized approach—that while the approach is decentralized, there is still a body of authority comprising player representatives. MMORPGs that could benefit most from such city-states would be those whose virtual worlds are intended to be "fully-realized", as Burke (2004) calls it. These worlds would have a range of playable character classes that are interdependent, for example raw resource gatherers to artisans and craftsmen to adventurers, which in turn drives an economy to expedite their transactions. In other words, these games are designed to benefit from law and order. In contrast, highly PvP-centric games like *Shadowbane* may benefit less from the implementation of such city-states.

---

[134] The role played by the bounty hunter here is different from the bounty hunter profession *in Star Wars Galaxies* (remarked by respondent [R46] in Chapter 4). The bounty hunter in *Stars Wars Galaxies* is a profession that any player can adopt. It also does not have the control community-instituted mechanisms suggested in Rogers' city-state government.

Empowering participants through decentralized approaches

There are advantages to decentralized approaches of managing grief play that do not rely too much on the game operator. A key advantage is that it changes player perceptions of grief play. This can occur in two ways. Firstly, the absence of fair-play—for example the aggressor is vastly more powerful than the victim—is a condition for players to believe grief play is taking place. Assuming that the methods of response are equally accessible to all players and the systems have not been abused (for example by griefers themselves), players are less likely to view an incident as grief play if they can seek recourse on their own. Secondly, players will derive satisfaction in seeing their systems work in 'punishing' the griefer. Even in the event that these systems do not ultimately change the griefer's propensity to grief, players are less likely to experience a sense of helplessness and inability to respond against the griefer—and they will be less likely to complain about grief play.

Decentralized approaches when administered properly are also unlikely to incite player protests. The EULAs allow game operators to discipline their users as they deem necessary. However, when the perceived imbalance of power between user and administrator is coupled with instances where there is an absence of community-wide agreement on the punishment meted out, it can result in dissident behavior among users (Smith 1999, p. 146). By empowering players to manage and respond to disputes themselves with the game operator adopting a purely technical role through making available those tools of dispute resolution, the risk of protests can be lessened. MUD administrators in *LambdaMOO* certainly saw this when they confined themselves to purely technical roles after they became tired of having to adjudicate player disputes for years (Dibbell 1993).

Having said this, the communities in MMORPGs are now so large that the efficacy of decentralized approaches to grief play may be somewhat diminished. Players are accorded high degrees of anonymity in MMORPGs, and this layer of anonymity will grow as a player base gets larger. In a smaller community, for example a small discussion forum or MUD, people will know who the troublemakers are. This in turn expedites possibilities for them to respond. For example a participant who knows who the troublemaker is through word of mouth can add him to his ignore list. In MMORPGs like *EverQuest* or *World of Warcraft*, player bases are so big that only the most widely publicized offenders are ever heard of. That there are so many players in these games may even provide incentive for a player to grief, since there is notoriety to gain and many players to

218

impress[135]. While decentralized approaches to managing grief play can be useful, there will still be a need to employ other approaches. Game operator punishment continues to be a deterrent for bad behavior. When community-driven punishment or social pressure to behave fails, punitive systems that employ technological means to disallow or inhibit a griefer's ability to disrupt can work. In reference to Bruckman et al.'s (1994) model, I argue that both decentralized and social, and centralized and technological approaches can be coupled to provide a comprehensive approach to managing grief play.

In summary, grief play is a social issue with technological implications. The circumstances present in an MMORPG can also limit the efficacy of managing grief play if only decentralized and social approaches of management are employed. Some scholars, for example Preece (2004, p. 60), argue that it would be ideal for managerial processes to bring together the best sociological and technological approaches. Keeping these considerations in mind, Bruckman et al.'s (1994) model can be used to propose a multi-method model to manage grief play:

1. *Centralized and technological approaches*. Current punitive systems that either surgically remove or limit a player's ability to grief (for example disabling the ability to use chat channels), or remove the player altogether (for example player account suspension or banning).

2. *Centralized and social approaches*. The employment of player volunteers to act as advisors to new players to help instill the appropriate implicit rules of behavior. Incentives for good behavior can be instrumental too—for example the identification and publicity of player exemplars.

3. *Decentralized and technological approaches*. The continued empowerment of players to deal with griefers using in-game mechanisms. These would include player justice mechanisms, or more precise mechanisms to limit the contact a griefer can impose on another player, for example instancing, ignore lists, and removal of specific players from communities or establishments.

4. *Decentralized and social approaches*. These include social networks, player judiciaries or if implemented as a more comprehensive and authoritative fashion, a player city-state government.

Finally, it would be possible to implement the full array of approaches in this model only for a PvP-centric MMORPG. PvE-centric games like *EverQuest*, or games which are primarily designed to be

---

[135] See the reputation motivation in Chapter 5.

social simulations, for example *The Sims Online*, may find it less appropriate to create a culture where players are encouraged to employ player justice or violent methods of recourse to manage grief play. In these cases, there may need to be greater reliance on social approaches if decentralized mechanisms are to be employed.

Conclusion

If nothing else, players do not like feeling helpless when griefed. While players recognize that the game operator has administrative powers over the game, they still expect to be able to directly engage griefers. Developers themselves agree that player-driven methods are the best ways of managing grief play.

The devil, as one may say, is in the implementation. Each player-driven method of managing grief play brings about different challenges. Player justice may be immediately satisfying to many players. However, it requires equal if not better skill in PvP to be effective. This means that the ability to administer justice can be unequal. Moreover, not every player is disposed towards combative play styles. PvP-centric methods also require the best players of it to behave themselves, but there are no such guarantees. Game operators also tend to be less responsive if PvP-centric methods of response are available, with game masters seemingly reluctant to arbitrate when disputes occur. Some problems of fair-play can be eliminated through game design; for example, players cannot attack others who are in particularly vulnerable states. Other problems are more difficult to address. For example, it is not easy to create a meticulously balanced PvP system where players win encounters by skill and not by character class deficiencies. The balance of a PvP system itself is also highly contentious among players. A casual observation of discussion forums reveal many players who constantly complain about how their class is deficient compared to others, even when it may not be.

Player judiciaries are more methodical. They also are accessible to all players, unlike player justice methods which require some measure of individual skill on the part of players. However, player judiciaries require game operator support and endorsement, and can be abused by players themselves. Moreover, they are not methods that provide immediate gratification. They take time to work.

Higher level systems of managing grief play that involve players are player volunteers and social networks. Both of these methods are social in nature and can exert peer pressure for players to behave. Informal reputation systems however operate on the basis of public awareness. It is easy for a badly behaving player to disappear in the large body of players that make up an MMORPG. Formal reputation systems can also encourage rather than deter griefers intent on gaining for themselves a title of notoriety. Player volunteers can also be effective as they attempt to inculcate implicit rules into players at the onset. However, such a system is susceptible to players who abuse their given powers, and thus require time investment on the part of the game operator to train and monitor these volunteers.

Game operator-driven punitive systems are devoid of player involvement and thus less vulnerable to player abuse, or the issues of differing skill and game knowledge in using game mechanisms to expedite grief play. However, whether punishment can be well received or not depends on player perceptions of whether the game operator can assess a grief play incident fairly and render appropriate judgment. If this can be achieved, then punishment can be surgical (in-game) or broad (out-of-game), and meted out to good effect in grief play management.

This chapter concludes the substantial discussion of the five research objectives of this study. The next chapter presents the general observations of grief play in view of these discussions.

CHAPTER 9: STUDY OUTCOMES

The overall research objective of this study was to investigate grief play and its management mechanisms. This objective was operationalized into five more focused objectives: to investigate what grief play means, what motivates players to engage in it, how it affects the game, what players expect from grief play management, and how grief play can be managed. Each objective was discussed as the topic of interest in the five chapters—Chapters 4 to 8—in which grief play was characterized.

As a result of data analysis, 17 'categories' were identified. The conceptual framework below was presented in Chapter 3, and shows the organization of categories into their respective topics of interest.

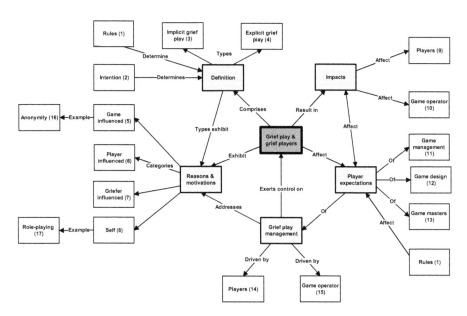

Figure 7: Conceptual framework of grief play (revisited)

The final chapter of this book considers each of these five topics and its relevant categories, and associates where appropriate a general observation of grief play to each. To aid in the reading of this chapter, statements of the general observations will be presented first. They are:

1. Players use implicit rules when they determine if an activity is grief play.

2. The factors motivating griefers directly or indirectly result in their enjoyment of the game.

3. Grief play constitutes problematic player behavior in view of the negative impacts it causes.

4. The feelings of distress that players feel when griefed can be circumvented by empowering players to respond in technological and social ways.

Where appropriate, the categories in Figure 7 are related via its number into each section.

What grief play means

While there is a substantial body of knowledge already existing on anonymity, deindividuation and disinhibited behavior in computer-mediated communication, there is comparatively less study of bad behavior in online role-playing environments like MMORPGs. The limited literature on grief play has defined griefers as players who derive enjoyment by intentionally engaging in activities that disrupt other players' gaming experiences. While participants of MMORPGs seem familiar with such characterizations, debate continues on grief play. Disagreement is often centered on these two issues:

1. When an activity becomes grief play.

2. If grief play is allowed or disallowed in the game.

For the first issue, existing studies have characterized grief play as intentionally disruptive activities. However, players view grief play in a different way compared to that proposed in literature. While some players recognize that there is often a clear *intention* (2) to disrupt play experiences in *explicit* (4) types of grief play, this—alongside enjoyment of having caused disruption—is not the only criteria in their determination of when an activity becomes grief play. For them, grief play is also characterized by other things, including the absence of fair-play and that the actor is not directly benefiting from the act. For example, a player who attacks a vulnerable player repeatedly may be perceived to be griefing. This is regardless of whether or not the aggressor is role-playing or is involved in faction-based PvP that is designed into the game. Other players do not view the presence of a clear intention to disrupt as a key criteria. For them, some of these acts are driven by the desire to get ahead despite inconveniences caused. The study regards these activities as *implicit* (3) subtypes of grief play, with greed play an example of such an implicit subtype.

The second issue of whether grief play is allowed or disallowed in the game is pertinent, because if there are *rules* (1) disallowing a play style or activity, there is an immediate basis for players to expect certain responses from the game operator, and for the game operator to enforce rules. In practice, what is allowed or disallowed in the game is ultimately in the purview of the game operator, which in turn depends on what their rules state. These rules would be expressed as Law of code and game rules. Law of code continues to be sacrosanct, no matter what type of game it is. Engaging in activities that are exploitative of game design or code will also render irrelevant the intention behind the activity. These activities are punishable, regardless of intent. Games that allow players to aggressively respond against griefers commonly also see the game operator less likely to intervene. In PvP-centric games, game operators do tend to expect players to resolve player disputes on their own. In these cases, whether grief play is allowed or disallowed is moot—game masters simply may not respond. Such levels of involvement and commitment to respond on the part of the game operator are commonly either implied, or stated as game rules.

The scene becomes less clear when aggressive responses are not available, for example in non-PvP-centric games. Recognizing that disruptive intention can be difficult to determine, many non-PvP-centric games identify specific play activities, and state in game rules that they are disallowed. If the act is still committed, they will be ruled as disallowed activities regardless of the intention behind the activity. This does not however stop arguments from occurring among players on the activity's permissibility. There are two reasons for this. Firstly, the kind of activities possible in an MMORPG heightens the importance of context. It is already difficult to qualify every disruptive activity possible in the game, the more so considering the dynamic nature of content in the MMORPG. Many activities may be legitimate play styles but when used in certain ways can still constitute bad behavior. Other activities disallowed by game rules (but technically possible under Law of code) may be reasonable depending on context, as the 'invis' incident showed. Hence, as difficult as intention or other circumstances in the context can be to determine, there is still a strong case for considering it in any activity assessment. Secondly, grief play is an imposition of one's play style on others and is perceived to be disruptive. In a multi-player game where players interact with each other in a myriad of ways, it is difficult for every player not to impose their play styles on each other to some minimal degree, and many of these impositions will be disruptive. A player who chats in a certain way may not think it is offensive, but it may be for others. A player who engages a mob first before another player may simply be faster or more highly skilled. Both of these reasons create fertile ground for players to argue about grief play.

For many players, what separates grief play from normative play styles is when grief play passes the boundaries of 'acceptable' behavior. Such boundaries may differ from player to player, but there is often a somewhat broad consensus on what is acceptable behavior in each game. Such a consensus is manifested as implicit rules that exist among players of that game. Thus, the first general observation of this study is this: *players use implicit rules when they determine if an activity is grief play.* For many, the general rule is this: if an activity is disruptive to them, beyond the boundaries of acceptable behavior for that game, it is grief play regardless of what the game rules may say. When this kind of grief play happens, and there is no in-game recourse, they will demand a response from the game operator. Conversely, if they perceive the disruptive acts to be part of 'normal' game play, they will be less likely to complain or seek attention when grief play happens.

The importance of implicit rules in player perception brings about the question of how its adoption among players can be nurtured. It was explained in Chapter 4 that the catch all statement governing general conduct in itself is limited in utility. I argue that the game operator should not merely rely on a catch all statement governing general conduct, but to embrace these implicit rules into game governance. The game operator should encourage the adoption of implicit rules. This inclusion is in addition to the already existing game rules governing the use of game mechanisms. Implicit rules are already influenced by game rules that inform players what to expect in the game. Such support can be improved by inviting player representation to prepare a list of frequently asked questions regarding conduct, and incorporating it in governance alongside game rules. An example of an implicit rule that is stated within this governance could be the camp check in *EverQuest*. Rather than stating that all players must share and that no players have exclusive access to an area (which is behavior currently required by *EverQuest*'s game rules), players can be encouraged in the governance to do camp checks. In doing so, the occurrence of disputes over rights to a game area that may require game master arbitration can be forestalled. Finally, these implicit rules do not need to be binding and punishable if they are broken. Rather, they are intended to create in players the kind of culture that the game operator would like players to adopt in their game.

What motivates players to engage in grief play

Factors in a game can affect a person's inclination to grief. The factors themselves may be a 'reason' that facilitates or expedites the occurrence of grief play, or a 'motivation' that is a compelling circumstance that drives or stimulates the occurrence of grief play. Some factors are *game influenced* (5), and cannot be easily changed. The game is online and there is the absence of visual cues and a layer of *anonymity* (16) among participants, characteristics that are common to virtual communities. The existence of decreased inhibition for engaging in bad behavior is also similar to that found in virtual communities (Lea et al. 1992; Spears & Lea 1992; Thompsen 1997; O'Sullivan & Flanagin 2003). Other factors are *player influenced* (6), *griefer influenced* (7) or stemming from *self* (8). On the latter, some griefers claim to be *role-playing* (17). However, more often than not, role-playing seems to be an excuse rather than a genuine motivator for grief play.

Some factors are within the sphere of control of the game operator. For example, with regards to 'game premise', game rules coupled with rule enforcement can affect the level of griefing. Other factors stem from more personal circumstances: for example, moods that occur as a consequence of events from the real-world, or the goals a player has when playing.

When harassment, power imposition and scamming occur because of a motivation, it will result in activities that many players tend to view as intentional grief play. In comparison, when greed play occurs because of a reason, it is less likely to be viewed as intentional grief play.

Relationships among factors are observed as well. In particular, the second general observation of this study is illustrated via a model representing these relationships: *the factors motivating griefers directly or indirectly result in their enjoyment of the game*. All players—including griefers—act in the game because they ultimately seek to derive enjoyment from the activities. A player can engage in grief play to meet his personal goals for the game, for example achievement-centric goals. When that goal is met, for example through implicit grief play subtypes, he derives enjoyment from his success in having met that goal.

How grief play affects the game

Grief play can impact *player* sentiments, behavior and communities (9). It can also impact the design and service aspects of the *game operation* (10). The most commonly observed negative effects on players are that grief play is annoying, distressing, and can propagate. It also creates dissension among players, and dissatisfaction with the game operator. When grief play affects players, they take their grievances to public forums. This in turn pressures the game operator to address those grievances, either through conflict resolution, rule enforcement, or effecting design changes. Game developers have to create code to address exploitation or place restrictions on player interaction, and game operators have to devote resources to a costly customer service operation to address complaints and arbitrate disputes.

There are also many more negative impacts of grief play observed than positive or neutral ones. This leads to the third general observation of this study: *grief play constitutes problematic player behavior in view of the negative impacts it causes.* Impacts can also be interrelated through cause and effect. Some impacts are observed to be immediate outcomes of grief play, for example annoyance, or emotional distress. Other outcomes seem to occur only after an extended period of griefing or other intermediary impacts have first taken place.

What players expect from grief play management

The impacts of grief play on players are also observed to be influenced by four factors, one of which is the expectations players have of the game operator. Player expectations are arranged into three aspects of the game operation; namely *game management* (11), *game design* (12), and *game masters* (13).

Rules (1) govern the permissibility of the environment, which affect player expectations. Players themselves expect game rules to be clear and to be enforced. These expectations seem reasonable, but there is less congruity on player expectations of game master involvement in relation to the permissibility of activities players can impose on each other. Specifically, even in PvP-centric games, players still expect game master involvement when grief play occurs. This can happen because there are occasionally surrounding circumstances in a grief play incident that can result in unequal ability to use PvP as a method of resolving the dispute.

Nonetheless, such PvP methods are cited by developers and player proponents as means by which players can manage grief play on their own. According to the belief held by some, grief play should be lessened in PvP-centric games. However, grief play was rampant in early *Ultima Online*, and continues to exist in more current PvP-centric games like *Shadowbane*. This is also an almost paradoxical situation: grief play already exists when players have no recourse. However, PvP which will allow players to respond against griefers may or may not lessen the amount of grief play. Some developers in fact believe there is more grief play in games like *Shadowbane* than in non-PvP-centric games. The research methods employed in the study cannot draw conclusions on whether players are more likely to grief in PvP-centric games or not. What it can show, however, is that players feel satisfaction in aggressively responding (via PvP) against griefers, and this mitigates their propensity to complain against the game operator when griefed.

As a general rule, the more players are aware that their participation in the game world will result in their getting exposed to violent and imposing types of game play from others, the less they will experience the negative emotions of annoyance and distress after being griefed.

While game operators do listen to feedback provided by players, the terms of use that players are required to agree to are favorable towards the operator. However, while players are powerless as individuals in effecting the changes in game content or mechanisms they may desire, as a disgruntled collective they possess more leverage. It is in the game operator's interest to ensure players possess the proper expectations of their game. Their setting of expectations is by no means an easy task, given the size of the player base, the constantly evolving game content, and the influence from other MMORPGs players participate in.

Grief play management

For game operators, the real benefit of better understanding grief play lies in how they can better manage it. Several methods that can be or have been used to manage grief play have been discussed in the last chapter. Some methods already see implementation in games, while others have only seen limited use or are hypothetical. The methods themselves are either driven by *players* (14), or by the *game operator* (15).

One prominent method of management is related to the expectation players have of responding or retaliating against griefers. When players cannot retaliate, players invariably feel helpless, and that seems to exacerbate the feelings of annoyance, frustration and distress. An important component of grief play management is thus this empowerment of players to respond or retaliate against griefers. These are player-driven and decentralized approaches, and are an important aspect of grief play management.

In many cases where players can respond directly against griefers, while the initial feelings of annoyance are still present, many remark on the satisfaction felt as a consequence. This can be very well the driving thrust of any kind of response opportunity that is made available by the game operator to players, which in turn brings about the fourth and final general observation of this study. The game operator cannot stop any player from feeling griefed no matter how game rules or

228

implicit rules are stated. However, *the feelings of distress that players feel when griefed can be circumvented by empowering players to respond in technological and social ways.* In one sense, it does not matter if a player's enjoyment is disrupted, particularly if the disruption remains within the play context of the game. However, it matters to the game operator if he is sufficiently distressed to complain and leave the game. The two areas that the game operator can exert some control over are player expectations, and empowering players to respond against their griefers. By doing so, players are less likely to feel the adverse effects, and therefore distress. The idea in grief play management, in other words, is not to eliminate grief play. Rather, it is to manage its effects, and these two areas are the key.

CONCLUSION

If nothing else, the spectrum of perceptions, arguments and counterarguments pertaining to what is grief play in MMORPGs, expectations of its participants and how it should be dealt with all point to the subjectivity of grief play. With the play activities permissible in MMORPGs, it is inevitable that players impose on each other—and these impositions in many cases (outside strongly abusive harassment) are in reality small steps away from the activities becoming grief play. Where conflict is an expected part of game play, whether the act of aggression is driven by the desire to ruin enjoyment or not becomes a moot issue. The case for perceiving grief play as non-normative behavior lies in games where violent conflict or aggressive play among players is not intended by game design. And even in these games, grief play for many griefers themselves remain symbolic acts where either disruption is a consequence rather than the intention; or if disruption is intentional, it is merely their way of imposing legitimate play activities on others. Grief play remains bad and problematic behavior. Its impacts on participants are not trivial and griefer behavior must be managed. However, whether grief play is non-normative behavior or not continues to depend on context and other subjective circumstances.

The subjectivity of grief play and that it means different things to MMORPG participants also brings about questions and issues deserving of further study. The first point for further research is suggested by the qualitative nature of this study. This study has been intended to be a first and substantial explorative exercise in our understanding of grief play. From this juncture, one avenue of further work could be to identify specific concepts discussed here and to employ quantitative methods to detect how representative are some of these concepts. For example, Pizer (2003, p. 431) notes that just 3 percent of players grief. A quantitative study could investigate the proportion of players belonging to a player type that grief in a certain way. It would be interesting to see statistics on 'achiever' players (Bartle 1996) and their propensity towards greed play to further explore the relationships between player types and grief play subtypes. Another potential area of study could be to find out if players are more likely to grief in PvP than in PvE-centric games—such a study would certainly provide further illumination on whether PvP decreases or increases the level of grief play in the game.

The second potential research area stems from comparisons between MMORPGs and other virtual communities. There are characteristics of the MMORPG that set it apart from other virtual communities like Usenet, which in turn provide fertile ground for further work. For example, the player base in an MMORPG does not form a single unified collective but is instead fragmented into smaller communities, each with their unique identity and infrastructure. The interaction among player communities in an MMORPG can be high. Investigation into its social dynamics, for example community bullying between griefer and other player communities[136], could provide insights into how aggressive virtual communities interact with each other. Axelsson & Regan's (2002) statistically-based study of player attitudes in *Asheron's Call* also reveals that players are more likely to demonstrate good behavior with people they are familiar with. It would be interesting to employ similar methods to see if players in a community that ferments bad behavior in an MMORPG are encouraged to exhibit the same behavior. Another characteristic of an MMORPG is the interplay among game rules, implicit rules and Law of code. The grey area among what is technically permitted by Law of code, allowed by service rules, and expected by implicit rules coupled with the difference in power between a paying user and the service operator is in itself a fascinating dimension to study in reference to virtual communities. This is regardless of whether the environment in question is an MMORPG, or if the context is bad behavior at all. Other research could consider the larger reasons purported for bad behavior in virtual communities—for example, the reduction of social cues noted by Lea et al. (1992), Spears & Lea (1992), Thompsen (1997) and O'Sullivan & Flanagin (2003), or anonymity noted by Smith (1999), Utz (2000), Finn (2004) and Suler (2004)—and investigate how representative are these reasons for motivating a player to behave badly in online role-playing environments. Further research on the management of virtual communities in light of this study could also be pursued. This study made use of existing knowledge on virtual communities and applied it to grief play and its management. An investigation of how the methods of managing grief play in an MMORPG in turn can be adopted in other virtual communities would be very worthwhile.

A third point for further research is to relate what has been said about grief play to problematic behavior in the real-world. On this, Will Wright, who designed *The Sims Online*, when interviewed in September 2003[137] had this to say:

> We've been talking to people in homeland security that want to know if we could simulate a terrorist network. I keep telling them they don't have to; they just need to come study the griefers in a multi-player game, because they are exactly that. They always figure out how

---

[136] See Chapter 8 – 'Might is right'.

[137] The transcript of the interview is at http://www.mallofthesims.com/newsproarchives/arc8-2003.html.

to get by every little loophole, they hide in the cracks, they respond very fast to whatever new policies you put in place. It is like the perfect simulator for a terrorist organization.

Without getting into a detailed discussion of terrorism itself, the parallels between grief play and real-world equivalents that Varney (2005) describes in *The Escapist* magazine spring to mind again. Will Wright's reference of grief play to real-world terrorism is interesting. This relation is also highly arguable, as any discussion attempting to relate the two needs to consider the many deeply weighted issues of terrorism, including its roots in history, the clash of ideologies, and the devastating effects of a terrorist act. It is an area that lies outside the immediate scope of this study, and hence for the moment, I have stayed clear of drawing substantial relationships between the two in this work. Still, from a cursory glance, if there is any arguable relation between grief play and terrorism, I venture that the griefer motivator that seems most comparable to Wright's reference would be 'protest'. Beyond this, the intention of this explorative study has not been to provide a better understanding of global terrorism in light of grief play behavior in MMORPGs. However, that some industry watchers and game developers have observed the existence of similar characteristics is noteworthy.

Afterword

Part of the motivation for this study came from my own experience playing *Ultima Online*. Prior to my getting involved as a player of MMORPGs, I was familiar with role-playing—having played Dungeons & Dragons on the tabletop—and with computer gaming, *Ultima* being one of the first computer games I was exposed to in the early 80s. The later *Ultima* single-player games were known for strong narratives and NPCs that conversed and behaved like real persons. Like others who were familiar with the world of Britannia, I was excited when I learnt that *Ultima Online* was in development. The very idea of playing with other real-world persons in a world I was already familiar with through the single-player games was captivating. I participated in *Ultima Online* firstly as an alpha-phase tester, then properly as a player in 1997 shortly after the game's public release. My association with MMORPGs continued thereafter, particularly in *EverQuest*, *Dark Age of Camelot*, *Star Wars Galaxies*, and *EverQuest 2.* Alongside *Ultima Online,* these are the five MMORPGs I have spent the most time in, advancing to fairly high-level characters and play areas in each.

Of these games, it is *Ultima Online* that has left an indelible impression on me. As fascinating as was the whole experience of playing in a virtual world populated by other people, and where every one of my actions was impacting the world in some way, I was shocked at the level of aggression of player-killers who hung just outside the cities. While I was fortunate enough not to be harassed too much by these griefers, the very thought of being at great risk whenever I left the safe havens of the cities made me a nervous player. It was not a pleasant experience.

Initially, my feelings about grief play immediately after my experience as an *Ultima Online* player bordered on contempt and hostility against those who perpetrated it. But my participation in *EverQuest*, particularly as a leader of a high-level community from 1999, gave me an early and alternative insight into not just why some players play the way they do, it also impressed upon me that every participant in the very large virtual world has different perceptions and needs. My experiences as a community leader led to my first academic foray into MMORPG research in 2001. It was centered on the establishment of player communities in *EverQuest*, and the outcome was a qualitative research study involving interviews with many community leaders of the game.

So, while I continued to dislike getting griefed, I became intrigued by the player behavior and found the subject interesting for several reasons. Firstly, in light of my realizing the huge variety of perceptions and needs from players, I was curious about my own reactions to getting griefed, and wanted to reconcile this to how others were feeling about grief play. Secondly, I followed the threads of discussion in forums and the debates, and it became apparent that there was consensus only on that grief play was disruptive. Players were divided over when an activity became grief play, whether it should be considered normal game play or not, why players were engaging in it, and their expectations of the game operator in managing the behavior. Thirdly, I grew admiration for the players who sought to respond against griefers. I observed their sentiments of annoyance, followed by frustration, then finally resolve and action. I remember the Skara Brae Rangers[138] of *Ultima Online*, and how players applauded and cheered them on as they fought griefers.

On all these counts, I was more interested in learning about the feelings and perceptions of what were clearly subjective experiences for players than seeking quantifiable representations on what players thought about grief play or producing a magic solution to eliminate grief play. Even if the general finding is that some degree of grief play has to be expected in every MMORPG, this work on grief play has tried to shed some light into the experiences of players involved in it from both

---

[138] See Chapter 6 – 'Player communities'.

sides of the picture. It has also been a personal journey of discovery that has led to a better understanding of the feelings I experienced in 1997 as a player of a virtual world populated with griefers and players who tried to counter it.

In closing, I would like to bring us back to a player sentiment noted at the start of this book: that "It's just a game." But no matter what people may say about computer 'gaming', the fact remains that the players in each game take it *very* seriously. MMORPG players would not be putting in so much time into the game and sharing their experiences and perceptions on public forums if they were not taking their games seriously. When players are confronted with social situations in the game comparable to that of the real-world, they exhibit the same reactions, beliefs and values. Whether they are griefers or non-griefing players, they meet social needs through interaction with other participants. They organize themselves into smaller groups for self-support. They feel a sense of achievement in meeting in-game challenges and solving its problems, whether they do this independently of other participants or collaboratively. When they suffer loss or defeat from game constructs or in activities against other participants, they experience emotions from the same pool if those activities had taken place in the real-world. Dourish (1998, p. 6) puts it in a particularly apt way when he remarks in his introduction to MUD research that:

> Whether they're in the Corporate Boardroom or the Forest of Eternal Gloom, people are people and interact in much the same way—and the technologies they depend on are much the same.

Researchers, for example Williams (2000, p. 101) and Sternberg (2001), have argued that the actions people in the virtual world undertake have effects on the persons in their real-world equivalents, and I agree. There is indeed nothing unreal about the experiences of participants even in a virtual world. As long as experiences are so real to players, MMORPGs will continue to be a fascinating area of study that provides insight into the ways we interact and socialize with each other.

REFERENCES

Aarseth E J 1997, *Cybertext: perspectives on ergodic literature*, The John Hopkins University Press, Baltimore.

Adrianson, L & Hjelmquist, E 1999, 'Group processes in solving two problems: face-to-face and computer-mediated communication', *Behaviour & Information Technology, vol. 18*, no. 3, pp. 179-198.

Alberts, J K, Kellar-Guenther, Y & Corman, S R 1996, 'That's not funny: understanding recipients' responses to teasing', *Western Journal of Communication*, vol. 60, no. 4, pp. 337-357.

Andrews, D C 2004, 'Audience-specific online community design', *Communications of the ACM*, vol. 45, no. 4, pp. 64-68.

Au, W J 2002, 'Showdown in cyberspace: Star Wars vs. The Sims', *Salon.com*, July 9 2002. From http://www.salon.com/tech/feature/2002/07/09/mmorpg/

Axelsson, A-S & Regan, T 2002, How belonging to an online group affects social behavior-a case study of Asheron's Call, Microsoft Research. From ftp://ftp.research.microsoft.com/pub/tr/tr-2002-07.pdf

Bakardjieva, M & Feenberg, A 2001, 'Involving the virtual subject', *Ethics and Information Technology*, vol. 2, no. 4, pp. 233-240.

Bakardjieva, M 2003, 'Virtual togetherness: an everyday-life perspective', *Media, Culture & Society*, vol. 25, no. 3, pp. 291-313.

Bargh, J A, McKenna, K Y A & Fitzsimons, G M 2002, 'Can you see the real me? Activation and expression of the "true self" on the Internet', *Journal of Social Issues*, vol. 58, no. 1, pp. 33-48.

Bartle, R 1996, 'Hearts, clubs, diamonds, spades: players who suit MUDs', *Journal of MUD Research*, vol. 1, no. 1. From http://www.mud.co.uk/richard/hcds.htm

Bartle, R 2004, *Designing virtual worlds*, New Riders, Indianapolis, Indiana.

Bassett, E H & O'Riordan, K 2002, 'Ethics of Internet research: contesting the human subjects research model', *Ethics and Information Technology*, vol. 4, no. 3, pp. 233-247.

Beaubien, M P 1996, 'Playing at community: multi-user dungeons and social interaction in cyberspace', in L Strate, R Jacobson & S B Gibson (eds), *Communication and cyberspace: social interaction in an electronic environment*, Hampton Press, New Jersey, pp. 179-188.

Becker, D 2004, 'Inflicting pain on 'griefers', *CNET News.com*, 13 December. From http://news.com.com/2102-1043_3-5488403.html?tag=st.util.print

Besag, V E 1989, *Bullies and victims in schools*, Open University Press, Milton Keynes, Philadelphia.

Blizzard Entertainment Inc. 2005a, *World of Warcraft(R) terms of use agreement*. From http://www.worldofwarcraft.com/legal/termsofuse.html

Blizzard Entertainment Inc. 2005b, *World of Warcraft(R) surpasses five million customers worldwide*. From http://games.techwhack.com/307-201211-world-of-warcraftr-surpasses-five-million-customers-worldwide

Bogdan, R C & Biklen, S K 1992, *Qualitative research for education*, 2nd edn, Allyn and Bacon, Boston.

Bollmer, J M, Harris, M J, Milich, R & Georgesen, J C 2003, 'Taking offence: effects of personality and teasing history on behavioral and emotional reactions to teasing', *Journal of Personality*, vol. 71, no. 4, pp. 557-604.

Bosworth, K, Espelage, D L & Simon, T R 1999, 'Factors associated with bullying behavior in middle school students', *The Journal of Early Adolescence*, vol. 19, no. 3, pp. 341-362.

Branscomb, A W 1996, 'Cyberspaces: familiar territory or lawless frontiers', *Journal of Computer-Mediated Communication*, vol. 2, no. 1. From http://jcmc.indiana.edu/vol2/issue1/index.html

Bromberg, H 1996, 'Are MUDS communities? Identity, belonging and consciousness in virtual worlds', in R Shields (ed), *Cultures of Internet: virtual spaces, real histories, living bodies*, SAGE Publications Ltd., London, pp. 143-152.

Bromseth, J C H 2002, 'Public places—public activities?', in *Association of Internet Researchers*, Maastricht. From http://www.intermedia.uio.no/konferanser/skikt-02/docs/Researching_ICTs_in_context-Ch3-Bromseth.pdf

Brown, B & Bell, M 2004, 'CSCW at play: 'There' as a collaborative virtual environment', in *ACM conference on computer supported cooperative work*, pp. 350-359.

Bruckman, A 1992, 'Identity workshop: emergent social and psychological phenomena in text-based virtual reality'. From http://www.cc.gatech.edu/fac/Amy.Bruckman/papers/index.html

Bruckman, A 2002, *Ethical guidelines for research online*. From http://www.cc.gatech.edu/~asb/ethics

Bruckman, A, Curtis, P, Figallo, C & Laurel, B 1994, 'Approaches to managing deviant behavior in virtual communities', in *Conference on Human Factors in Computing Systems*, Boston, Massachusetts, pp. 183-184.

Burke, T 2004, *Play of state: sovereignty and governance in MMOGs*. From http://www.swarthmore.edu/SocSci/tburke1/The%20MMOG%20State.pdf

Capurro, R & Pingel, C 2002, 'Ethical issues of online communication research', *Ethics and Information Technology*, vol. 4, no. 3, pp. 189-194.

Charmaz, K 1994a, '"Discovering" chronic illness: using grounded theory', in B G Glaser (ed), *More grounded theory methodology: a reader*, Sociology Press, Mill Valley, California, pp. 65-94.

Charmaz, K 1994b, 'The grounded theory method: an explication and interpretation', in B G Glaser (ed), *More grounded theory methodology: a reader*, Sociology Press, Mill Valley, California, pp. 95-115.

Cloutier, R E 2004, 'Online gaming: the new social circle?' In *Mass High Tech.*, vol. 22, no. 38, p. 16.

Collins, M 1992, *Flaming: the relationship between social context cues and uninhibited verbal behavior in computer-mediated communication*. From http://www.emoderators.com/papers/flames.html

Colvin, G, Tobin, T, Beard, K, Hagan, S & Sprague, J 1998, 'The school bully: assessing the problem, developing interventions, and future research directions', *Journal of Behavioral Education*, vol. 8, no. 3, pp. 293-319.

Constas, M A 1992, 'Qualitative analysis as a public event: The documentation of category development procedures', *American Educational Research Journal*, vol. 29, no. 2, pp. 253-266.

Cornett, S 2004, 'The usability of massively multiplayer online roleplaying games: designing for new users', in *SIGCHI conference on Human factors in computing systems*, Vienna, pp. 703-710.

Crothers, L M & Levinson, E M 2004, 'Assessment of bullying: a review of methods and instruments', *Journal of Counseling and Development*, vol. 82, no. 4, pp. 496-503. Retrieved from ProQuest.

Curtis, P 1992, 'Mudding: social phenomena in text-based virtual realities', in *Conference on the Directions and Implications of Advanced Computing*, Berkeley California. From ftp://ftp.lambda.moo.mud.org/pub/MOO/papers/DIAC92.txt

Davis, J P 2002, 'The experience of "bad" behavior in online social spaces: a survey of online users', *Social Computing Group, Microsoft Research*. From http://research.microsoft.com/scg/papers/Bad%20Behavior%20Survey.pdf

Davis, J P, Steury, K & Pagulayan, R 2005, 'A survey method for assessing perceptions of a game: the consumer playtest in game design', *Game Studies*, vol. 5, no. 1. From http://gamestudies.org/0501/davis_steury_pagulayan/

Davis, S B 2005, *The cost of insecurity: griefing, from anonymity to accountability*. From http://www.skotos.net/articles/guestvoices2.phtml

de Moor, A & Wagenvoort, J 2004, 'Conflict management in an online gaming community', in *Community Informatics Research Network 2004 Conference*, Prato, Italy. From http://www.communitysense.nl/papers/cirn04.pdf

Delwiche, A 2003, 'MMORPG's in the college classroom', in *The State of Play: Law, Games, and Virtual Worlds*, New York City. From http://www.nyls.edu/docs/delwiche.pdf

Denegri-Knott, J 2003, 'Consumers behaving badly: deviation or innovation? A conceptual exploration of empowered communications online-the case of consumer-producer relationships on the web', in *HOIT 2003 The Networked Home and the Home of the Future Conference*, Irvine,

California. From
http://www.crito.uci.edu/noah/HOIT/HOIT%20Papers/consumers%20behaving%20badly.pdf

Dey, I 1999, *Grounding grounded theory: guidelines for qualitative inquiry*, Academic Press, San Diego, California.

Dibbell, J 1993, 'A rape in cyberspace. How an evil clown, a Haitian trickster spirit, two wizards, and a cast of dozens turned a database into a society', in *The Village Voice*, 23 December. From http://www.juliandibbell.com/texts/bungle_vv.html

Dodig-Crnkovic, G & Larsson, T 2005, 'Game ethics—Homo Ludens as a computer game designer and consumer', *International Review of Information Ethics*, vol. Special Issue. From http://www.idt.mdh.se/personal/gdc/work/Homo_Ludens_Ethics-IJIE.pdf

Donath, J 1999, 'Identity and deception in the virtual community', in P Kollock & M Smith (eds) *Communities in cyberspace,* Routledge, London, pp. 29-59.

Dourish, P 1998, 'Introduction: the state of play', *Computer Supported Cooperative Work*, vol. 7, no. 1-2, pp. 1-7.

Ducheneaut, N & Moore, R J 2004, 'The social side of gaming: a study of interaction patterns in a massively multiplayer online game', in *ACM conference on computer supported cooperative work*, Chicago, Illinois, pp. 360-369.

Einarsen, S 2000, 'Harassment and bullying at work: A review of the Scandinavian approach', *Aggression and Violent Behavior*, vol. 5, no. 4, pp. 379-401.

Electronic Arts Inc. 2003a, *What is Origin's policy regarding harassment?* From http://support.ea.com/cgi-bin/ea.cfg/php/enduser/std_adp.php?p_faqid=45

Electronic Arts Inc. 2003b, *What is physical harassment?* From http://support.ea.com/cgi-bin/ea.cfg/php/enduser/std_adp.php?p_faqid=59

Electronic Arts Inc. 2003c, *Ultima Online Service Rules of Conduct.* From http://support.ea.com/cgi-bin/ea.cfg/php/enduser/std_adp.php?p_faqid=347

Evans, R D 2001, 'Examining the informal sanctioning of deviance in a chat room culture', *Deviant Behavior*, vol. 22, no. 3, pp. 195-210.

Farmer, M 2001, 'Games for girls going...going...gone?' *Game Developer*, vol. 8, no. 7, pp. 64-65.

Finn, J 2004, 'A survey of online harassment at a university campus', *Journal of Interpersonal Violence*, vol. 19, no. 4, pp. 468-483.

Flicker, S, Haans, D & Skinner, H 2004, 'Ethical dilemmas in research on Internet communities', *Qualitative Health Research*, vol. 14, no. 1, pp. 124-134.

Foo, C Y & Koivisto, E M I 2004, 'Defining grief play in MMORPGs: player and developer perceptions', in *SIGCHI International Conference on Advances in computer entertainment technology*, Singapore, pp. 245-250.

Fox, C L & Boulton, M J 2005, 'The social skills problems of victims of bullying: self, peer and teacher perceptions', *British Journal of Educational Psychology*, vol. 75, pp. 313-328.

Friedman, E & Resnick, P 2001, 'The social cost of cheap pseudonyms', *Journal of Economics and Management Strategy*, vol. 10, no. 2, pp. 173-199. From http://www.si.umich.edu/~presnick/papers/identifiers/index.html

Froomkin, A M 1995, 'Anonymity and its enmities', *Journal of Online Law*, vol. art. 4. From http://www.wm.edu/law/publications/jol/95_96/froomkin.html

Fullerton, T, Swain, C & Hoffman, S 2004, *Game design workshop: designing, prototyping, and playtesting games*, CMP Books, San Francisco, California.

Genender, L 2005, 'Griefing for the greater good', In *The Escapist*, pp. 29-30. From http://www.escapistmagazine.com/issue/19

Glaser, B G & Strauss, A L 1967, *Discovery of grounded theory: strategies for qualitative research*, Aldine de Gruyter, New York.

Glaser, B G 1992, *Basics of grounded theory analysis*, Sociology Press, Mill Valley, California.

Gorriz, C M & Medina, C 2000, 'Engaging girls with computers through software games', *Communications of the ACM*, vol. 43, no. 1, pp. 42-49.

Goslin, M, Shochet, J & Schell, J 2003, 'Toontown Online: building massively multiplayer games for the masses', in T Alexander (ed), *Massively multiplayer game development*, Charles River Media, Hingham, Massachusetts, pp. 3-19.

Gotved, S 2002, 'Spatial dimensions in online communities', *Space & Culture*, vol. 5, no. 4, pp. 405-414.

Grabosky, P N 2001, 'Virtual criminality: old wine in new bottles?', *Social Legal Studies*, vol. 10, no. 2, pp. 243-249.

Grimmelmann, J 2004, 'Virtual worlds as comparative law', *New York Law School Law Review*, vol. 47, pp. 147-184.

Grimmelmann, J 2005, 'Virtual power politics', *Social Science Research Network*. From http://papers.ssrn.com/sol3/papers.cfm?abstract_id=707301

Grudin, J 1994, 'Groupware and social dynamics: eight challenges for developers', *Communications of the ACM*, vol. 37, no. 1, pp. 92-105.

Gupta, P & Pu, P 2003, 'Social cues and awareness for recommendation systems', in *International Conference on Intelligent User Interfaces*, Miami, Florida, pp. 245-247.

Hall, W A & Callery, P 2001, 'Enhancing the rigor of grounded theory: incorporating reflexivity and relationality', *Qualitative Health Research*, vol. 11, no. 2, pp. 257-272.

Hallford, N & Hallford, J 2001, *Swords & circuitry: a designer's guide to computer role-playing games*, Prima Publishing, Roseville, California.

239

Hardin, G 1968, 'The tragedy of the commons', *Science*, vol. 162, no. 3859, pp. 1243-1248.

Harmon, A 2004, 'Internet gives teenage bullies weapons to wound from afar', in *The New York Times*, 26 August 2004.

Haumersen, T 2000, 'Ultima Online lawsuit', in *GameSpy.com*, 1 September. From http://www.gamespy.com/articles/492/492177p1.html

Henderson, S & Gilding, M 2004, '"I've never clicked this much with anyone in my life": trust and hyperpersonal communication in online friendships', *New Media & Society*, vol. 6, no. 4, pp. 487-506.

Herring, S C 2004, 'Slouching toward the ordinary: current trends in computer-mediated communication', *New Media & Society*, vol. 6, no. 1, pp. 26-36.

Hiltz, S R, Turoff, M & Johnson, K 1989, 'Experiments in group decision making, 3: disinhibition, deindividuation, and group process in pen name and real name computer conferences', *Decision Support Systems*, vol. 5, no. 2, pp. 217-232.

Holland, N N 1996, *The Internet regression*. From http://www.rider.edu/~suler/psycyber/holland.html

Huff, C, Johnson, D G & Miller, K 2003, 'Virtual harms and real responsibility', *Technology and Society Magazine, IEEE*, vol. 22, no. 2, pp. 12-19.

Huizinga, J. 1955, *Homo Ludens: a study of the play-element in culture*, The Beacon Press, Boston.

Hunicke, R, LeBlanc, M & Zubek, R 2004, 'MDA: A formal approach to game design and game research', in *Challenges in Game AI Workshop, Nineteenth National Conference on Artificial Intelligence*. From http://www.cs.northwestern.edu/~rob/publications/MDA.pdf

Igbaria, M 1999, 'The driving forces in the virtual society', *Communications of the ACM*, vol. 42, no. 12, pp. 64-70.

Ito, M 1997, 'Virtually embodied: the reality of fantasy in a multi-user dungeon', in D Porter (ed), *Internet culture*, Routledge, New York, pp. 87-109.

Jakobsson, M & Taylor, T L 2003, 'The Sopranos meets EverQuest: social networking in massively multiplayer online games', in *Digital Arts and Culture Conference*, RMIT University, Melbourne, Australia, pp. 81-90.

James, D, Walton, G, Robbins, B, Dunin, E, Mills, G, Welch, J, Valadares, J, Estanislao, J & DeBenedictis, S 2004, '2004 persistent worlds whitepaper', *IGDA Online Games SIG*. From http://www.igda.org/online/IGDA_PSW_Whitepaper_2004.pdf

Järvinen, A 2003, 'Making and breaking games: a typology of rules', in *Level Up: Digital Games Research Conference*, Utrecht.

Järvinen, M 2000, 'The biographical illusion: constructing meaning in qualitative interviews', *Qualitative Inquiry*, vol. 6, no. 3, pp. 370-391.

Jensen, C, Davis, J & Farnham, S 2002, 'Finding others online: reputation systems for social online spaces', in *Conference on Human Factors in Computing Systems*, Minneapolis, Minnesota.

Johnson, D G 1997, 'Ethics online', *Communications of the ACM*, vol. 40, no. 1, pp. 60-65.

Joinson, A 1998, 'Causes and implications of disinhibited behavior on the Internet', in J Gackenbach (ed), *Psychology and the Internet*, Academic Press, San Diego, California, pp. 43-60.

Joinson, A N & Dietz-Uhler, B 2002, 'Explanations for the perpetration of and reactions to deception in a virtual community', *Social Science Computer Review*, vol. 20, no. 3, pp. 275-289.

Kautz, H, Selman, B & Shah, M 1997, 'Referral web: combining social networks and collaborative filtering', *Communications of the ACM*, vol. 40, no. 3, pp. 63-65.

Kayany, J. M. 1998, 'Contexts of uninhibited online behavior: flaming in social newsgroups on usenet', *Journal of the American Society for Information Science*, vol. 49, no. 12, pp. 1135-1141.

Keith, S & Martin, M E 2005, 'Cyber-bullying: creating a culture of respect in a cyber world', *Reclaiming Children and Youth*, vol. 13, no. 4, pp. 224-228.

Ketlner, D, Capps, L, Kring, A M, Young, R C & Heerey, E A 2001, 'Just teasing: a conceptual analysis and empirical review', *Psychological Bulletin*, vol. 127, no. 2, pp. 229-248.

Kiesler, S, Siegel, J & McGuire, T W 1991, 'Social psychological aspects of computer-mediated communication', in C Dunlop & R Kling (eds), *Computerization and controversy: value conflicts and social choices*, Academic Press, San Diego, California, pp. 330-349.

Kim, A J 1998, 'Killers have more fun', in *Wired News,* May 1998. From http://www.wired.com/wired/archive/6.05/ultima_pr.html

Kim, A J 2000, *Community building on the web*, Peachpit Press, Berkeley, California.

King, S A 1996, 'Researching Internet communities: proposed ethical guidelines for the reporting of results', *The Information Society*, vol. 12, no. 2, pp. 119-127.

Koivisto, E M I 2003, 'Supporting Communities in Massively Multiplayer Online Role Playing Games by Game Design', in *Seminar of Game Studies*, Tampere, Finland. From http://www.digra.org/dl/db/05150.48442

Kolbert, E 2001, 'Pimps and dragons: how an online world survived a social breakdown', in *The New Yorker*, May 28. From http://www.newyorker.com/fact/content/?010528fa_FACT

Kollock, P & Smith, M 1996, 'Managing the virtual commons: cooperation and conflict in computer communities', in S C Herring (ed), *Computer-mediated communication: linguistic, social, and cross-cultural perspectives*, John Benjamins, Amsterdam, pp. 109-128.

Kollock, P 1998, 'Design principles for online communities', *PC Update*, vol. 15, no. 5, pp. 58-60. From http://www.sscnet.ucla.edu/soc/faculty/kollock/papers/design.htm

Kosak, D 2002, 'What's this world coming to? The future of massively multiplayer games', in *GameSpy.com*. From http://www.gamespy.com/gdc2002/mmog/

Koster, R. (n.d.), *'A philosophical statement on playerkilling'*. From
http://www.raphkoster.com/gaming/pkphilosophy.shtml

Kowalski, R M 2000, '"I was only kidding!": victims' and perpetrators' perceptions of teasing',
Personality and Social Psychology Bulletin, vol. 26, no. 2, pp. 231-241.

Kvale, S 1996, *Interviews: an introduction to qualitative research interviewing*, SAGE
Publications, London.

Laber, E 2001, 'Men are from Quake, women are from Ultima', in *The New York Times*, Jan 11.

Land, D 2003, 'Teasing apart secondary students' conceptualizations of peer teasing, bullying and
sexual harassment', *School Psychology International*, vol. 24, no. 2, pp. 147-165.

Landau, S, Milich, R, Harris, M J & Larson, S E 2001, '"You really don't know how much it
hurts:" children's and preservice teachers' reactions to childhood teasing', *School Psychology
Review*, vol. 30, no. 3, pp. 329-343.

Lastowka F G & Hunter, D 2004, 'Virtual crime', *Social Science Research Network*. From
http://papers.ssrn.com/sol3/papers.cfm?abstract_id=564801

Laurel, B 2004, 'Narrative construction as play', *Interactions*, vol. 11, no. 5, pp. 73-74.

Lazzaro, N 2004, 'Why we play games: four keys to more emotion in player experiences', in
Games Developers Conference, San Jose, California. From
http://xeodesign.com/xeodesign_whyweplaygames.pdf

Lea, M, O'Shea, T, Fung, P & Spears, R 1992, '"Flaming" in computer-mediated communication',
in M Lea (ed), *Contexts of computer-mediated communication*, Harvester Wheatsheaf,
Hertfordshire, pp. 89-112.

Lea, M, Spears, R & de Groot, D 2001, 'Knowing me, knowing you: anonymity effects on social
identity processes within groups', *Personality and Social Psychology Bulletin*, vol. 27, no. 5, pp.
526-537.

Lee, H 2005, 'Behavioral strategies for dealing with flaming in an online forum', *The Sociological
Quarterly*, vol. 46, no. 2, pp. 385-403.

Lee, K S 2002, *The online identity and deviant behavior: who are you in massively multiplayer
online role playing game?*, Human-Computer Interaction Institute, Carnegie Mellon University.
From http://www.cs.cmu.edu/~sangl/papers/MMORPG-deviantbehavior-paper.pdf

Lessig, L 1999, 'The code is the law', In *The Industry Standard,* April 9. From
http://www.lessig.org/content/standard/0,1902,4165,00.html

Levander, M 2001, 'Where does fantasy end?', in *Time Magazine*, vol. 157, no. 22, June 4.

Lin, H & Sun, C-T 2003, 'Problems in simulating social reality: observations on a MUD
construction', *Simulation Gaming*, vol. 34, no. 1, pp. 69-88.

242

Lin, H & Sun, C-T 2005, 'The 'white-eyed' player culture: grief play and construction of deviance in MMORPGs', in *DiGRA 2005 Conference*, Vancouver, British Columbia. From http://www.digra.org/dl/db/06278.21161.pdf

Luff, I 2000, '"I've been in the Reichstag": rethinking roleplay', *Teaching History*, pp. 8-17.

Ma, X, Stewin, L L & Mah, D L 2001, 'Bullying in school: nature, effects and remedies', *Research Papers in Education*, vol. 16, no. 3, pp. 247-270.

MacKinnon, R C 1997, 'Punishing the persona: correctional strategies for the virtual offender', in S G Jones (ed), *Virtual culture: identity and communication in cybersociety*, SAGE Publications, London, pp. 206-235.

MacKinnon, R C 1998, 'The social construction of rape in virtual reality', in F Sudweeks, M L McLaughlin & S Rafaeli (eds), *Network and netplay: virtual groups on the Internet*, Menlo Park, California:AAAI Press; Cambridge, Massachusetts:MIT Press, pp. 147-172.

Manninen, T 2002, 'Towards communicative, collaborative and constructive multi-player games', in *Computer Games and Digital Cultures Conference*, Tampere University Press, Tampere. From http://www.tol.oulu.fi/~tmannine/publications/CGDC2002_CCC_Multi-player_Games.pdf

McKenna, K Y A, Green, A. S. & Gleason, M. E. J. 2002, 'Relationship formation on the Internet: what's the big attraction?' *Journal of Social Issues*, vol. 58, no. 1, pp. 9-31.

Mills, C B & Babrow, A S 2003, 'Teasing as a means of social influence', *The Southern Communication Journal*, vol. 68, no. 4, pp. 273-286.

Mnookin, J L 1996, 'Virtual(ly) law: the emergence of law in LambdaMOO', *Journal of Computer-Mediated Communication*, vol. 2, no. 1. From http://jcmc.indiana.edu/vol2/issue1/lambda.html

Morningstar, C & Farmer, F R 1991, 'The lessons of Lucasfilm's Habitat', in M Benedikt (ed), *Cyberspace: first steps*, MIT Press, Cambridge, Massachusetts, pp. 273-301.

Mulligan, J & Patrovsky, B 2003, *Developing online games: an insider's guide*, New Riders, Indianapolis, Indiana.

Myers, D 2005, '/hide: The aesthetics of group and solo play', in *DiGRA 2005 Conference*, Vancouver, British Columbia. From http://www.loyno.edu/~dmyers/F99%20classes/Myers_PlayAesthetics.doc

Mythic Entertainment Inc. 2001, *End user access and license agreement*. From http://support.darkageofcamelot.com/kb/article.php?id=072

Neuman, W L 2003, *Social research methods: qualitative and quantitative approaches*, Allyn and Bacon, Boston.

Nunkoosing, K 2005, 'The problems with interviews', *Qualitative Health Research*, vol. 15, no. 5, pp. 698-706.

O' Sullivan, P B & Flanagin, A J 2003, 'Reconceptualizing "flaming" and other problematic messages', *New Media & Society*, vol. 5, no. 1, pp. 69-94.

Olavsrud, T 2002, 'NCsoft, SINA team to bring Lineage to China', in *Asia.internet.com*, November 22. From http://asia.internet.com/news/article.php/1546831

Oliveira, M & Henderson, T 2003, 'What online gamers really think of the Internet', in *2nd workshop on Network and system support for game*, Redwood City, California, pp. 185-193.

Oliver, J 2002, 'The similar eye: proxy life and public space in the MMORPG', in *Computer Games and Digital Cultures*, ed. Mäyrä, F., Tampere. From http://www.digra.org/dl/db/05164.45486

Olweus, D 1993, *Bullying at school: what we know and what we can do*, Blackwell, Oxford.

Ostrom, E 1990, *Governing the Commons*, Cambridge University Press, Cambridge.

Papargyris, A & Poulymenakou, A 2004, 'Learning to fly in persistent digital worlds: the case of massively multiplayer online role playing games', *ACM SIGGROUP Bulletin: Special issue on online learning communities*, vol. 25, no. 1, pp. 41-49.

Pawluk, C J 1989, 'Social construction of teasing', *Journal for the Theory of Social Behavior*, vol. 19, no. 2, pp. 145-167.

Pham, A 2002, 'The nation; online bullies give grief to gamers; Internet: troublemakers play to make their peers cry, driving away customers and profit', in *Los Angeles Times*, Sep 2, p. A-1.

Phillips, D J 1996, 'Defending the boundaries: identifying and countering threats in a Usenet newsgroup', *The Information Society*, vol. 12, no. 1, pp. 39-62.

Pizer, P 2003, 'Social game systems: cultivating player socialization and providing alternate routes to game rewards', in T Alexander (ed), *Massively multiplayer game development*, Charles River Media, Hingham, Massachusetts, pp. 427-441.

Porter, C E 2004, 'A typology of virtual communities: a multi-disciplinary foundation for future research', *Journal of Computer-Mediated Communication*, vol. 10, no. 1. From http://jcmc.indiana.edu/vol10/issue1/porter.html

Postmes, T & Spears, R 2002, 'Behavior online: does anonymous computer communication reduce gender inequality?' *Personality and Social Psychology Bulletin*, vol. 28, no. 8, pp. 1073-1083.

Postmes, T, Spears, R, Sakhel, K & de Groot, D 2001, 'Social influence in computer-mediated communication: the effects of anonymity on group behavior', *Personality and Social Psychology Bulletin*, vol. 27, no. 10, pp. 1243-1254.

Powers, T M 2003, 'Real wrongs in virtual communities', *Ethics and Information Technology*, vol. 5, no. 4, pp. 191-198.

Preece, J 2001, 'Sociability and usability in online communities: determining and measuring success', *Behaviour & Information Technology*, vol. 20, no. 5, pp. 347-356.

Preece, J 2002, 'Supporting community and building social capital: Introduction', *Communications of the ACM*, vol. 45, no. 4, pp. 37-39.

Preece, J 2004, 'Etiquette online: from nice to necessary', *Communications of the ACM*, vol. 47, no. 4, pp. 56-61.

Preece, J & Maloney-Krichmar, D 2005, 'Online communities: design, theory, and practice', *Journal of Computer-Mediated Communication*, vol. 10, no. 4, p. 2005. From http://jcmc.indiana.edu/vol10/issue4/preece.html

Pritchard, M 2000, 'How to hurt the hackers: the scoop on Internet cheating and how you can combat it', in *Gamasutra*, July 24. From http://www.gamasutra.com/features/20000724/pritchard_01.htm

Randall, P 1997, *Adult bullying: perpetrators and victims*, Routledge, London & New York.

Rasmussen, T 1997, 'Social interaction and the new media: the construction of communicative contexts', *The Nordicom Review*, vol. 2, no. 2. From http://www.nordicom.gu.se/common/publ_pdf/29_rasmussen.pdf

Reid, E 1994, *Cultural formations in text-based virtual realities* (MA Thesis), University of Melbourne. From ftp://ftp.lambda.moo.mud.org/pub/MOO/papers/CulturalFormations.txt

Reid, E 1999, 'Hierarchy and power: social control in cyberspace', in M A Smith & P Kollock (eds), *Communities in cyberspace*, Routledge, London, pp. 107-133.

Resnick, P, Zechhauser, R, Friedman, E, & Kuwabara, K 2000, 'Reputation systems', *Communications of the ACM*, vol. 43, no. 12, pp. 45-48.

Rheingold, H 2000, *The virtual community: homesteading on the electronic frontier, revised edition*, MIT Press, Cambridge, Massachusetts. From http://www.rheingold.com/vc/book/

Ridings, C M, Gefen, D & Arinze, B 2002, 'Some antecedents and effects of trust in virtual communities', *Journal of Strategic Information Systems*, vol. 11, no. 3-4, pp. 271-295.

Roberts, T L 1998, 'Are newsgroups virtual communities?' in *SIGCHI conference on human factors in computing systems*, Los Angeles, California, pp. 360-367.

Rogers, A 2003, 'City-state governments—their roles in online communities', in T Alexander (ed), *Massively multiplayer game development*, Charles River Media, Hingham, Massachusetts, pp. 464-476.

Rossignol, J 2005, 'A deadly dollar', In *The Escapist*, pp. 18-22. From http://www.escapistmagazine.com/issue/19

Rouse III, R 2005, *Game design: theory and practice, 2 edn*, Wordware Publishing, Plano, Texas.

Rozak, M 2005, *Differentiation*. From http://www.mxac.com.au/drt/Differentiation.htm

Sage, P D 2003, 'Customer support and player reputation: it's all about trust', in T Alexander (ed), *Massively Multiplayer Game Development*, Charles River Media, Hingham, Massachusetts, pp. 90-99.

Salem, D A, Bogat, G A & Reid, C 1997, 'Mutual help goes on-line', *Journal of Community Psychology*, vol. 25, no. 2, pp. 189-207.

Salen, K & Zimmerman, E 2004, *Rules of play: game design fundamentals*, The MIT Press, Cambridge, Massachusetts.

Salin, D 2003, 'Ways of explaining workplace bullying: a review of enabling, motivating and precipitating structures and processes in the work environment', *Human Relations*, vol. 56, no. 10, pp. 1213-1232.

Salmivalli, C & Voeten, M 2004, 'Connections between attitudes, group norms, and behaviour in bullying situations', *International Journal of Behavioral Development*, vol. 28, no. 3, pp. 246-258.

Sassenberg, K & Boos, M 2003, 'Attitude change in computer-mediated communication: effects of anonymity and category norms', *Group Processes & Intergroup Relations*, vol. 6, no. 4, pp. 405-422.

Scholder, A & Zimmerman E 2003, *Game design+game culture,* Peter Lang, New York.

Schrum, L 1997, 'Ethical research in the information age: Beginning the dialog', *Computers in Human Behavior*, vol. 13, no. 2, pp. 117-125.

Scott, J U, Hague-Armstrong, K & Downes, K L 2003, 'Teasing and bullying: what can pediatricians do?' *Contemporary Pediatrics*, vol. 20, no. 4, pp. 105-111.

Shapiro, J P, Baumeister, R F & Kessler, J W 1991, 'A three-component model of children's teasing: aggression, humor, and ambiguity', *Journal of Social and Clinical Psychology*, vol. 10, no. 4, pp. 459-472.

Siegel, J, Dubrovsky, V, Kiesler, S & McGuire, T W 1986, 'Group processes in computer-mediated communication', *Organizational Behavior and Human Decision Processes*, vol. 37, no. 2, pp. 157-187.

Smith, A D 1999, 'Problems of conflict management in virtual communities', in M A Smith & P Kollock (eds), *Communities in cyberspace*, Routledge, London, pp. 134-166.

Smith, C B, McLaughlin, M L & Osborne, K K 1998, 'From terminal ineptitude to virtual sociopathy: how conduct is regulated on Usenet', in F Sudweeks, M L McLaughlin & S Rafaeli (eds), *Network and netplay: virtual groups on the Internet*, Menlo Park, California:AAAI Press; Cambridge, Massachusetts.:MIT Press, pp. 95-112.

Smith, J H 2004, 'Playing dirty—understanding conflicts in multiplayer games', in *5th annual conference of The Association of Internet Researchers*, Sussex. From http://www.itu.dk/people/smith/texts/playing_dirty.pdf

Smokowski, P R & Kopasz, K H 2005, 'Bullying in school: an overview of types, effects, family characteristics, and intervention strategies', *Children & Schools*, vol. 27, no. 2, pp. 101-110.

Sony Online Entertainment Inc. 2003, *EverQuest continues exponential growth after four years with record setting 118,000 simultaneous users*. Press Release, March 5 2003. From http://goliath.ecnext.com/coms2/summary_0199-2532997_ITM

Sony Online Entertainment Inc. 2004a, *EverQuest rules of conduct*. From http://help.station.sony.com/cgi-bin/soe.cfg/php/enduser/std_adp.php?p_faqid=16204

Sony Online Entertainment Inc. 2004b, *Policies: community standards*. From http://starwarsgalaxies.station.sony.com/en_US/players/content.vm?page=Policies%20Community%20Standards&resource=policies

Sony Online Entertainment Inc. 2005, *Sony Online Entertainment announces official online game auction site*. Press Release, April 20 2005. From http://www.gameinfowire.com/news.asp?nid=6210

Sorrell, J M & Redmond, G M 1995, 'Interviews in qualitative nursing research: differing approaches for ethnographic and phenomenological studies', *Journal of Advanced Nursing*, vol. 21, no. 6, pp. 1117-1122.

Spears, R & Lea, M 1992, 'Social influence and the influence of the 'social' in computer-mediated communication', in M Lea (ed), *Contexts of computer-mediated communication*, Harvester Wheatsheaf, Hertfordshire, pp. 30-65.

Spears, R, Postmes, T, Lea, M & Wolbert, A 2002, 'When are net effects gross products? The power of influence and the influence of power in computer-mediated communication', *Journal of Social Issues*, vol. 58, no. 1, pp. 91-107.

Sproull, L & Kiesler, S 1986, 'Reducing social context cues: electronic mail in organizational communications', *Management Science*, vol. 32, no. 11, pp. 1492-1512.

Stern, P N 1994, 'The grounded theory method: its uses and processes', in B G Glaser (ed), *More grounded theory methodology: a reader*, Sociology Press, Mill Valley, California, pp. 116-126.

Sternberg, J 2001, *Misbehavior in cyber places: the regulation of online conduct in virtual communities on the Internet* (Ph.D thesis), New York University.

Strauss, A & Corbin, J 1994, 'Grounded Theory Methodology', in N K Denzin & Y S Lincoln (eds), *Handbook of qualitative research*, SAGE Publications, Thousand Oaks, California.

Suler, J 1997, *The bad boys of cyberspace: deviant behavior in online multimedia communities and strategies for managing it*. From http://www.rider.edu/~suler/psycyber/badboys.html

Suler, J 2002, 'Identity management in cyberspace', *Journal of Applied Psychoanalytic Studies*, vol. 4, no. 4, pp. 455-459.

Suler, J 2004, 'The online disinhibition effect', *CyberPsychology and Behavior*, vol. 7, no. 3, pp. 321-326. From http://www.rider.edu/~suler/psycyber/disinhibit.html

Taylor, S J & Bogdan, R 1984, *Introduction to qualitative research methods: the search for meanings*, John Wiley & Sons, New York.

Taylor, J & MacDonald, J 2002, 'The effects of asynchronous computer-mediated group interaction on group processes', *Social Science Computer Review*, vol. 20, no. 3, pp. 260-274.

Taylor, T L 1999, 'Life in virtual worlds: plural existence, multimodalities, and other online research challenges', *American Behavioral Scientist*, vol. 43, no. 3, pp. 436-449.

Taylor, T L 2002, 'Whose game is this anyway? Negotiating corporate ownership in a virtual world', in *Computer Game Developers Conference Proceedings,* San Jose, California. From http://www.itu.dk/~tltaylor/papers/Taylor-CGDC.pdf

Thompsen, P A 1997, 'What's fueling the flames in cyberspace? A social influence model', in L Strate, R Jacobson & S B Gibson (eds), *Communication and cyberspace: social interaction in an electronic environment*, Hampton Press, Cresskill, New Jersey, pp. 297-315.

Thomsen, S R, Straubhaar, J D & Bolyard, D M 1998, 'Ethnomethodology and the study of online communities: exploring the cyber streets', *Information Research*, vol. 4, no. 1. From http://informationr.net/ir/4-1/paper50.html

Tito, G 2005, 'Dood, it's part of the game', In *The Escapist*, pp. 23-28. From http://www.escapistmagazine.com/issue/19

Tragesser, S L & Lippman, L G 2005, 'Teasing: for superiority or solidarity?' *The Journal of General Psychology*, vol. 132, no. 3, pp. 255-266.

Tresca, M 1998, *The impact of anonymity on disinhibitive behavior through computer-mediated communication*, (MA Thesis), Michigan State University. From http://www.msu.edu/user/trescami/thesis.htm

Turkle, S 1995, *Life on the screen*, Simon & Schuster, New York.

Turkle, S 1999, 'Identity in the age of the internet', in H Mackay & T O'Sullivan (eds), *The media reader: continuity and transformation*, SAGE Publications, London, pp. 287-304.

Utz, S 2000, 'Social information processing in MUDs: the development of friendships in virtual worlds', *Journal of Online Behavior*, vol. 1, no. 1. From http://www.behavior.net/JOB/v1n1/utz.html

Varney, A 2005, 'Real world grief', In *The Escapist*, no. 19, pp. 34-38. From http://www.escapistmagazine.com/issue/19

Vorderer, P, Hartmann, T & Klimmt, C 2003, 'Explaining the enjoyment of playing video games: the role of competition', in *Proceedings of the second international conference on Entertainment computing*, Pittsburgh, Pennsylvania, pp. 1-9.

Vrooman, S S 2002, 'The art of invective: performing identity in cyberspace', *New Media & Society*, vol. 4, no. 1, pp. 51-70.

Wadhams, N 2003, 'Griefers' form harassing mob in Sims game', in *Baltimore Sun*, July 10.

Walther, J B 1997, 'Group and interpersonal effects in international computer-mediated collaboration', *Human Communication Research*, vol. 23, no. 3, pp. 342-369. Retrieved from ProQuest.

Waskul, D & Douglass, M 1996, 'Considering the electronic participant: some polemical observations on the ethics of on-line research', *The Information Society*, vol. 12, no. 2, pp. 129-139.

Wellman, B & Gulia, M 1999, 'Virtual communities as communities: netsurfers don't ride alone', in M A Smith & P Kollock (eds), *Communities in cyberspace*, Routledge, London, pp. 167-194.

Werry, C 1999, 'Imagined electronic community: representations of virtual community in contemporary business discourse', *First Monday*, vol. 4, no. 9. From http://www.firstmonday.org/issues/issue4_9/werry/index.html

Williams, D & Skoric, M 2005, 'Internet fantasy violence: a test of aggression in an online game', *Communication Monographs*, vol. 72, no. 2, pp. 217-233.

Williams, M 2000, 'Virtually criminal: discourse, deviance and anxiety within virtual communities', *International Review of Law, Computers & Technology*, vol. 14, no. 1, pp. 95-104.

Williams, R B & Clippinger, C A 2002, 'Aggression, competition and computer games: computer and human opponents', *Computers in Human Behavior*, vol. 18, no. 5, pp. 495-506.

Wilson, J Q & Kelling, G L 1982, '*Broken windows*', in The Atlantic Monthly, vol. 249, pp. 29-38.

Wimpenny, P & Gass, J 2000, 'Interviewing in phenomenology and grounded theory: is there a difference?' *Journal of Advanced Nursing*, vol. 31, no. 6, pp. 1485-1492.

Wisebrod, D 1995, 'Controlling the uncontrollable: regulating the Internet', *4 Media & Communications Law Review*, vol. 331. From http://www.wisebrod.com/docs/dw-inet.htm

Wolz, U, Walker, H, Palme, J, Anderson, P, Chen, Z, Dunne, J, Karlsson, G, Laribi, A, Männikkö, S & Spielvogel, R 1997, 'Computer-mediated communication in collaborative educational settings', in *Annual Joint Conference Integrating Technology into Computer Science Education*, Uppsala, Sweden, pp. 51-69.

Yan, J 2003, 'Security design in online games', in *19th Annual Computer Security Applications Conference*, Las Vegas, Nevada. From http://www.acsac.org/2003/papers/114.pdf

Yee, N 2001, *The Norrathian Scrolls: a study of EverQuest (Version 2.5)*. From http://www.nickyee.com/eqt/home.html

Yee, N 2002, *Facets: 5 motivational factors for why people play MMORPG's*. From http://www.nickyee.com/facets/home.html

Zapf, D & Einarsen, S 2001, 'Bullying in the workplace: Recent trends in research and practice— an introduction', *European Journal of Work and Organizational Psychology*, vol. 10, no. 4, pp. 367-373.

APPENDIXES

Appendix 1: A section of an interview with a player [R29]

D1-NP-Q1. How would you define grief play?

[R29]: Provided the game is an online multi-player game (hence referred to as MMORPG) where anonymity is mostly conserved, I define grief play as an action in-game that deliberately and negatively affects one or more players in the game (i.e., *Ultima Online*). To be very blunt: "I am a grief player - I will do what I please when I please even if it involves explicitly upsetting you and/or ruining your gaming experience."

The details... grief play is not limited to simply killing a player and taking all of his hard-earned virtual items as many would be quick to assume; in a dynamic online world there are dynamic instances of grief play. One form I deem as "resource hoarding." An example: a fairly over-powered player or, more likely, a group of players that is over-powered "camp" or "hog" the only monster spawning area where a rare and/or unique item can be found. These players will horde the items and create even more of a demand for them in-game aside from the fact that they are already rare and/or unique. Because they horde most of these items (and therefore have a vast supply), they have a great control on the price of the aforementioned item in the game's player-economy. Their drive is to suckle the most game currency (or nowadays real-life currency) from other players, instead of sharing the spawning grounds, taking turns, and essentially allowing others a chance at getting the item. The main forms of grief play I would include in the definition would be: Player abuse (this includes a broad sub-groups: verbal abuse, ethnic and/or racial attacks, randomized player-killing/player hunting - i.e., killing the Xth player to walk down a certain road while the killers wait in hiding as a game, and so on); Resource hoarding (mentioned above); and Exploitation (includes code hacking programs, scamming, and taking advantage of known/unknown bugs).

D1-NP-Q1(a). About resource hoarding, is this activity carried out with the deliberate intention of negatively affecting players in the game?

[R29]: I must refine my definition of "grief playing." One may take an action within a MMORPG that affects another player negatively, but it does not necessarily have to be deliberate. Grief playing actions are those that a player takes having a visible and obvious negative effect (usually an intense one) on another player or group of players. Despite the griever's awareness as well as the victims', the grieving player continues with the negative action and thus becomes, in a sense, deliberate. The grief action of resource hoarding falls more correctly under this new definition because (for the most part), resource hoarding is not deliberate, but has an obvious negative effect on player(s) also attempting to gather the resource besides the griever. The grief player knows his actions are negatively affecting others, yet he usually continues to hoard despite the comments of upset players. To be cursory, the grief player's actions are not initially or fully deliberate, but lean heavily towards deliberate once it has been acknowledged by others directly to the player that his actions are negatively affecting their gaming experience.

D1-NP-Q1(b). You've made an interesting proposition. Just to quickly clarify; in your assessment, grief play may not be with the specific intention of negatively affecting other

players, but if the player persistently chooses to continue in his actions with the full knowledge that his play style is having that effect on others, it is griefing then?

[R29]: Yes, I do believe this to be a more correct definition of griefing. I support my definition because an extremely similar feeling is felt by the negatively affected player through this sort of behavior than, say, a player just behaving that way to savor the joy of ruining his/her experience in-game. Although a little more extreme in the completely deliberate/sadistic way, in both situations the victim loses out by: 1. getting upset by being able to do little about the other player's behavior 2. having his/her plans or well intentions (i.e. sharing a resource but still getting much in the end) ruined by this behavior and finally 3. reaching a stage closer to not wanting to play the game and/or resorting grief-play to deliberately affect the original griefer to "teach them a lesson." I realize that this definition is more loose and open to some degree of interpretation; for instance, suppose the griefer isn't really griefing or is even aware of his/her "Behavior - maybe he/she is foreign, can't speak the majority of other players' language, and simply doesn't understand that he/she is griefing due to a language barrier. This situation may be especially the case if he/she were hoarding resources; in a behavior such as "res-killing" though, no language is necessary to understand the action is intentionally harmful to a player's gaming experience. Diversity among MMORPGs is increasing daily with the introduction of overseas servers, and with cross-server character transfers in the works for at least one MMORPG, I believe diversity will explode. Ultimately, although it may leave some room for players to apply its definition to more situations than probably necessary, I still stick with it based on the fact that: 1. the griefer knows he is negatively affecting the other player(s) - sans the exception mentioned and 2. the victim of the action is wholly and negatively affected.

D1-NP-Q2. Can you describe a strong instance of grief play you have encountered in an MMORPG you play in?

[R29]: Personally, the strongest instance I have had to deal with as a player of *Ultima Online* is player-killing. Before the implementation of a player killing facet (Felucca) and a non-player killing facet (Trammel) rather than just a player-killing facet, and nearly any lucrative "spawning ground" was littered with player-killers eager to earn their living at the cost of other player's lives and dignity. But I eventually found a friend that introduced me to some great, remote NPC monster "hunting grounds" located within a dungeon that were supposedly player killer free. From then on, I decided this area would become my hunting grounds that I would visit on a regular basis until I had enough game currency accumulated to buy a house in-game. The next day I visited the grounds, I made my time very lucrative fighting the monsters alone. I did not have the ability to "Recall" out of the dungeon (a spell that could, when targeted on a small rune "marked" for a certain location, teleport you immediately out of an area). Upon leaving the dungeon to run back to town with my hard-earned items and gold, a group of 3 players in the same guild came out of hiding, cast a paralyzing spell on me, and used other powerful spells to kill me within 10 seconds. They took all of my items, including some wood which was easily attainable by using an axe on a tree not more than 3 gaming tiles away from where my body lay. Each day after this happened, I would have to assume the risk of dying by this particular guild of player killers should I desire to return to the hunting ground. In fact, I died many times, even after summoning help from anti-player killers. Ultimately, I found that I was barely breaking even and could knew finding other areas to hunt would lend only five times the misery I had experienced at the mentioned hunting grounds. My other option was to become a merchant, most entirely bound within the safety of the city walls. I could not stand the repetitiveness of being a merchant character, so I cancelled my account and quit the game weighing the cost of the monthly service and enjoyment of the game versus the misery caused by player killers without in-game "morals."

D1-NP-Q2(a). In this instance, were the griefers breaking established game-rules, or social "play-nice" rules, or both?

[R29]: The players were not breaking established games rules, but that doesn't mean the established rules were correct in my mind. One might say the players were harassing me, which they very well might have intended to do; "hey, let's go wait for that one guy to leave the dungeon again to see how many more times we can kill him and loot all his stuff!" would illustrate a harassment-type behavior. On the other hand, the murdering players may have only been using my gains to save for their own in-game desires such as a bigger house or an elite weapon, and not intending to harass me whatsoever. Social rules are different for every player. The murderers may have formed their own set of rules regarding this behavior such as: "if you're willing to venture out of town then you have to risk anything can happen to you at any time" (in this case outside the dungeon). The victim's social rules might appear as: "It's harassment to repeatedly kill the same successful player for personal gain rather than naturally accumulate wealth by hunting monsters or being a merchant." All in all, the game's rules were not broken in this case, but according to MY social "play-nice" rules, I was harassed and therefore negatively affected by grief actions.

D1-NP-Q2(b). I see. Given that each player's set of social rules differ, do games define a "general" set of social rules they expect all players to abide by?

[R29]: Games do define a "general" set of social rules they expect all players to abide by, as with most games. For example, a player is considered "breaking the social rules" if he/she is verbally assaulting another player. "I'm going to find you and kill you in real life" or "I want to fondle your (insert body part)" sorts of phrases would fall under this ruleset, but obviously there are many more greatly offensive ways of saying things players could conjure up. Perhaps the most obvious sign of "general social rules" games set is evident their "player age rating," which indeed is the "Rated For (insert categorized age group here)" label one finds on a game box. For example, *Ultima Online* switched from a "17 year old +" rating to a general "Teen +" rating with the last expansion. I have become aware of both many player's anguish and relief, and both are substantial. Some older players who, well, took advantage of the older rating are now being slapped with harassment complaints for the actions they previously performed prior to the rating change. Parents of younger players are relieved because they can better control what their children "see" in the game.

Regardless of these situations, grief play takes a role in the social world of MMORPG games, and should therefore take up a rule in the general social rule set, at least to a certain degree. It is interesting that most grief play actions are NOT in any rule set, because the definition, causation, and consequence isn't clearly understood. A separate, "recommended" social rule set on player etiquette should exist aside from the rating rule set (verbal assault, etc.). This social rule set should address grief play, the situations it arises in, and what to do if it begins to affect you, the player. This rule set, however, would not be able to take action against a griefer as griefers themselves would surely exploit such a system to their benefit. It would simply be the "10 commandments" of MMORPG play. On a personal basis, I believe game makers should map out and acknowledge openly the entire deal of "grief play" - within the instructions manual, at the account setup, or even more forwardly the first X number of times a player logs in so that players are very aware. By being aware of grief play, players would better understand its causes and would be able to take some action themselves to thwart it.

Appendix 2: A section of an interview with a developer [R33]

D1-D-Q1. How would you define grief play?

[R33]: I would say any player behavior which ruins the enjoyment of others and is no directly supported by the game design. For instance, on a MMORPG where player vs player combat is explicitly allowed, having one player kill another is okay (even if a little annoying). However, on a MMORPG where player combat is not possible directly (for example, you could lure a big monster close to a newbie and have the monster kill him), it would be.

A lot of people consider griefing to be the use of exploits, but it has been my experience that most people who do it aren't always that crafty. In City of Heroes, a common problem is people killing the mob you had whittled down to near death. They get all the credit for none of the work. It's not an exploit, and in fact, it is even encouraged by a game system which rewards the last hit instead of all hits.

I think griefing is someone working within the confines of the system without understanding the moral implications of their actions. In the CoH example, stealing kills is allowed and even encouraged by the game system. If you want to level fast with minimal danger, that is the best option you can take. However, from a moral standpoint, it isn't very nice and tends to piss people off.

A lot of multiplayer games use things like "common sense" to control players when they've created a wide open system with a variety of ways to play. I don't think griefers are exactly bad people. They just owe more to gameplay than common sense as far as what actions are good or bad. And there are lot of people who grief the game system, if not the game players. For example, people who take advantage of AI flaws by hiding behind certain types of level geometry. It's just that AI doesn't complain :)

D1-D-Q1(a). You've noted that griefing would be an act that isn't directly supported by the game design. Could I get your opinion on this scenario: a player with vendors somehow succeeds in cornering an important resource needed by players and is normally sold on NPC vendors, so that it no longer becomes available for sale on NPCs. Players can only buy the resource at hugely inflated prices, and the seller does this for the purpose of making large profits. Would you consider such an act griefing?

[R33]: Only if you consider Microsoft Windows griefing... :) What you've described is basically "winning" capitalism - a monopoly. It's not morally correct, nor is it beneficial to the bigger picture, but using the rules available to you, it is the best way to guarantee the largest profits with the least amount of risk. In short, it is the best way to make lots of money.

In a single player game, that kind of behavior is how you assure victory. However, in a multiplayer game, you cannot ever have "victory". No one player can ever have complete dominance over all the other ones. It is unfair and the potential for screwing other players over is quite high. That's why we have anti-monopoly laws in real life. Even if the "gameplay" supports and encourages it, we need additional rules to enforce moral correctness as well.

I don't really consider it griefing because it is something one would most likely do without really appreciating the affect it has on other players. Griefing to me seems to be something which intentionally ruins the other player's experience. Even if it was an accident, after the event occurred it would be quite obvious who you were hurting and why. If you did it again knowing those affects, then you aren't very nice. Monopolies are just the way capitalism tends towards and is usually far enough removed from the negative effects that most people wouldn't notice the individual's plight.

D1-D-Q1(b). You've also suggested that people grief the game system. As an aside, do players grief the game as a means for protesting against the system (of rules for example?) or its management?

[R33]: It's not that they grief the system, they just use the system. If you look at the game system from a practical standpoint, anything which isn't directly disallowed is explicitly allowed. However, the game system is no alone and requires social and moral guidelines which further define the good and bad actions - only those tend to not be quite so explicitly defined.

Once an exploit is found, management is typically aware of it and have explicitly forbid it already. However, perhaps they are taking their time fixing the problem and some players think it is a high priority that is being ignored. They sometimes indulge in the behavior to bring attention to the developers. It's kind of like saying "Look, no police show up when I shoot someone, so I'm going to shoot people until it is a big enough problem that police start showing up on time".

I run a forum community myself, which is not a game but definitely a social arena with specific rules. These rules have been broken on purpose by some members who had a problem with me or the other moderators. What it boils down to is that they wanted attention. It sounds like a child throwing a tantrum, but they had what they considered a legitimate beef with the management and felt that that beef was being ignored or suppressed. So they made the biggest stink they could before it could be suppressed, and large enough so that it couldn't be ignored. They anger was felt by everyone. Whether their anger was justified or not is a different story.

D1-D-Q1(c). You've suggested that the game system requires social and moral guidelines which further define good and bad actions. Many MMORPGs include "catch all" rules requiring all participants to play harmoniously and fairly, alongside more specific rules on specific actions (e.g. kill-stealing, training). Have these two types of rules been effective in managing player behavior?

[R33]: No way. We've got anti-jay walking rules in real life and I have yet to see that stop anyone - and that's a specific rule. These abstract and general rules are WAY too easy to bend. If you don't define the boundaries, you spend more time arguing about what fits inside than doing anything about it.

D1-D-Q2. Do you think it is possible for grief play to be accidental at all?

[R33]: Absolutely. I've accidentally stolen kills in CoH just because I didn't know someone else was working on a mob. They could've been doing projectiles from behind a corner and I'd run up an kill it not seeing that. And there have been cases where I've found an exploit accidentally, only to repeatedly return to it even after I realized it was one. I think most types of griefing start out by accident, though they quickly become publicized and picked up by others who think it is funny.

D1-D-Q3. Are there types of grief play that are particularly difficult to deal with by game design?

[R33]: It doesn't matter what you design, it is ALWAYS possible. It comes from the inherent limitation of what we do as people and what we do as gamers. When playing Monopoly, winning involves screwing over your opponents and sending them to the poor house. As friends, you would never do something like that, but the game introduces pressures to do such a thing and the rules which dictate how and why.

Any time you've got a competitive goal, and that could be something as stupid as who has the best looking hat, the players will look for the best approach to victory that is allowed by the game. Cheating is bad, but creatively using the rules is indisputable. You can't yell at a Scrabble player with a bigger vocabulary, so many competitive Scrabble players go memorize dictionaries.

I think that MMORPGs are all kind of generically the same at this point, all revolving around the killing of monsters and leveling up. As such, I think there are common techniques to grief which are encouraged by such a system that can only be completely eradicated by removing core concepts.

For example, if you kill a monster, it leaves a corpse filled with loot. To prevent people from stealing from the corpse, only you can access it for a limited time. When you die, only you can access your own corpse. This removes the major incentives for player killing but at the sake of destroying the metaphor of the world. Certainly a real barbarian would not wait 30 seconds to loot a lone yak corpse.

To beat the grief, more and more special rules are created which apply only to the players. They are no longer part of the world, but special entities which visit the world and are practically devoid of any real danger because of it. This is a good thing and a bad thing.

But, like I said, it doesn't matter what kind of online game you make, there will be exploits to take advantage of, and rules which can be used amorally to your advantage.

D1-D-Q4. Could I get your opinion on a scenario about role-playing and griefing. A player's character is a thief, and this is visibly tagged on this character for all to see. What if this person scams another player, but when queried by the game master, he insists he was role-playing in a manner consistent to that of a thief?

[R33]: I don't consider that griefing. It seems to me that all the signs were there that the scammed player should've been a little more careful. You can't regulate trust - that is something which is earned between two players. You can't make rules which forces everyone to behave in such a manner that trust is implicit.

What you can do is create rules and guidelines which have repercussions for breaking trust. For instance, if a thief steals from someone in real life, you tell the police and they try to track them down, and hopefully, put them in jail. In a game with paying customers, you can't have a player get put into jail because they'll quit the game. So it is an interesting decision.

Ultimately, if you don't want people roleplaying thieves, don't have thief classes. It is a class which revolves around shady deals and deception and law breaking - yet the rules of the game implicitly deny all those things. If you want to control the social situation, the best thing is by doing it implicitly and explicitly through the gameplay mechanics and metaphors.

Griefing, to me, seems like someone who breaks the metaphor of the world to take advantage of the game. In real life, you don't have people shooting arrows through walls or monsters getting caught on trees. A roleplaying thief scamming someone neither breaks the world nor the game - it would even be required on some roleplaying heavy MUDs.

D1-D-Q5. I'd like to get your opinion on this statement: "if there was no grief in this game, the game would become boring (for players)".

[R33]: That depends on your definition of "grief". I don't really see grief as something you can't have. It is something which goes along with EVERY social system, no matter how large or small. It isn't something you can get rid of, only encourage better behavior and punish the worst behaviors.

We have a society where it is easier to break into a house and steal a tv than it is to work a job and buy a tv (especially the plasma screen ones). The thing which prevent us all from doing that is that there are laws involved and the punishment is significant enough to defer most reasonable minded people. But people still steal TVs. People will ALWAYS steal TVs. You can't eradicate the behavior - you just make it so difficult to do that people find an easier, and perhaps less damaging, way of succeeding.

D1-D-Q6. Ultima Online has Trammel and Felucca aspects, which have separated players into PvE and PvP environments. In your assessment, has this been effective in managing griefing to more acceptable levels?

[R33]: I don't think it affects griefing at all. If PvP is outlawed, able minded individuals will find something else to amuse them. What it does is separate two distinct playing styles for people who aren't actually griefers. You see, there are people who want to play a PvP game because it is more challenging and more realistic. It isn't that they want to screw over other players (though I'm sure some of them prefer to keep their options open). That's just how they want to play.

But that playing style may not appeal to less demanding players who prefer escapism and cooperation to the challenge of living in constant fear and mistrust of the other players. These are two genres of gaming styles and I don't think that they imply any sort of predisposition towards griefing at all.

I think too many game designers look at griefing as any playing style contrary to what they intended, typically in the destructive way. PvP is, in general, not griefing. It is designed into the system. In a game with no PvP at all (like City of Heroes), teleporting an unwilling participant into a group of 30 high level enemies is griefing. It is unfair, unprotectable, and unpunishable. PvP, by the same criteria, is as fair as the combat system, protectable through planning, and punishable by higher level players hunting down problem characters (vigilantes).

D1-D-Q6(a). On a related note, have frontier justice systems in which players are allowed to attack their tormentors actually been effective in reducing grief play?

[R33]: Probably not. I think most people who intentionally grief other players already know what they are doing is probably not right. It's funny, enjoyable, and a boost to the old self esteem, but they tend to know that what they are doing is not strictly legal. As such, they are already taking a certain risk in the first place.

For instance, in the recent SWG scandal, you know the people who figured out the credit duping exploit knew that they were doing something unethical and wrong. However, the benefits were worth the perceived risk. Of course, the admins came down HARD on them to prevent such a thing from happening again. In short, the perceived risk must outweigh the perceived gain for an action to be prevented.

Players being able to protect themselves will just cause intentional griefers to target easier targets. Do you rob the big burly guy carrying the gun, or the teenage girl in the flowery skirt? They will attack newbies because even though the option to defend themselves is present, they are not likely experienced enough to know how to handle the situation, or socially viable to know others to take the risk on their behalf.